D0457336

49 MYTHS ABOUT CHINA

49 MYTHS ABOUT CHINA

Marte Kjær Galtung and Stig Stenslie

Foreword by Andrew J. Nathan

ROWMAN & LITTLEFIELD
Lanham • Boulder • New York • London

Published by Rowman & Littlefield
A wholly owned subsidiary of The Rowman & Littlefield Publishing Group, Inc.
4501 Forbes Boulevard, Suite 200, Lanham, Maryland 20706
www.rowman.com

Unit A, Whitacre Mews, 26-34 Stannery Street, London SE11 4AB, United
Kingdom

British Library Cataloguing in Publication Information Available

Library of Congress Cataloging-in-Publication Data

Galtung, Marte Kjær, 1976–
[49 myter om Kina. English]
49 myths about China / Marte Kjær Galtung and Stig Stenslie.
pages cm
Includes bibliographical references and index.
ISBN 978-1-4422-3622-6 (cloth : alkaline paper) — ISBN 978-1-4422-3623-3 (electronic)
1. China—Miscellanea. I. Stenslie, Stig. II. Title. III. Title: Forty-nine myths about China.
DS706.G3413 2015
951—dc23
2014024511

∞ ™ The paper used in this publication meets the minimum requirements of
American National Standard for Information Sciences Permanence of Paper for
Printed Library Materials, ANSI/NISO Z39.48-1992.

Printed in the United States of America

CONTENTS

FOREWORD

Andrew J. Nathan

The more important China becomes to us, the harder it seems to be to grasp its reality. Everyone is his own China expert today, thanks to the surge in Western businessmen, students, and tourists traveling to that country. Along with more experts, we have more confusion. Now, along come two highly qualified, learned, and entertaining Norwegian experts to set the rest of us straight.

Norway might seem an unexpected source of expertise on China—but such a view would express a myth about Norway: that it is a remote, inward-looking place. In fact, as a geographically large, but demographically small, and highly prosperous country, heavily dependent on oil exports to the rest of the world, Norway has a large stake in global stability. It is a staunch American ally in NATO and maintains a sophisticated, elite defense establishment. It has a cosmopolitan culture and integrates refugees from around the world into its citizenry. Norway takes a strong interest in trends all around the world, including in China, and its Peace Prize Committee (which is not part of the government) has awarded two peace prizes to people from China—His Holiness the Dalai Lama (who was born in Tibet but fled into exile in 1959) in 1989 and rights advocate Liu Xiaobo in 2010.

So it should not be surprising that Norway's foreign policy and security establishment keeps a close eye on global affairs. For a small country, security policy is less about hardware and more about understanding other countries' languages, cultures, and histories in order to learn what drives their policies and how they might best be either accommodated or resisted. Marte Kjær Galtung and Stig Stenslie—members of the Norwegian Defence Staff—draw on their humanistic training in anthropology and political science, as well as on their area-studies expertise, to give us a brisk, pointed introduction, in the form of short commentaries on prevalent myths, to what makes China tick. In doing so they speak for themselves, not for their government. But their insights reflect the fact that they come from a country that needs an unencumbered view of the world and that neither competes with China nor depends on it, but which takes seriously the implications of its rise.

Along with the Arab world, China has often served as the classic "Other" for an ever-changing West struggling to define and redefine itself. Coming from the ambitious but insecure commercial-military power of thirteenth-century Venice, Marco Polo portrayed China as infinitely affluent and powerful. For the Enlightenment thinker François-Marie Arouet Voltaire, as he argued against religious obscurantism, China was the home of secular rationality. For Adam Smith, during the early industrial revolution, China was a warning example of economic stagnation. For Georg Wilhelm Friedrich Hegel, writing in the Napoleonic era, China exemplified a country without heroes, revolution, or progress, relegated to a status outside history. Over the years we have seen China as poor or rich, superstitious or rational, barbarous or civilized, passive or warlike. In effect, the West has defined its own identity by creating an image of China as its imaginary opposite.

Today, we are in a period—not the first—of supposed Western decline. The West feels disunited, indecisive, inefficient, and weak. Portrayals of a "rising China" as united, decisive, efficient, and strong give concrete meaning to those characteristics.

Not that China is not really rising. Its gross domestic product (GDP) has increased by doubt digits for three decades, and its military budget has gone up along with it. It asserts its "core national interests" with increasing vigor. The question is, however, whether China's rise is really equivalent to the West's decline—its natural accompaniment or even its cause. When we see China as a threat, are we seeing China as it really is?

The so-called China threat is such a shape-shifter—to borrow a phrase from Karl Marx, a "specter haunting" the post–Cold War world of American dominance—that it is hard to pin down what China threat theorists really fear. One can summarize the discourse as expressing three kinds of worries, sometimes in combination:

> *Economic:* China will become the world's biggest economy; it will soak up all our technology and flood us with products; its currency will become the world's reserve currency; it will set standards for technology and consumer products; it will force the whole world to adopt the Chinese way of doing business.
>
> *Military:* China's economic growth will cause it to have more and more military power to pursue its existing territorial claims and

expand its regional influence, while also expanding its strategic interests overseas, such as workers, oil fields, investments, and so on, and it will find itself constrained to project military power to protect these interests. It will dominate first its own region and then the world.

Normative: The success of the Chinese model will bring an end to the soft-power dominance of democracy and human rights. China will rewrite existing international norms on free trade, human rights, humanitarian intervention, development assistance, and so on, and will use its financial clout to influence not only domestic but foreign media, academia, and public culture.

There are two ways to evaluate such fears. First, one can project existing trends into the future—what we might call "on-trajectory" forecasting. This kind of prediction is correct most of the time because most of the time trends usually do continue to develop in the same direction. But such a forecast is guaranteed eventually to be wrong because sooner or later history surprises us.

The second approach is to think about all the unlikely ways in which things could go off trajectory and try to identify the "most likely unlikely" scenarios. This type of prediction is wrong most of the time but sooner or later has a good chance of being correct because, in the long run, the only sure thing is the occurrence of something unexpected.

If we think about the China threat in the first way, we should incorporate the following facts and trends into our analysis: China's regime remains in stable control of the country, despite many diverse challenges to its rule. As long as political disorder does not break out, the economy will continue to grow. But that economy has already started to slow, as all fast-growing economies have eventually done, and we should expect the rate of growth to continue to moderate. China's government will face a complex internal and external security agenda into the distant future. It must manage domestic challenges arising from rapid social change, ideological skepticism, and dissatisfaction among ethnic and religious groups. It must deal with the complaints of rural dwellers whose land is being either seized or polluted and with those of urban residents who oppose polluting factories and unsafe consumer products.

Taiwan will continue to resist integration into the People's Republic of China. China's major neighbors—Japan, India, and Russia—and its strong midsized neighbors, like South Korea, Vietnam, and Indonesia, will continue to resist Chinese domination. The United States will not pull out of Asia. China's prosperity will continue to depend on its interdependence with the global economy as a source of raw materials and energy and as a market for Chinese manufactures. China will continue to have a strong stake in regional and global peace and stability so that its economy is not disrupted. If all this is true, then it is unlikely in the foreseeable future that China will seek, or be able, either to push the United States out of Asia or to overthrow the global system.

This does not mean that the rise of China presents no challenges to the status quo. We should expect continued friction between China and many of its neighbors as it tries to improve its position in territorial disputes. China will continue to challenge the US claim that it can legally conduct naval surveying and intelligence operations up to twelve nautical miles off the Chinese coast. It will continue to pressure Taiwan for reunification. So we can expect friction between China on one side and the United States and its regional allies on the other. Such frictions carry the risk of escalation, leading to armed clashes. But it would be an exaggeration to conflate this risk of local conflict with a risk of China taking over the world.

What about off-trajectory change? The longer the time frame, the more likely the occurrence of something dramatically different. (Think of the fall of the Soviet Union or the Arab Spring.) Of course, this unexpected type of change is inherently unpredictable. But we should be able to identify some kinds of radical historical shifts as less improbable than some others.

For example, looking at China's domestic situation, we can identify key vulnerabilities in the economic model. These include the heavy toll that environmental degradation is taking on the land, water, air, and public health, rendering the current growth model unsustainable. Another economic vulnerability is the demographic structure of an aging population. Third is the stimulation of rapid growth by heavy, and often unproductive, state investment in infrastructure and (through loans from state banks) real estate. Considering such factors, we can rule out a resurgence of double-digit growth and rule in the possibility—although not the inevitability—of a dramatic growth decline or economic crisis occurring sooner or later.

Politically, too, the Chinese system is vulnerable. It lacks the sense of long-term stability found even in poorly performing democracies like those of Japan, France, and—sad to say—our own American system. The Chinese leadership itself states officially that it must "reform" and "improve" its political system, create "socialist-style democracy," and build "socialist rule of law"—that is, that the Chinese political system remains under construction. Even though the broad public gives the regime high marks for performance, it too sees the current system as a way station on the road of political evolution toward an unknown future form of government. Despite muscular repression, as old dissidents are jailed or exiled new dissidents keep cropping up, demanding fundamental change. Political change may be peaceful and gradual, or it may emerge in the midst of a crisis—but change does seem likely. Again one must add the qualifier "sooner or later."

China's international environment is potentially turbulent as well. Right on its border lies one of the most unstable countries in the world, North Korea, run by an anachronistic personal dictatorship, riven with factional strife and armed with nuclear weapons, that rules over a destitute population. If that regime collapses or unleashes war, China will pay a big price one way or another. Other unstable regimes bordering China include those in Burma, Pakistan, Afghanistan, Tajikistan, Kyrgyzstan, and Kazakhstan. Ethnic strife or the rise of extremist movements could produce refugee flows or terrorist havens in these places that would threaten China's security. Further afield, disorder in Africa or the Middle East could threaten China's supplies of oil, copper, and other commodities. Polarization of relations with Europe and the United States could threaten its export markets and financial stability.

By contrast, it is hard to think of plausible off-trajectory changes in China's foreign policy environment that would enhance China's security. It is unlikely, for example, that any of China's larger neighbors will decide to ally themselves with Beijing because distrust runs high throughout the region. Off-trajectory change, in short, which is likely to occur sooner or later, is more likely to diminish than enhance the China threat.

Of course, some myths about China are actually true. China is located in a different part of the world from us. It has its own priorities, security needs, and vision of the future, and it does not always see the world in the same way that we see it. It is increasingly closely linked to us and is not going away. So we need to understand it.

Galtung and Stenslie offer a spirited, enjoyable way to improve our insight. It will be a rare reader who doesn't believe, perhaps unconsciously, in quite a few of the myths skewered in this book. Test yourself by looking at the table of contents and asking how you would disprove these propositions before you go on to read what the authors say. Then see how Galtung and Stenslie correct your mistakes. But don't worry. They will not make you feel stupid, because they offer not opposing myths but nuanced truths. Their deft approach will be fun for beginners and informative for experts. At the end of reading their forty-ninth essay, one will stand disabused of a bonus, fiftieth myth: the dangerous idea that outsiders cannot understand China.

ACKNOWLEDGMENTS

Many people have supported us throughout the writing process. First and foremost, our thanks go to Arne Jon Isachsen, who read and commented on earlier versions of the entire text. Moreover, big thanks to all those who shared their knowledge of China and made suggestions for parts of the book, including Ane Bislev, Jo Inge Bekkevold, Harald Bøckman, Tore Linné Eriksen, Ole Fossgård, Heidi Østbø Haugen, Gørild Heggelund, Huang Jing, Asbjørn Lode, Otto Malmgren, Cecilia Milwertz, Truls Mossman, Andrew J. Nathan, Qian Jiwei, Jørgen Randers, Unn Målfrid H. Rolandsen, Tehmina Sarwar, Christina M. Smikop, Iselin Stensdal, Rune Svarverud, Elin Sæther, Monika P. Thowsen, Brigt Harr Vaage, Wang Luyao, Wang Yi, and Zheng Yongnian. Any errors and shortcomings are to be blamed on us alone. Many thanks to our literary agent Peter W. Bernstein for his invaluable advice, enthusiasm, and steadfast trust in our project. Thanks also go to Susan McEachern and Carrie Broadwell-Tkach for excellent guidance and support with the publication of this book and to the Freedom of Expression Foundation for generous support. Last but not least, a big thanks to friends and family. And Amber and Steve!

—Marte Kjær Galtung and Stig Stenslie

MAP OF CHINA

INTRODUCTION

There are numerous Western myths about China. This book challenges some of them, hopefully without creating too many new ones in the process.

By "myth" we mean a widespread perception that is not true. Some of the myths we discuss are well known; others exist within more exclusive groups of people concerned with China in one way or another. In some cases, the Chinese themselves—the people in general or the government—encourage our mistaken perceptions about them. But most of these myths are really about how we Westerners see ourselves, inasmuch as China or the Chinese people are depicted as what we are not. Such myths foster alienation. Western perceptions of the empire in the East have for centuries oscillated between sinophilia and sinophobia, influenced as much by historical changes in the West as by the development of China.

Ever since the Middle Ages, China has had a prominent place in the European mind. Marco Polo, the Venetian merchant traveler and explorer who lived from 1254 to 1324, first fueled the Europeans' dreams of an empire far to the east. Venice was captivated by the stories of the man who had met the mighty Kublai Khan, then ruler of China, and who also wrote a book about his years in the Middle Kingdom.

Polo was nicknamed "Millione," perhaps because the word "million" appears over and over again in his stories of China: Kublai Khan had 1 million horsemen; he had millions of ships; his kingdom had millions of cities. The Europeans of Polo's time could not imagine such large numbers, and thus many dismissed them as exaggerations or pure fantasy. Nevertheless, for centuries Polo's intriguing stories shaped the European

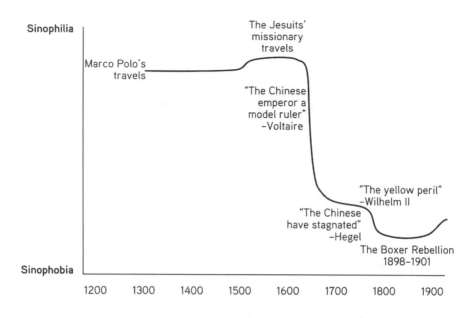

Western Views of China from Marco Polo to World War II

understanding of China: the luxury and affluence; the exotic culture; the women's sensual, servile, and manipulative nature; the knowledge and new inventions. All this made China—in the Western mind—an unknown, distant, mysterious, and exceedingly attractive place.[1]

Whether Polo actually set foot in China has been fiercely debated ever since his return to Venice in 1298. Frances Wood, a sinologist and curator at the British Museum in London from 1977 to 2013, is among those who argue that Polo's trip to China is itself mere myth.[2] Wood says obvious gaps in Polo's account make it doubtful that he ever got that far. Why did he not mention the Great Wall? Chinese writing? The Chinese passion for tea? The practice of binding women's feet? All these things would at that time have made an indelible impression on a European visitor. Furthermore, Wood notes that Polo's travel book is characterized by numerous factual errors and exaggerations. Most likely, the skeptics say, Polo never ventured past Constantinople, or he may have settled somewhere near the Black Sea, at that time an important link between West and East. Some surmise he spent twenty-four years there, listening to the tales of the endless stream of travelers.

Almost two centuries later, in the late fifteenth century, Vasco da Gama discovered the sea route to East Asia, which allowed for more contact between the Europeans and the Chinese. Goods and ideas began to flow between the continents. Beginning with Francisco Xavier, who traveled to India, Japan, and China from 1542 to 1552, Jesuit missionaries provided Europeans with the first reliable accounts of the kingdom of the East. After much effort, the missionaries gained a foothold in the Chinese imperial court, often serving as astronomers, engineers, and artists. They thereby acquired an in-depth knowledge of the Chinese language and insights into Chinese culture.

One of the missionaries, Father Matteo Ricci—known as Li Madou among the Chinese—won the emperor's favor. An intellectual and cultivated man from a noble Italian family, he soon spoke fluent Chinese and devoted himself to the study of China's rich history, culture, and religion. Father Ricci's *De christiana expeditione apud Sinas* (*The Christian Expedition to China*), published after his death in 1610, was translated into all the major European languages and shaped Western understanding of the Chinese for more than a century. Ricci described them as humane and friendly. During the 1600s Jesuit missionaries published several other books on China, all very favorable. Wanting to justify their missionary activities and methods, the Jesuits had a vested interest in creating a positive image.[3] And they were quite successful in China—largely due to their adaptation of "infidel" native customs and beliefs, many of which were sharply criticized in Europe. Enlightenment intellectuals embraced the Jesuits' accounts. Thinkers such as Gottfried Wilhelm Leibniz, François-Marie Arouet Voltaire, and Christian Wolff considered the Chinese wise bearers of a proud and ancient tradition, much older and in many areas more developed than European civilization. Confucianism was especially well thought of by European intellectuals. It was in sync with Enlightenment ideals, which were critical of existing European institutions such as absolute monarchy, the aristocracy, and the dogmas of the Christian church. Confucius was praised for his common sense and clarity—the latter because he did not surround his moral philosophy with a mystical aura. These European thinkers portrayed China as a country ruled by venerable, philosophically minded rulers whose advisors were appointed on the basis of their intellectual abilities, respect for the law, and high moral standards—all prerequisites for stability in a realm as vast as China.

Leibniz collected Jesuit narratives and described China as an ideal society in his book *Novissima sinica* (*News from China*). He stated that the kingdom of the East surpassed Europe in population, agricultural production, and respect for the law. In his *Dictionnaire philosophique*, Voltaire called the Chinese imperial government the most admirable ever developed by mankind and went further than most in his praise of Confucius. Similarly, the German philosopher Christian Wolff praised Chinese moral philosophy in his lectures at the Institute of Oriental Studies in Halle—a Prussian university city—to an extent that incurred the wrath of local Christian theologians. The issue became so controversial that Emperor Friedrich Wilhelm I had to intervene, firing Wolff for his "heresy." Wolff was given the choice of leaving Prussia within forty-eight hours or dangling from the gallows. He packed his suitcase.

Just when every self-respecting European monarch had built his own Chinese garden, tearoom, or a pagoda, European sinophilia reversed course. By the mid-eighteenth century, a new bout of sinophobia had emerged. This had more to do with developments in Europe than in China. The pope condemned the Jesuit missionaries' controversial methods in 1742. Before long the emperor had kicked the missionaries out of China anyway. Enlightened Europeans were increasingly inspired by the idea of rationality, especially as it related to advances in moral philosophy. China's vaunted stability was now seen as stagnation.

"The [Chinese] empire is an embalmed mummy painted with hieroglyphs and shrouded in silk; its internal life is like that of animals in hibernation," wrote German philosopher Johann Gottfried Herder in 1787.[4] Herder believed that Chinese culture had not evolved for centuries and consisted of remnants of the distant past. This view became prevalent among European thinkers from the late eighteenth century until the late nineteenth. The idea of a stagnating China was reproduced and elaborated in the works of intellectuals such as Adam Smith and Karl Marx.

Georg Wilhelm Friedrich Hegel (1770–1831) was another European thinker who shaped his contemporaries' views of China. According to Hegel, who equated history with change, the Chinese were passive, not inquisitive, and developmentally stalled—and therefore had no history. "The History of the World travels from East to West, for Europe is absolutely the end of History, Asia the beginning,"[5] he wrote. Hegel believed that China's character had been shaped early on, once and for all. This notion of a stagnating China remained prevalent among Europeans for decades. It is the mother of all myths about the Middle Kingdom.

In the nineteenth century, Europeans called China the "Sick Man of Asia" (to parallel the "Sick Man of Europe," the weakened Ottoman Empire). The West was considered active, whereas China was passive. A common perception was that only the West could "save" China from stagnation and ruin—a useful idea for anyone who wished to excuse European and American colonialism in Asia. China was never directly colonized, but military force and occupation were used to open the Chinese market up to trade. Goods manufactured in Europe were exchanged for spices, silk, and porcelain.

At the same time, some Western voices challenged this highly Eurocentric—and distinctly racist—view of China. Western sinologists, missionaries, diplomats, and officials with firsthand knowledge of China sought to make the country and its culture the subject of academic study. Oxford University was the first Western academic institution to offer training in Chinese language. In 1876, Professor James Legge undertook an extensive project to translate the major Chinese literary classics, becoming a prime example of a European who approached Chinese culture with deep respect and passion. Although Legge and others had a positive image of China, they lived and worked in a time when imperialism—which ran on the notion of the Western world's intellectual and moral supremacy—was a powerful force in the world. Thus Western influence was regarded as the key to bringing backward China into the modern world, for instance by promoting Western technology and science in the East.

The winds shifted again at the end of the nineteenth century. The Boxer Rebellion from 1898 to 1901 initially targeted Chinese and Western Christian missionaries but eventually aimed to eliminate all or most Western political and economic influence in China. In the summer of 1900, 189 Western missionaries and more than thirty-two thousand Chinese converts to Christianity were massacred across China. Churches were burned.[6] The West now viewed China as a menacing place full of bald, squinty-eyed, creepy people.

The notion of the "yellow" race (Chinese and Japanese) as an insidious threat to the "white" race spread. The Boxer Rebellion was only one of several elements fanning the flames. Japan's rapid expansion and militarization around the turn of the twentieth century added further fuel to the notion of a "yellow peril," as did extensive Chinese and Japanese immigration to the sparsely populated parts of the "white" race's territories—particularly Australia, South Africa, and the West Coast of the United States. Many Chinese had already immigrated to California during the 1848 Gold Rush, and more would follow. China's growing population was a source of awe and fear in the West. In 1910 Jack London published the short story "The Unparalleled Invasion," in which he describes a future with China as a military superpower.[7] Kaiser Wilhelm II of Germany was particularly concerned by what he perceived as a threat from the east; he is often said to have coined the term "yellow peril" (*die gelbe Gefahr*).[8] All the ships of the Hamburg America Line had a statue of the Archangel Michael onboard, symbolizing Germany's leadership in resisting the Asian threat, represented by a golden Buddha. By all accounts, the emperor himself designed the symbol.[9]

Dr. Fu Manchu—introduced in 1913 in a series by the British novelist Sax Gabriel Rohmer—came to personify the "evil Chinaman."[10] Dr. Fu was a prominent member of the mandarin class, the highly educated bureaucrats who served the Chinese emperor, and a creepy criminal. He had a clean-shaved head, catlike eyes, a fantastic physique, and an ingenious brain. He harbored an intense hatred of Western culture in all its forms and aimed to dominate the world. To reach this immodest goal, the doctor sought the support of both the "Young China" movement and unscrupulous Indian bandits.

Dr. Fu was, however, not the only Chinese supervillain. He was joined by another doctor, Dr. Yen How. Matthew Phillips Shield created this character in 1898. The book was an immediate best seller. The character was supposedly based on newspaper articles about the real Chinese revolutionary leader Dr. Sun Yatsen, who lived at the same time. Dr. Yen shared Dr. Fu's personal traits: a bald head, yellow skin, piercing eyes, and superhuman abilities. But Dr. Yen was cosmopolitan. Educated in Germany and the United States, he harbored an intense hatred of Western civilization. He was nicknamed the "Yellow Peril."

There was the occasional good Chinese character, like the Honolulu police officer Charlie Chan, created by Earl Derr Biggers in 1919, although his heyday lasted from the 1930s to the 1950s. He appeared first in a series of short stories, then subsequently in a number of films, radio plays, and cartoons. Chan was intelligent and thoroughly honest.

In 1942, four months after the Japanese attack on Pearl Harbor, a national survey revealed that 60 percent of Americans were unable to place China on the world map.[11] But toward the end of the war, Americans knew more about China, and many had a positive view. The Chinese had, after all, once again fought with the Allies.

The People's Republic of China was established in 1949; since then, Western perceptions of China have changed rapidly. In the Cold War atmosphere of the 1950s and 1960s, China was seen as an agent of the Soviet Union and therefore in a negative light. The perception that the standoff between the West and the Communists would lead to a third world war was prevalent. China's participation in the Korean War, from 1950 to 1953, cemented its partnership with the Soviet Union. China also provided military support to the Communists in Vietnam, Cambodia, and Laos, making relations with the United States and the West difficult. Between 1965 and 1970, 320,000 Chinese soldiers fought side by side with the North Vietnamese army against the Americans.[12]

At the end of the 1950s, the Belgian author Henri Verne created yet another Chinese supervillain, the horrific Mr. Ming, alias the "Yellow Shadow." Ming claimed to be a direct descendant of the powerful Ming emperors who ruled China from 1368 to 1644. The opium-smoking bad guy was the leader of a criminal sect called the "Old China" and aimed to revitalize ancient Chinese traditions. Like the other Chinese villains, he was clean shaven, athletic, possessed of a hypnotic gaze, and very intelligent. Naturally, he aspired to world domination. To reach this goal, Ming invented, among other marvels, robots, deadly lasers, and a quantum

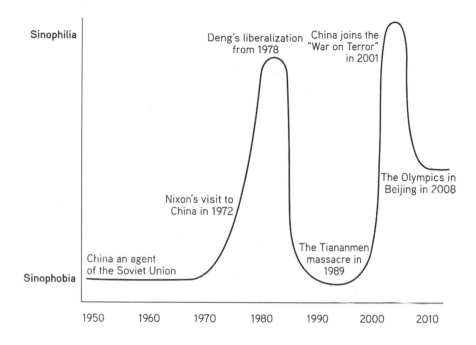

Sinophilia

Deng's liberalization
from 1978

China joins the
"War on Terror"
in 2001

The Olympics in
Beijing in 2008

Nixon's visit to
China in 1972

China an agent
of the Soviet Union

The Tiananmen
massacre in
1989

Sinophobia

1950 1960 1970 1980 1990 2000 2010

Western Views of the People's Republic of China

mechanical machine that transported him to an obscure location in the
Himalayas every time he was killed by his nemesis, the American Bob
Morane.

During his lifetime, Mao Zedong appealed to some leftist individuals
and groups in the West who admired his efforts to liberate the Chinese
people from imperialism and poverty. Nevertheless, the dominant view of
Mao in the West was negative. The People's Republic existed for more
than twenty years before it was formally recognized by the United States.
Until 1971, the United States considered the government on Taiwan to be
China's legitimate government.

Western views of China became more positive during the 1970s and
the 1980s as relations between the People's Republic and the United
States improved. The breakthrough came in 1972 when President Richard
Nixon surprised the world by meeting with Mao in Beijing. China and the
United States wanted normal relations; they now regarded the Soviet
Union as a greater threat than each other. The year before, the United
Nations had recognized the Communist government in Beijing as China's
legitimate government, and the People's Republic had taken over Tai-
wan's seat on the UN Security Council. In 1976, Mao died, and Deng
Xiaoping emerged as China's new leader. Deng guarded the Communist

Party's monopoly on power but initiated gradual economic reforms, including opening up the Chinese economy to the outside world. The Western view of China improved. The Chinese seemed more like us, no longer a threat—not to mention a huge potential market.

The Tiananmen Square massacre in June 1989 changed all that. It coincided with the crumbling of the Soviet Union and the Eastern Bloc, and China no longer appeared as the lesser of two evils. Now Beijing was viewed as the main opposition in the global fight for freedom and democracy. Western attention shifted to massive human rights violations in China.

But the tide turned yet again at the beginning of the twenty-first century—once more as a result of improved relations between China and the United States. China entered the World Trade Organization (WTO) in 2001 and eagerly joined the "war on terror" after the September 11 attacks on the United States that same year. In the West, the security discourse changed: the main threat to Western civilization was now militant Islamism, not communism. President George W. Bush had a grim reputation in Europe and the Middle East, but he eventually gained popularity in China after a bumpy start. He worked with Beijing to safeguard the status quo in the Taiwan Strait and cooperated with Chinese authorities to find diplomatic solutions to North Korea's menacing nuclear program.

At the time of this writing, sinophobia once again dominates in the West. China is regarded by many Europeans and Americans as a danger—a fear reflected in the titles of a number of best sellers, such as Martin Jacques's *When China Rules the World: The Rise of the Middle Kingdom and the End of the Western World*, Stefan Halper's *The Beijing Consensus: How China's Authoritarian Model Will Dominate the Twenty-First Century*, and Arvind Subramanian's *Eclipse: Living in the Shadow of China's Economic Dominance*.[13]

The backdrop for these rather alarmist titles is the global financial crisis, which started in the United States in 2008 and quickly spread to Europe. China also felt the impact of the crisis—exports fell for the first time in many years. But the Chinese managed to keep their economy going through large-scale investments in new infrastructure. Economic growth remained robust. China's confidence in its own model of economic management grew. Many Chinese enterprises have thrived by investing in internationally famous brands, advanced technology, and firms involved in the production of oil and other commodities. In the West, Chinese acquisitions are often perceived as threats rather than contributions to making the world's economic wheels spin faster.

As the West wallowed in economic crisis, China overtly demonstrated its great power ambitions through grand celebrations like the 2008 Olympics in Beijing and the sixtieth anniversary of the People's Republic in

2009. Many predict that the Chinese economy will be larger than that of the United States within a few years. As if this was not enough, the Chinese have been flexing their military muscle, acting more assertively than before, particularly in territorial disputes at sea.

Negative impressions of China have been exacerbated by the government's harsh repression of ethnic unrest in Tibet and Xinjiang, corruption scandals involving members of the senior leadership, and the treatment of high-profile dissidents such as Chen Guangcheng (the blind campaigner for laborers' rights who fled into exile in the United States in 2012) and Liu Xiaobo (currently serving an eleven-year sentence in a Chinese prison for his human rights activities). When Liu Xiaobo was awarded the Nobel Peace Prize in 2010, the Chinese government froze all political dialogue with Norway. Negotiations on a trade agreement were stopped, and some Norwegian exports to China were halted. The Chinese interpreted the prize as an attack on their legal and political system by the Norwegian authorities. In official Chinese eyes, it confirmed the West's arrogance, reawakening memories of the "Century of Humiliation" that began with the Opium Wars in the mid-nineteenth century.

The West's views of China and the Chinese are, however, far from black-and-white. There is still room for sinophilia. Although official China is difficult to understand and like in many cases, the Chinese people are easier to appreciate. International companies court Chinese consumers. Famous Chinese actors are increasingly featured in global advertising campaigns. Watch manufacturer TAG Heuer has hired Chen Daoming, a star of *Hero*, known as an "emperor of Chinese drama," while Omega has Zhang Ziyi, the beauty known from films such as *House of Flying Daggers*, *Memoirs of a Geisha*, and *Crouching Tiger, Hidden Dragon*. Art and culture have renewed the country's prestige. The world recognizes regime critics Ai Weiwei, mastermind behind Beijing's magnificent "Bird's Nest" stadium, and Liu Xiaobo, widely admired for his poetry and prose, for their work as much as for their outspokenness. Other artists who are not dissidents—for instance, the filmmakers Ang Lee, the Taiwanese known for international blockbusters such as *Hulk*, *Brokeback Mountain*, *Life of Pi*, and *Crouching Tiger, Hidden Dragon*, and Zhang Yimou, the man behind *Hero*, *Raise the Red Lantern*, and *House of Flying Daggers*—also attract broad international attention.

At the moment, the regime in Beijing is struggling with a worse reputation than the people as a whole. The following chapters discuss myths related to various aspects of contemporary China: politics, culture, economy, the country's relations to the outside world, and history. Altogether, we highlight forty-nine myths. Since China is huge and this book is small, we don't discuss any of the myths in great depth, but we hope that in unpacking these central myths we give readers a clearer understanding of fact and fiction regarding today's China.

Notes

1. Marco Polo, *The Travels of Marco Polo, the Venetian* (London: Forgotten Books, 2012).
2. Frances Wood, *Did Marco Polo Go to China?* (Boulder, CO: Westview Press, 1995).
3. Gianni Guadalupi, *China: Through the Eyes of the West* (Vercelli, Italy: White Star Publishers, 2003), 103–4.
4. J. G. Herder cited in R. J. Goebel, "China as an Embalmed Mummy: Herder's Orientalist Poetics," *South Atlantic Review* 60, no. 1 (January 1995): 111–29.
5. Georg Wilhelm Friedrich Hegel, *Philosophy of History* (New York: Barnes & Noble, 2004), 13.
6. Larry Clinton Thompson, *William Scott Ament and the Boxer Rebellion: Heroism, Hubris, and the Ideal Missionary* (Jefferson, NC: McFarland, 2009), 184.
7. For the full text of the short story, see "The Unparalleled Invasion," World of Jack London on the Web, http://www.jacklondons.net/writings/StrengthStrong/invasion.html.
8. G. G. Rupert, *The Yellow Peril; or, the Orient versus the Occident as Viewed by Modern Statesmen and Ancient Prophets* (Choctaw, OK: Union Publishing, 1911), 9.
9. Daniel C. Kane, introduction to A. B. de Guerville, *Au Japon: Memoirs of a Foreign Correspondent in Japan, Korea, and China, 1892–1894* (West Lafayette, IN: Parlor Press, 2009), xxix.
10. For the book where the character Dr. Fu is first introduced, see Sax Gabriel Rohmer, *The Insidious Dr. Fu Manchu* (1913; rpt. London: Forgotten Books, 2008).
11. Zhang Longxi, "The Myth of the Other: China in the Eyes of the West," *Critical Inquiry* 15, no. 1 (autumn 1988): 123.
12. John Pardos, *The Blood Road: The Ho Chi Minh Trail and the Vietnam War* (New York: John Wiley & Sons, 2000), 363.
13. Martin Jacques, *When China Rules the World: The End of the Western and the Birth of a New Global Order* (New York: Penguin Press, 2009); Stefan Halper, *The Beijing Consensus: How China's Authoritarian Model Will Dominate the Twenty-First Century* (New York: Basic Books, 2010); Arvind Subramanian, *Eclipse: Living in the Shadow of China's Economic Dominance* (Washington, DC: Peterson Institute for International Economics, 2011).

Part I

The Party

Myth 1

COMMUNISM IS DEAD IN CHINA

To get rich is glorious!

—Deng Xiaoping

If Mao Zedong came back to life today, he would be blown away when he stepped out of his mausoleum in Tiananmen Square.[1] The chairman would see a transformed Beijing: skyscrapers, luxury cars, art and antiques galleries, businesspeople rushing around in Italian designer shoes. The political rhetoric, too, would surprise him. In 1978, Mao's successor, Deng Xiaoping, removed "class struggle" from the official ideology of the People's Republic of China and introduced "socialism with Chinese characteristics." The goal was to replace rigid central planning with commercially oriented state enterprises, existing alongside a dynamic private sector. As a result, in 2013 there were 168 US dollar billionaires in China—only the United States had a higher number.[2] The same year, China's number of dollar millionaires hit 1 million. Only the United States and Japan had more.[3] According to HSBC Bank, Chinese consumers accounted for 25 percent of global sales of luxury brands in 2012.[4] Louis Vuitton, Gucci, Burberry, and Prada together have as many as 179 stores in China,[5] serving a market that barely existed around the turn of the millennium. The young people of China seem to have only one goal in life: to get rich.

The superrich have even joined the Communist Party.

In the late 1990s, Jiang Zemin allowed the middle class—entrepreneurs and business owners—to hold seats in the National People's Congress, China's parliament and formally the highest state organ. By 2012 there were several dollar billionaires among the nearly three thousand delegates, and the total private wealth of the seventy richest delegates was

estimated at $500 billion. By comparison, the total assets of all members
of the US Congress, the judges of the Supreme Court, all government
ministers, and President Barack Obama equaled $45 billion the same
year.[6] The billionaires' incentive to hold seats in the National People's
Congress is largely related to China's inadequate legal protection and
poorly developed property rights. They join the system to protect themselves from being overrun by business rivals.

"With more than 80 million members, China's Communist Party is the
world's largest chamber of commerce!" "The Politburo works just like
the board of the investment bank Goldman Sachs!" "China's ideology
today? Yes, it's McKinsey-Leninism!" "Communism has been the longest road from capitalism to . . . capitalism!" There are loads of jokes about
China's "communism," famously nicknamed "Market-Leninist" two
decades ago by Nicholas D. Kristof.[7]

Very few believe in the trio Lenin, Marx, and Mao—may they rest in
peace—any longer. "It doesn't matter whether a cat is white or black; as
long as it catches mice, it's a good cat," Deng said at the Guangzhou
conference in 1961.[8] Mao's successor was highly pragmatic. He liberal-
ized the economy and, to a certain degree, politics, granting the individual
in private life more freedom. If they can afford it, the Chinese can buy
what they want, do what they want for a living, and send their children to
schools in the United States.

And yet the legacy of communism remains, despite the rapid economic, social, and political changes of the last thirty years. Consider the
position of Christianity in Europe today. Many Europeans say that they
do not believe in God, but Christian ideas have shaped their beliefs to
some extent. Likewise, although people in China do not believe in communism, the ideology has left its mark on them. The idea of aristocracy,
for example, is as remote and unacceptable to the Chinese as it is to
Americans, despite its having been intact less than one hundred years
ago.

Moreover, China still has a Leninist political system, as Richard
McGregor shows in his book *The Party*.[9]

All appointments to senior positions in ministries, state-owned enterprises, universities, and the media—virtually every important institution
in the People's Republic—must go through the Organization Department
of the Communist Party. All state enterprises still have party committees
as the top decision-making body, and many neighborhoods still have
neighborhood committees. Media is monitored through the Party's Propaganda Department, which issues daily directives to the media. These
often painfully detailed guidelines—delivered formally on paper or less
formally in e-mails, text messages, and phone calls—explain which current issues the party regards as sensitive. They make clear whether and

how these issues should be discussed in the news. The People's Liberation Army (PLA) belongs to the party, not to the nation. The Central Military Commission, the military's top leadership, is led by the party's general secretary. All officers holding the rank of colonel or higher must be party members. Political commissars permeate the military on all levels. And last, but not least, the party has neutralized all political rivals, established control over the courts, limited religious groups and civil society, composed an extensive network of internal monitoring and security services, and carried out "political reeducation" of detainees in labor camps.

Mao's spirit lives.

In addition, the state still plays a very important role in the economy, although China is often cited as a pioneer in market reforms and globalization. China has resisted traditional market capitalism with regard to privatization, property rights, and deregulation. Recognizing this, the conservative Heritage Foundation ranked China 135 (out of 183 countries) in "economic freedom" in 2011. According to Heritage, China is one of the least economically free countries—one of the countries where market forces are given the least leeway.[10] The Fraser Institute, which also assesses the degree of economic freedom in various countries, notes the same. In its report for 2011, China was ranked 92 of 141.[11]

Furthermore, the party still takes ideology dead seriously. The people may not care about ideology, but for the elite it retains great significance—the cat must be white. Communism is sacred and cannot be touched. This is because the regime uses ideology to legitimize its right to rule. The worst crime in China today is organizing political opposition to the party, and the second worst is questioning the party's ideological stances. These stances are constantly evolving; Communist ideas adapt to the country's changing needs. The party's dogmas are developed by the Central Party School and numerous governmental think tanks, such as the Chinese Academy of Social Sciences (CASS), with its more than two thousand employees.[12] The party also invests considerable resources in solid ideological training for its millions of members. Before each promotion within their jobs, all party members are sent to the party schools, where they are updated on the latest ideological guidelines from the top leadership. Marxist-Leninist ideology is woven into the Chinese education system, from primary schools to universities. Ideological education of the PLA is particularly important to ensure its loyalty to the party. While Western media often express concerns about the politicization of the Chinese military, Chinese media on the contrary worry about its depoliticization.

On 26 December 2013, the 120th anniversary of the chairman's birth was marked with high-profile festivities, exhibitions, and Mao-themed luxury goods. Obviously, today's Chinese are not Communists. Never-theless, our revived Mao would recognize the political and economic system he set spinning.

Notes

1. To illustrate the tremendous upheavals that have taken place in China over the past few decades, many observers have toyed with the idea that "Mao rose from the dead," including Jeffrey N. Wasserstrom, *China's Brave New World: And Other Tales of Global Times* (Bloomington: Indiana University Press, 2007); Rana Mitter, *Modern China: A Very Short Introduction* (Oxford: Oxford University Press, 2008).

2. "Inside the 2013 Forbes China 400: A Record 168 Billionaires," *Forbes Magazine*, 21 October 2013, http://www.forbes.com/sites/russellflannery/2013/10/21/inside-the-2013-forbes-china-400-a-record-168-billionaires.

3. Kanis Li and Jeanny Yu, "China Likely to Overtake US as Richest Coun-try as Number of Dollar Millionaires Hits 1m," *South China Morning Post*, 10 October 2013, http://www.scmp.com/business/economy/article/1328125/china-likely-overtake-us-richest-country-number-dollar-millionaires.

4. Cited in Andrew Roberts, "Louis Vuitton Risks Logo Fatigue as Chinese Tastes Mature," *Bloomberg*, 24 September 2012, http://www.bloomberg.com/news/2012-09-24/vuitton-gucci-risk-first-mover-disadvantage-in-china.html. See also "Luxury in China: To Get Rich Is Glorious," PSFK Consulting, 26 May 2009, http://www.psfk.com/2009/05/to-get-rich-is-glorious-trend-report-on-luxury-in-china.html.

5. *Dagens Næringsliv*, 26 September 2012, 30.

6. "China's Billionaire People's Congress Makes Capitol Hill Look like Pauper," *Bloomberg*, 26 February 2012, http://www.bloomberg.com/news/2012-02-26/china-s-billionaire-lawmakers-make-u-s-peers-look-like-paupers.html.

7. Nicholas D. Kristof, "China Sees 'Market-Leninism' as Way to Future," *New York Times*, 6 September 1993, http://www.nytimes.com/1993/09/06/world/china-sees-market-leninism-as-way-to-future.html.

8. Quoted in Li Zhisui, *The Private Life of Chairman Mao: The Memoirs of Mao's Personal Physician* (New York: Random House, 1994), 376.

9. Richard McGregor, *The Party: The Secret World of China's Communist Rulers* (New York: HarperCollins, 2010).

10. "2011 Index of Economic Freedom," Heritage Foundation and *Wall Street Journal*, 2011, http://www.heritage.org/index/country/China.

11. "Economic Freedom of the World 2011: Annual Report," Fraser Institute, 2011, http://www.freetheworld.com/cgi-bin/freetheworld/getinfo.cgi.

12. Figures from the homepage of the Chinese Academy of Social Sciences, http://bic.cass.cn/english/infoShow/Arcitle_Show_Cass.asp?BigClassID=1&Title=CASS.

Myth 2

CHINA IS CENTRALLY CONTROLLED

Because China is a one-party state, it is easy to assume that the central government in Beijing makes all political decisions for the whole huge country and that the provincial governments and local authorities abide by its every word. One imagines that the central level of the party makes detailed plans for every part of the country—plans that cover economics, political reforms (or the lack thereof), and relations with other countries. No sane local politician, one might think, would contemplate going against these plans, local political institutions being merely the long arms of Beijing reaching into the provinces. There is no room, one might further believe, for independent political thinking. Chinese people supposedly put the common good before their own self-interest, so it is natural to assume that local authorities have the interests of the whole country in mind in their every move.

But the relationship between the center and the provinces is far more complex.

Like a supreme being, China's top leadership is omnipresent—but it is not all-powerful. China is indeed controlled by the central government, according to its constitution. When it comes to issues of urgent national interest such as Taiwan and Tibet, there is little room for deviation from what Beijing has decided. But in many other matters, provinces do have substantial autonomy to pursue their own agendas and interests. Party secretaries at the provincial level have ministerial ranks. This provides them with considerable political power. When Beijing announces new laws or policies, provincial governments see these as starting points for negotiation; rather than following central edicts to the letter, they consider what is appropriate in their provinces.

There is a long tradition of local leaders dismissing instructions from the capital, instead letting local conditions and needs dictate what should be done. Chinese proverbs practically recommend such a practice: "The sky is high and the emperor is far away" (*Tian gao, huangdi yuan*), and "When policies arrive from above, there are countermeasures on the ground" (*Shang you zhengce, xia you duice*).

China is in effect a federal state, says Professor Zheng Yongnian, director of the East Asian Institute at the National University of Singapore. Power is decentralized, and the provinces have considerable autonomy.[1]

When it comes to the financial matters of the provinces, Beijing imposes few constraints. A flexible system benefits the central government because it lets the various provinces experiment with different economic models. Some provinces have full market economies; other provinces' local economies rely on state-owned enterprises. The city of Wenzhou in Southeast China is known for its skilled businessmen. Already in the early 1980s, when the rest of China still had a planned economy, the local government encouraged and supported Wenzhou's private economic actors despite criticism from Beijing. Today Wenzhou receives 75 percent of its tax revenue from private enterprises. In the industrial province of Liaoning, in the northeast on the North Korean border, the relationship between private and state-owned enterprises is reversed: the private sector creates only 25 percent of the province's wealth.

Provinces also experiment with political reforms independently of the central government. The most extreme example is Hong Kong, which so distinguishes itself from the rest of China in political, legal, economic, and financial affairs that they say, "One country—two systems" (*Yiguo liangzhi*). Another example is Sichuan province, where local authorities have tested several means of strengthening local democracy. For instance, the people of the Buyun Township have been allowed to choose their own leaders since 1999, and a representative committee in Shizhong elects that district's leaders. The real litmus test of democracy is of course how the list of candidates is made, and they are usually subject to party approval. In the city of Wenling in the Zhejiang province, randomly selected people are consulted when the local government makes the budget. After being presented with a number of projects that the county authorities are considering, these representatives vote for the ones they like best. None of these procedures are established by Beijing or regulated in the constitution.

Many provinces even have their own agendas when it comes to relations with other states. An example is Yunnan province's relationship with Myanmar. The initiative for oil and gas pipelines from Myanmar to China—adopted by the central government in 2007—originally came from the government of Yunnan. In order to win support for the project, local academics were asked to depict the pipelines as essential to national energy security. The strategy proved successful: the message got through to Beijing, and the authorities of Yunnan got what they wanted. The pipeline will end up in Yunnan's capital, Kunming. Occasionally Yunnan even defies Beijing's interests. The business community of Yunnan has major investments in Myanmar in mining, timber, and infrastructure. Local Yunnanese businesspeople have personal, ethnic, and economic ties to minority groups in Myanmar, as well as to the armed militias fighting the central government. Yunnan's priorities are thus on a collision course with those of Beijing, which attaches great importance to its relationship with the central government in Myanmar. Myanmar wants Beijing to force Yunnan to end its support for rebel groups, but Yunnan goes its own way. It is noteworthy that provinces have their own foreign policy, traditionally a concern of the state and the state alone. One definition of a state is that it has a monopoly on the country's foreign policy—and the Chinese central government somewhat surprisingly does not.

The balance of power between central and local in China is dynamic. There is a constant tug-of-war over who should control what. As we have seen, the provinces largely govern themselves, but the central government often tries to rein in local power brokers. In the 1980s, local authorities received greater freedom in economic matters under the decentralization policy called "decentralizing power and transferring profits" (*fang quan rang li*). In 1994, the central government decided local freedom was too great and introduced a number of reforms to regain power. Tax reforms, for example, subjected tax collection throughout the country to centrally determined policies, not provincial guidelines. [2]

Beijing has neither the ability nor the incentive to micromanage the provinces.

China's sheer size makes it impossible for the central government to implement all decisions effectively. To put things in perspective, three provinces have populations larger than Germany's: Guangdong, Shandong, and Henan. [3] Eight Chinese cities have more than 10 million inhabitants; ninety-three have more than 5 million. In the United States, only New York has more than 5 million inhabitants. China's biggest city, Chongqing, is home to 30 million people. If it were a country, it would be the forty-first largest in the world, and 150 countries would be smaller. [4] In 2020, six provinces will probably have gross domestic products (GDPs) of more than US$1 trillion, as large as the GDPs of Russia and Canada. [5] On this scale, many decisions simply must be made locally.

Economic freedom and responsibilities provide local authorities with greater incentive to create local economic growth. When a model or experiment proves successful in one place, others can learn from it; when it fails, central authorities need not take responsibility. Crucially, provincial governments that enjoy greater freedom are more likely to continue supporting the central leadership.

And Beijing needs the support of its provinces.

Notes

1. Zheng Yongnian, *De Facto Federalism in China: Reforms and Dynamics of Central-Local Relations* (Singapore: World Scientific, 2007).

2. Tsang Shu-ki and Cheng Yuk-shing, "China's Tax Reforms of 1994: Breakthrough or Compromise?" *Asian Survey* 34, no. 9 (1994), http://www.sktsang.com/ArchiveIII/China_tax_1994.pdf; Hwa Erh-Cheng, "Progress in Reforming China's Banks" (paper presented during the "China's Policy Reforms: Social Services, Regulation and Finance" conference, Stanford University, Stanford, California, 22–24 October 2008), http://scid.stanford.edu/group/siepr/cgibin/scid/?q=system/files/shared/Hwa_10-3-08.pdf.

3. "Communiqué of the National Bureau of Statistics of the People's Republic of China on Major Figures of the 2010 Population Census," National Bureau of Statistics of China, 29 April 2011, http://www.stats.gov.cn/english/newsandcomingevents/t20110429_402722516.htm.

4. William Antholis, "New Players on the World Stage: Chinese Provinces and Indian States," *Brookings Essay*, 22 October 2013, http://www.brookings.edu/research/essays/2013/new-players-on-the-world-stage.

5. Zhang Zhiming, "Inside the Growth Engine: A Guide to China's Regions, Provinces and Cities," HSBC Global Research, December 2010, http://www.research.hsbc.com/midas/Res/RDV?p=pdf&key=nmMuQ3lvVa&n=284797.PDF.

Myth 3

THE LEADERSHIP IS DEEPLY DIVIDED

> In contrast to the history of the Communist Party of the Soviet Union,
> the record of the Chinese Party is one of chronic factionalism, even at
> times when a dominant figure such as a Mao or a Deng was present.
> —Arthur Waldron[1]

In March 2012, a political earthquake shook China. Bo Xilai—party secretary of Chongqing, member of the Politburo, and son of one of the founders of the People's Republic—was stripped of all his party positions and arrested, accused of "serious disciplinary violations." Not only was his bright political career shattered, but his wife, Gu Kailai, was accused of poisoning and killing the British businessman Neil Heywood. Bo had been a candidate for promotion to the Politburo's Standing Committee, the small group that governs China, which was to be renewed at the Eighteenth Party Congress in the autumn of the same year.

Several top leaders in Beijing had undoubtedly wanted to get rid of him. Bo was an ambitious, charismatic, and populist politician who had violated the party's unwritten rules by promoting himself through public campaigns. He was digging his own grave. Nonetheless, for the party his downfall came at an unfortunate time, just ahead of the important party congress. China's new leadership was to be named, and the appearance of unity was crucial.

The Bo case gained huge attention both in China and abroad. Those who see the top of the Communist Party as a "Byzantine court" characterized by Machiavellian intrigues, power struggles, and dirty tricks took it as further proof of their view. There was much speculation about cracks within the elite—analytical sport for some, wishful thinking for others.

Regardless of the Bo scandal, however, there are good reasons to argue that unity within the party leadership is strong. Why?

The usual behavior of the leaders is to fall in line and follow established norms. Heads rolled during the first decades of the People's Republic, but remarkably few elite conflicts have reached the public since the 1989 protests. In the wake of that unrest, conservative leaders got the upper hand, and liberals were pushed out. Among the latter was Zhao Ziyang, the general secretary of the party. He was stripped of his post and put under house arrest because he opposed using the military to curb the protests. In recent years, there have been few serious conflicts within the party leadership; the Bo case is a rare exception. The power struggles are at times intense, especially in the run-up to the all-important party congresses. But the political game is regulated by certain rules. This was evidenced by the relatively orderly transfers of power from Deng to Jiang, Jiang to Hu Jintao, and Hu to Xi Jinping.

The leaders' attitudes also indicate elite cohesion. Disagreements do occur from case to case, but there seems to be broad agreement on the political course—that is, to continue the economic reforms initiated by Deng and, of course, to maintain the Communist Party's monopoly on power.

How should we understand the unity within the elite?

First, the leaders share identical backgrounds and socialization. When studying a picture of the members of the Politburo's Standing Committee, one might be forgiven for imagining that they are the results of a cloning project. All are men. All are dressed in dark suits, with neat ties. They all wear simple, square glasses and have the same oil-black hair, not a gray lock to be seen. They are all in their late fifties or sixties. Several are sons of former party veterans. They have different political networks, but they are all products of the party apparatus, a closed career system of more or less predetermined paths. These men have attained the top.

Second, the leadership is unified by norms, including the ideal of collective leadership. No individual—like Mao and Deng—or single faction should be allowed to dominate the party leadership. "Simply put," says Professor Zheng Yongnian, "Chinese politics was depersonified under Deng, collectivized under Jiang, and institutionalized under Hu."[2] Jiang introduced collective decision making based on consultation and compromise, whereas Hu took important steps to formalize political decision-making processes. Elite circulation is another important shared value. Deng worked to retire the old guard. He introduced a fixed retirement age of seventy (later reduced to sixty-eight) for Communist Party leaders and the principle that leaders could only serve for two five-year periods. Unlike the vast majority of the world's Communist leaders, Deng did not cling to power until he died. Being a descendant of one of the great Chinese revolutionary heroes can't hurt, but promotions are based on merit. This means that leaders must advance within the party gradually, without any serious political scratches. Those who reach the pinnacle have broad experiences, ranging from managing state-owned companies to serving as party secretaries at the provincial level, some with responsibility for more than 100 million people. Despite what nepotism does exist, the system produces rather competent leaders. Last but not least, internal discipline is an important norm, as expected in a Leninist party. Disagreements are ideally resolved behind closed doors and never aired in public. And everyone should obey the orders of his superiors, though the system is not directly authoritarian. Debate within the party leadership often gets intense prior to important political decisions, but as soon as a decision is made, everyone is expected to stand loyally behind it.

Third, the leaders are linked by common concerns. Most of all they worry that Chinese society will implode. Fear is deeply rooted within the leaders, who remember very well the riots of 1989 and the collapse of the Eastern Bloc in the early 1990s. The leadership is fully engaged in daily crisis management related to inflation, housing bubbles, corruption, environmental degradation, land disputes, and a myriad of other things. They are less concerned with developments outside China, although there are many sources of anxiety there as well. International crises can pop up suddenly and unexpectedly. China's civil war—between the Communists in Beijing and the Nationalists in Taipei—is not yet over, the Korean War has not yet formally ended, and China-Japan relations have never been normalized. The leaders are also troubled by what they perceive as an American containment strategy toward China, through military presence and alliance building in East Asia. Further, Chinese citizens are sometimes victims of persecution and abuse in countries like Indonesia and Zambia, Chinese vessels are hijacked by pirates in the Gulf of Aden, and Chinese workers may be kidnapped by rebels in Colombia or Pakistan. When the leaders wrap up their daily meetings in Zhongnanhai—a complex west of the Forbidden City that serves as Communist Party headquarters—they have many things to worry about. "Everyone knows that they are in the same boat, and that they must stand together," according to Professor Willy Lam.[3] If the ship sinks, everyone goes down with it.

Cohesion within the political elite is a prerequisite for effective and stable governance, and remaining united makes it easier for the Chinese leaders to manage the social forces that challenge the party. This is particularly important at a time when pressure on the government is building. Whether the new leaders will be able to stand together, however, is an open question.

On 22 September 2013, an intermediate people's court set up in the eastern city of Jinan found Bo Xilai guilty of bribery, abuse of power, and corruption. Bo was stripped of all his assets and sentenced to life imprisonment. The year before, his wife had been convicted of murdering Neil

Heywood and given a suspended death sentence. They learned the hard way that there are still serious consequences for testing the norms of China's political elite.

Notes

1. Arthur Waldron, "The Soviet Disease Spreads to China," *Far Eastern Economic Review* (October 2009): 27.
2. Interview with Professor Zheng Yongnian, Singapore, November 2011.
3. Interview with Professor Willy Lam, Oslo, November 2009.

Myth 4

THE COMMUNIST PARTY IS A MONOLITH

> A party is like a meat grinder; it grinds all the heads so they are mixed in a mush; and so they turn into mush heads and meatheads, all of them!
> —Henrik Ibsen's Dr. Stockman in *An Enemy of the People*

Seeing as how the leadership is not deeply divided, does that mean that the Communist Party is a monolith, as is often claimed? A popular assumption about the Communist Party is that its more than 85 million members are seamlessly united in Communist ideology. The top of the party makes all decisions and sends out directives that all members obey. Everyone marches in line—or else. The party owns all Chinese newspapers, and so no editorial runs without government knowledge and approval. The ruling party appears to be a monolith.

But this caricatured representation is not accurate and never has been.

Mao believed that there would always be either parties outside the ruling party or factions within. The chairman thus anticipated inevitable power struggles. His own reign was characterized by constant political wrangling. Times were tough, and in those days, many leaders died in prison. Since Mao, however, Chinese leaders have tended to die in bed. During the reform period the existence of different political opinions became more accepted, often even institutionalized. Today, there are obvious and significant differences within the party. No wonder—as the only legal political party with real influence, it attracts any and all who wish to engage politically. The party's millions of members naturally have different motives for joining, ranging from patriotism and political engagement to the desire for better career opportunities.

In China what we refer to as factions within the party tend rather to be stakeholders. These are social networks made up of people who share the same background, and they are not very stable. One group consists of those who came up through the Communist Party's youth league (*Tuanpai*), including former president Hu Jintao and former and current premiers Wen Jiabao and Li Keqiang. They prioritize a more equitable distribution of economic growth, the welfare of poor provinces, and environmental protection rather than overall market liberalism. Another group includes graduates of the prestigious Qinghua (Tsinghua) University in Beijing. Hu is an engineer from Qinghua and thus belongs to two interest groups. The categories are not airtight. A third group is the so-called princelings (*Taizi dang*). These are the children of revolutionary heroes, the first generation of leaders in China. President Xi Jinping and several of the new leaders belong to this group. There is also the group known as the Shanghai faction (*Shanghai bang*), which champions market deregulation and economic growth above all else. The group was strong when Jiang Zemin was president, Zeng Qinghong vice president, and Zhu Rongji prime minister, but it is less influential today.

Financial issues in particular create controversy. A close associate of former president Hu assures us that during budget negotiations, the extremes of the Communist Party find it harder to agree than do different political parties in the Norwegian parliament.[1]

Whether this is true, we do not know. But different provinces are governed according to fundamentally different models, demonstrating a great diversity of views on state and market. Take Chongqing and Guangdong. Chongqing is a city at the provincial level with more than 30 million residents. The government in Chongqing has strong control over the economy, the way one imagines Communist governments do. Half the budget is spent on public goods, such as education, social security payments, public housing, and health care. As much as 87 percent of growth takes place in the public sector. Mao quotations are broadcast to people's mobile phones and on television instead of commercial breaks. Guangdong is the exact opposite of Chongqing. Communism has left few traces in the economic policy of the province. The leaders prioritize economic growth over equal distribution. The public sector is kept as small as possible. Private companies have been the cornerstone of the economy since the 1980s, when the first foreign investors in China found their way there.[2]

Negotiations for membership in the World Trade Organization (WTO) at the end of the 1990s also revealed different agendas within the Communist Party. Opinions differed as to whether a system of free trade would be best for the country. The Chinese Ministry of Commerce, for example, wanted fewer barriers to foreign trade, while the organizations responsible for agriculture and telecommunications wanted to continue protecting these industries.

Disagreements at the top were even more obvious during the financial crisis that erupted in 2008. There were many different opinions about how to handle the crisis, particularly about how to distribute the huge stimulus package of 4,000 billion renminbi (RMB), or approximately US$650 billion. Some, believing that an even distribution nationwide was most important, emphasized building infrastructure and stimulating development in rural areas and poor provinces. Others believed that the money would provide better returns in the rich cities on the east coast: investments in these areas where industry was better developed, the thinking went, would benefit poor areas in the long term. The various camps debated this topic in editorials in national newspapers, a phenomenon as unusual as it is interesting. The fact that such different views were allowed to surface shows that disagreements reached high up in the party hierarchy. The stimulus package was, in the end, a compromise, a mix of support for rural areas and export-driven industry in east coast cities. State-owned enterprises were downsized—and bailed out. All factions won support for some of their pet causes.

This is how much of Chinese policy is made. Within the elite, coalitions are formed on a case-to-case basis, often crossing the borders of factions. Political decision making in China is consensus based and very complex. A wide variety of interest groups—the military, state-owned enterprises, and provincial governments, to name a few—work hard for their causes and political priorities. Despite political disagreements, everyone in the leadership agrees on the top political goal: to retain power. Disagreements—and they are often great—are about the best way to reach that goal. The elite have agreed to disagree, and they also agree on the rules for handling these differences.

Notes

1. Interview (name withheld) in Oslo, May 2010.

2. For more on the Chongqing and Guangdong models, see "One or Two Chinese Models?" European Council on Foreign Relations, November 2011, http://www.ecfr.eu/page/-/China_Analysis_One_or_two_Chinese_models_ November2011.pdf; Carolyn Cartier and Luigi Tomba, "Chapter 2: Symbolic Cities and the 'Cake Debate,'" *China Story Yearbook 2012: Red Rising, Red Eclipse.* Canberra: Australian National University, http://www.thechinastory. org/yearbooks/yearbook-2012/chapter-2-symbolic-cities-and-the-cake-debate.

Myth 5

THE MILITARY IS GAINING POLITICAL INFLUENCE

No doubt, the generals have hijacked the foreign policy!
—Troubled Western military attaché in Beijing[1]

In June 2010, in the wake of the Obama administration's announcement of a major arms sale to Taiwan, the Chinese government canceled a planned visit by US secretary of defense Robert M. Gates to Beijing. Western observers claimed that the "hawks" in the officer corps, unconcerned with the wishes of civil authorities, had decided that the meeting should not take place. On 11 January 2011, China's newest fighter aircraft with stealth technology (type J-20) took wing for the first time, on a day when Gates happened to be meeting with then president Hu Jintao in Beijing. The Chinese military leaders reportedly had not informed their chief about the test flight—an embarrassment for Hu. Similarly, the officers had apparently acted on their own initiative when they shot down one of China's own satellites in 2007—signaling their ability to pick American satellites from the sky as well. That same year, some PLA officers prevented the American aircraft carrier *Kitty Hawk* from making Hong Kong a port of call.

Because of such events, some China watchers believe that the military is gaining political influence.

In addition, colorful statements by military officers run counter to the country's official doctrine, which emphasizes China's "peaceful development" and a "harmonious world." Such bold contrariness is taken to indicate the officers' growing influence and political ambitions. According to General Liu Yuan, political commissar of the Academy of Military Science, an attack against Taiwan would "blot out the sky and cover up the earth."[2] Yang Yi, a naval officer at the Defense University, warns against assuming that China's rhetoric about "peaceful development" means that the country will never resort to force to secure its interests.[3] Colonel Dai Xu, author and commentator on strategic issues, informs us that "if the United States can light a fire in China's backyard, we can also light a fire in their backyard."[4] Such statements make China watchers choke on their green tea.

However, while the government allows officers at military educational institutions to vent their nationalist views, members of the Central Military Commission, China's top military leadership, rarely make such statements. Their public utterances adhere to the party line. Anything else would be a violation of their strict disciplinary codes—and would be career suicide. In some cases, officers down in the ranks have undoubtedly acted according to their own will. But this is more a result of poor information sharing and coordination than a desire to independently push foreign policy in a particular direction. Lack of coordination occurs primarily between the military and the Ministry of Foreign Affairs.

The reality is that the Chinese officer corps has gradually had its political wings clipped. It now has less political influence than before.

PLA officers have been pushed out of key positions in the party since the days of Mao and Deng, who were both politicians and officers; civilians dominate today's leadership. It was Deng who ordered the officers to stay away from politics and focus instead on building a professional military force. Since then, the number of military officers in the party's major organs has fallen dramatically. None of the members of the Politburo's Standing Committee—China's de facto top leadership—can boast a single day of operational military experience. The Politburo has not appointed a single officer to its Standing Committee since the party congress in 1992. At the end of the Cultural Revolution only fifteen years earlier, more than half of committee members were officers. The Politburo appointed in November 2012 had only 2 generals among its 25 members, while 65 officers were among the 371 selected members of the Central Committee. The only key body with heavy military representation is the Central Military Commission. Among the eleven members are ten generals, but the commission's chairman is a civilian, Xi Jinping. Somewhat ironically, Xi's wife, China's "First Lady" Peng Liyuan, holds the rank of major general in the PLA and is the country's highest-profile military person (though the title is an artistic rather than a military one).

Not only is the PLA poorly represented at the highest levels of government, but it is also given less priority than the People's Armed Police. It is this paramilitary police force, and not the PLA, that ensures the party's grip on power. The fact that army tanks were used against protesters during the massacre around Tiananmen Square in the spring of 1989 weakened the standing of—and morale within—the armed forces. The thankless task of ensuring internal security was transferred to the police in 1993. It was the People's Armed Police that handled the riots in Tibet's capital, Lhasa, in 2008 and in the Uyghur-dominated city of Urumqi in 2009. As social unrest grows, the paramilitary force has become more important and has thus been allocated more resources. In 2011, the National People's Congress adopted a budget for maintenance of internal order that exceeded the official defense budget for the first time.[5]

The military has become far more dependent on financial allocations from the civil authorities. This has strengthened civilian control over the military. Under Deng the military owned numerous industrial enterprises, and military units were largely self-sufficient. Thus the government kept defense spending down. The military's private business activities exploded in the 1980s, and a decade later the military controlled more than twenty thousand firms, which ranged from agriculture and mining via electronics to tourism and arms exports. This booming business activity ended in 1998 when Jiang forbade military officials from engaging in industrial enterprises and trade. He was worried that officers had become more concerned with their business empires than national security. Most of the officers accepted the prohibition, albeit reluctantly. To compensate for the lost income, the defense budget has skyrocketed. This has given the civilian government a powerful tool to ensure that officers remain satisfied and loyal.

Of course, the officers are among those setting the agenda when foreign policy is formulated. In China's relations with India, countries in Southeast and Central Asia, and the United States, military power is an instrument. Military leaders are accordingly included in the consultation process—and their advice is listened to. But, in the words of Mao, "The Party commands the gun, and the gun must never be allowed to command the Party." This mantra is still valid today—to a far greater extent than it was during the chairman's reign.

Notes

1. Interview (name withheld), Beijing, May 2010.

2. Cited in Russell Hsiao, "Hu Confers Hardliner Top Military Rank," *China Brief* 9, no. 15 (23 July 2009), http://www.jamestown.org/single/?no_cache=1&tx_ttnews%5Btt_news%5D=35306.

3. Quoted in Willy Lam, "PLA's 'Absolute Loyalty' to the Party in Doubt," *China Brief* 9, no. 9 (30 April 2009), http://www.jamestown.org/single/?no_cache=1&tx_ttnews%5Btt_news%5D=34920.

    4. "China PLA Officer Urges Challenging U.S. Dominance," Reuters, 28 February 2010, http://www.reuters.com/article/2010/03/01/us-china-usa-military-exclusive-idUSTRE6200P620100301.

    5. See, e.g., "Update 2—China Internal Security Spending Jumps Past Army Budget," Reuters, 5 March 2011, http://www.reuters.com/article/2011/03/05/china-unrest-idUSTOE72400920110305.

Myth 6

THE COMMUNIST REGIME LACKS LEGITIMACY

Simply put, legitimate governance means that people think it is okay for those in power to have power. Without legitimacy, leaders have a nasty tendency to resort to dirty tricks and brute force to cling to power. They might be motivated by true ideological conviction, or they might simply love the wealth and status power confers. Eventually, regimes stripped of legitimacy tend to fall. This was the case during the Arab Spring, when discontented masses overthrew their dictators. Thorbjørn Jagland, secretary-general of the Council of Europe and chairman of the Nobel Committee, referred to the "wall between the Communist Party and the people of China"[1] in a 2012 article in the Norwegian daily *Aftenposten*. Its headline, "New Walls Will Fall," demonstrated his belief that the rulers in Beijing would soon be history—perhaps even by the end of the year, he suggested.

Western observers often take the Communist Party's lack of legitimacy for granted, and there are undoubtedly many disgruntled Chinese. The Ministry of Public Security announced the annual number of "mass incidents"—protests, riots, and other forms of social unrest—until 2005, when the figure reached eighty-seven thousand.[2] Then the government reporting disappeared, at least from public view. The think tank CASS estimates that the number passed 90,000 the following year, while Professor Sun Liping at the Qinghua University claimed in 2010 that China sees as many as 180,000 such incidents every year.[3] If we are to believe these figures, then there are around five hundred protests, demonstrations, and riots in China every day. Most of these arise from local conflicts between employers and employees, as well as local authorities' aggressive expropriation of land—also known as landgrabs.[4]

The discontent is thus rarely directed at the authorities in Beijing—and there is little evidence that the regime is facing a crisis of legitimacy.

In the Pew Global Attitudes Project for 2010, the majority of Chinese responded that they were satisfied with their leaders.[5] As many as 87 percent were satisfied with the overall development of China, and the proportion of satisfied people has been stable at over 80 percent in recent years. In addition, 66 percent responded that they had experienced improvement in their lives over the past five years, 74 percent indicated that they were optimistic about the coming five years, and 91 percent expressed satisfaction with China's economy. The number of Chinese who responded that they were happy with the development of both the nation and the economy was unusually high (and significantly higher than the number of Americans and Europeans who were satisfied).

Bruce Gilley, a specialist on the comparative politics of China and Asia, classifies China as a country in which the government had "high legitimacy" at the beginning of the twenty-first century. He ranks China thirteenth in government legitimacy out of a total of seventy-two states. In Asia, only the government of Taiwan had greater support among its own population, he concludes.[6] He bases his conclusion on data measuring both attitudes (answers to questions about trust, support, and satisfaction with the government) and behavior (tax payments, voter turnout, political violence, demonstrations, and so forth). In authoritarian regimes, behavioral indicators have to be given more weight, since people are less likely to respond honestly about government legitimacy. Gilley found that Chinese authorities had the least support in rural and remote provinces, far away from the center of power. The weaker support in these areas was expressed in lower voter turnout and less willingness to pay taxes.[7]

The Communist Party's support among the Chinese can be attributed to several factors—all of which reflect the leadership's ability to govern.

First, the party ensures order and stability at home. There are obvious parallels between the ways in which people judge today's leaders and the ways they judged the ancient emperors, according to political scientist Vivienne Shue at Oxford University.[8] Stability (*wending*) has always been a prerequisite for both security and economic growth, which in turn was necessary to secure the resources needed for expanding the empire's influence. The fact that today's Chinese also value stability is confirmed by both Western and Chinese opinion polls. In 2003, the Roper Survey asked a sample of Chinese to rank a list of social values. The majority ranked stability second. In other states, stability ranked twenty-third on average.[9] In 2010, the Chinese Global Poll Center conducted a telephone survey in which 68.9 percent responded that stability should be the top priority for Chinese leaders. As many as 36.5 percent mentioned the Soviet Union's 1991 collapse as a horror scenario for China. [10]

Moreover, the party can claim credit for solid progress under its leadership. The ancient Chinese interpreted progress for the empire as a sign that the emperor was skilled; recessions were seen as sure signs that he was unfit. Rebellion was just, according to the Confucian ideology, to remove the incompetent emperor. The current leadership is also judged on its achievements. Under the party's leadership, the Chinese have experienced extraordinary economic growth. Although this growth has been unevenly distributed, most people have experienced progress. More and more Chinese have the chance not just to scrape by but to realize themselves—for example, to go on vacation or study abroad. These opportunities would have been unthinkable a few years back.

Last but not least, there is reason to argue that the nation's pride has been restored under the Communist Party's rule. In its own version of history, the party brought order after China had been humiliated by occupation, internal strife, and civil war—known as the "Century of Humiliation" among the Chinese. Furthermore, the leadership in Beijing cultivates "the nation's return" through symbol-laden and grandiose celebrations, such as the Olympics in Beijing in 2008 and the sixtieth anniversary of the People's Republic the following year. The country's technological progress is marked with status symbols like the space program and aircraft carriers. And party leaders seek to act with confidence on the international stage—and avoid at all costs appearing soft on the United States, the European Union countries, and Japan.

Contrary to Jagland's claims, then, there is ample reason to believe that many Chinese support the Communist Party. The leaders in Beijing must, however, be careful not to take the people's support for granted. The fact that many people support the party does not mean that the Chinese are blind to its weaknesses. Legitimacy must be reproduced continually and can vanish like dew before the sun. Especially dangerous for the party are corruption and nepotism, which exist at all levels of the political system right up to the top. Political elite families with economic interests have been unflatteringly nicknamed "the red nobility." There is in Chinese political culture a traditional distaste for corruption and nepotism that has hastened the collapse of several dynasties. Corruption and nepotism were also important reasons why the Chinese turned against the nationalist party Guomindang, making possible the success of the Communist Party. [11]

Notes

1. Thorbjørn Jagland, "Nye murer vil falle," *Aftenposten*, 2 January 2012, http://www.aftenposten.no/meninger/kronikker/Nye-murer-vil-falle-6731834. html.

2. See, e.g., Irene Wang, "Incidents of Social Unrest Hit 87,000 in 2005," *South China Morning Post*, 20 January 2006.

3. Will Freeman, "The Accuracy of China's 'Mass Incidents,'" *Financial Times*, 2 March 2010, http://www.ft.com/cms/s/0/9ee6fa64-25b5-11df-9bd3-00144feab49a.html#axzz1raquJDvr.

4. For an analysis of the causes of mass incidents, see Tong Yanqi and Lei Shaohua, "Large-Scale Mass Incidents in China," EAI Background Brief 520, 15 April 2010, http://www.eai.nus.edu.sg/BB520.pdf.

5. "22-Nation Pew Global Attitudes Survey," Pew Global Attitudes Project, 17 June 2010, http://www.pewglobal.org/files/2011/04/Pew-Global-Attitudes-Spring-2010-Report2.pdf.

6. Bruce Gilley, "The Meaning and Measure of State Legitimacy: Results for 72 Countries," *European Journal of Political Research* 45, no. 3 (2006): 499–525.

7. Other studies from the same period draw similar conclusions; see Jie Chen, *Popular Political Support in Rural China* (Washington, DC: Woodrow Wilson Center Press, 2004); Zhengxu Wang, "Political Trust in China: Forms and Causes," in *Legitimacy: Ambiguities of Political Success or Failure in East and Southeast Asia*, ed. Lynn White (Singapore: World Scientific, 2005).

8. Vivienne Shue, "Legitimacy Crisis in China?" in *Chinese Politics: State, Society, and the Market*, ed. Peter Hays Gries and Stanley Rosen (New York: Routledge, 2010), 46–51.

9. Cited in Joshua Cooper Ramo, *The Beijing Consensus* (London: Foreign Policy Centre, 2004).

10. *Beijing Global Times*, 1 November 2010.

11. See, e.g., "'Princelings' in China Use Family Ties to Gain Riches," *New York Times*, 17 May 2012, http://www.nytimes.com/2012/05/18/world/asia/china-princelings-using-family-ties-to-gain-riches.html; Shue, "Legitimacy Crisis in China?" 52–53.

Myth 7

THE FALUN GONG IS AN APOLITICAL MOVEMENT PERSECUTED FOR ITS RELIGIOUS BELIEFS

> Falun Gong has no political agenda or political aims whatsoever.
> —Falun Dafa (Falun Gong) in Europe[1]

In April 1999, around ten thousand members of the movement Falun Gong gathered outside Zhongnanhai near Tiananmen Square, where they did *qigong* (deep-breathing) exercises and demanded to speak with government representatives. The demonstration caught the authorities completely by surprise and caused great unease within the leadership. The movement was subsequently banned and many of its followers arrested. According to human rights organizations, thousands have since been persecuted for belonging to the Falun Gong.[2]

Proponents of the Falun Gong claim that the movement is peaceful and based on spiritual practice, with no formal organization. The US-based leader of Falun Gong, Li Hongzhi, stresses that the movement is apolitical and based on *qigong*, breathing exercises, and meditation. The movement's slogan is "Truth, Compassion, and Tolerance." Many Western human rights activists accept the Falun Gong's official representation of itself.

Falun Gong adherents are undoubtedly restricted in their religious practices, especially since 1999. It has also been well documented that they are persecuted, arrested, tortured, and sent to camps for so-called reeducation through labor—administrative detention without trial.

From the outside, it may seem illogical to persecute people simply because they practice meditation and *qigong*; indeed, this is not why

Falun Gong is banned. The reason is complex and unrelated in any significant way to religious practice.

Despite its supporters' claims to the contrary, Falun Gong does have a clear political agenda. The 1999 demonstration took place outside Zhongnanhai, the national headquarters of the Chinese Communist Party and government. It is difficult to interpret this as anything other than a clear political message addressed to the central government. The fact that the demonstration took place exactly ten years after the student demonstrations on Tiananmen Square began in April 1989 is also noteworthy. The websites of the Falun Gong voice strong criticism of the Communist Party, claiming, among other things, that the party is an evil cult that harms mankind (interestingly, the party says the same thing about the Falun Gong) and does everything it can to undermine the moral basis of the Chinese nation. The book *Nine Commentaries on the Communist Party—a Book That Is Disintegrating the Communist Party* has been published in many languages by the Epoch Group, which is associated with the Falun Gong. It is hard to see how the Falun Gong could claim to be apolitical after seeking in early 2000 to replace the portrait of Mao on Tiananmen Square with a portrait of Li Hongzhi and the Chinese flags with Buddhist flags.[3] Even though many practitioners probably have scant interest in politics, the movement as a whole has a clearly articulated political agenda.

Organizations outside official structures are not allowed in China. The Falun Gong claims that it is not an organization, but this is dubious. Official figures, also quoted on Falun Gong's websites, show that prior to the demonstration in 1999, the Falun Gong had between 70 and 100 million followers—about the same number as the Communist Party. Many of these members held high positions in the party and the military.[4] Before the movement was banned, it had a hierarchical organization much like the party's: members belonged to local chapters that followed guidelines from the level above, all the way up to the central level.[5] Ten thousand of these members were able to coordinate and plan the campaign of 1999. What's more, they managed to keep the plans secret from the authorities, despite China's highly developed security apparatus. When the thousands of protesters retreated, not a single piece of garbage was left behind. Anyone who has been to China knows that people there often simply throw garbage onto the street; even a few picnickers are likely to leave a mess behind. This was a disciplined bunch.

Is this discipline cultish? Chinese authorities and Western researchers have argued that it is.[6] There is evidence that Li Hongzhi requires total faith from his followers. On topics essential to Falun Gong, such as *qigong* and philosophy, members may read only books from an official list. Members are also discouraged from having contact with people outside the movement. Master Li stresses that his teachings are not open to interpretation.[7]

Followers are in some cases dissuaded from receiving life-sustaining medical treatment. According to Chinese authorities, 1,400 Falun Gong members have died as a result of this and other hazardous practices.[8]

Ask a Falun Gong member about this, and she will say that Li has never banned medical treatment. But Li's writings describe disease as a test of faith and taking medication or getting treatment as a sign that one's faith is weak. Consequently many people, including children, do not receive appropriate medical treatment.[9]

The fact that this organization has religious characteristics is a third reason why the Communist Party cannot accept it—not because of the members' religious practices, as the government has a very pragmatic view of religion and will allow for most actions as long as they do not undermine the government, but because the movement is so well organized. Authorities fear that religious organizations have even greater control over their members than do other types of organizations, diverting loyalty from the Communist Party. A powerful religious organization with no relation to the party-state is therefore alarming and totally unacceptable.

Official fear of religious movements has deep roots in Chinese history. Major religious movements have repeatedly contributed to or precipitated the overthrow of dynasties, so ruling regimes have good reason to feel threatened. An example from ancient history is the Daoist (Taoist) Yellow Turban Movement, which attempted to overthrow the Han Dynasty in 186 BCE. In 1368, the Buddhist White Lotus Movement was essential to the fall of the Mongol Yuan Dynasty. China's last dynasty, the Qing, fell in 1911 after several religious rebellions—a comeback of the White Lotus, the Taiping Rebellion (whose leader claimed to be the younger brother of Jesus Christ), and a number of Muslim uprisings. The members of these movements, which we would call cults today, had been so brainwashed by their charismatic leaders that many gladly died for their causes. In light of this history, the government can't feel good about the strong control Falun Gong seems to exert over its supporters.

The image of the Falun Gong as a meditative movement without formal organization or political agenda is a myth successfully created by the Falun Gong itself. It has succeeded in spreading this myth to the West in pursuit of international support. The idea that such a peaceful movement is prohibited for no apparent reason fits well into Western notions of a Chinese government that does little except suppress its citizens, quite randomly and by all means available. Take a look at the reality, and the suppression of this well-organized movement—with strong control of its members and a clear agenda to topple the Communist Party of China—

makes much more sense. An explanation for why the Falun Gong is persecuted, however, is in no way a defense of such persecution.

Notes

1. "Falun Gong Has No Political Agenda," Clear Harmony, 28 August 2002, http://www.clearharmony.net/articles/200209/7267.html.

2. See, e.g., "China: Falun Gong Practitioner Missing in China," Amnesty International, 10 May 2010, http://www.amnesty.org/en/library/asset/ASA17/021/2010/en/df9220a8-a89f-4d86-93a8-28ed2f15e915/asa170212010en.html.

3. Elizabeth J. Perry, *Challenging the Mandate of Heaven* (New York: M. E. Sharpe, 2002), xv–xxv.

4. Ibid.

5. Ibid.

6. See, e.g., Patsy Rahn, "The Falun Gong: Behind the Headlines," *Cultic Studies Journal* 17, no. 1 (2000): 168–86.

7. Ibid.

8. "What Are the Main Arguments of Falun Gong? Why Is It Deemed a Cult (Heresy)?" *Facts*, 13 November 2007, http://www.facts.org.cn/QandA/200711/t69238.htm.

9. See, e.g., Maria Hsia Chang, *Falun Gong: The End of Days* (New Haven, CT: Yale University Press, 2004), 101–2; Rahn, "The Falun Gong: Behind the Headlines."

Myth 8

CHINESE MEDIA IS MERELY A MOUTHPIECE OF THE COMMUNIST PARTY

> The [Chinese Communist Party]'s strict control of the media and the Internet has made China's broken society into a pressure cooker with no vents.
> —Wu Yisan, Independent Chinese Pen Center, Hong Kong [1]

There is no independent press in China, they say, since all Chinese media houses are owned by the party-state. The editor in chief of *People's Daily*, one of China's biggest newspapers, is a member of the Communist Party's Central Committee, and the media is the mouthpiece of the government and its policies. All the news is good; problems are reported only when the government is about to solve them—or has at least acknowledged them. Chinese reporters are said to be little more than government stenographers. Chinese media thus provide the antithesis of independent, investigative reporting—in many people's opinion.

Every year Reporters without Borders ranks the world's countries according to freedom of the press. In 2010 China placed 171 out of 178, in large part because all media is owned by the state and journalists risk arrest when they write. Thirty-one Chinese journalists and seventy Chinese netizens are in prison because of their statements, according to the organization. [2] One of them is the reporter Shi Tao, who is serving a ten-year sentence for leaking the authorities' guidelines for media coverage of the fifteenth anniversary of the massacre around Tiananmen Square.

The government regularly creates such guidelines for reporters. During the National People's Congress in 2012, journalists were sent a long list of topics not to be mentioned, ranging from the blossoming of the rare *youtan pulou* flower to a female district attorney driving a luxury car. Negative stories were not to appear on the front page.[3]

Yet it is not the case that Chinese reporters all live in fear of arrest; nor do newspapers and TV news broadcasts exclusively report how brilliantly everything is going in China. Today the role of the Chinese media is far more complex, and the average Chinese has access to more information, and more critical information, than before.

Chinese media have been run according to market principles since the 1990s, even though media houses are owned by the Communist Party. The media houses have been told to make profits as the government cuts subsidies. Therefore editors need high ratings and high circulation, which pure propaganda does not generate. Many editors have chosen a road without risks, focusing on entertainment and celebrity news. But some have chosen a more difficult route: investigative and critical reporting. Topics previously absent from the Chinese media—like environmental problems, corruption, the legal system, the health system, and violation of constitutional rights—are daily fare for Chinese readers and viewers today.

In some cases media show the government in a very unfavorable light and even defy government guidelines. Mainland newspapers' coverage of the disastrous train accident in Wenzhou in July 2011 was tantamount to that of Hong Kong newspapers, which enjoy a significantly higher degree of freedom.[4] The authorities, harshly criticized for their handling of the accident, quickly prohibited the media from conveying anything but official information. The prohibition was not observed, however—even the state news agency Xinhua printed critical questions. After the accident Chinese newspapers uncovered many transgressions in the top echelon of the Ministry of Railways, ranging from serious corruption to intimate missteps: then minister of railways Liu Zhijun was revealed to have eighteen mistresses. Eighteen is a lucky number in China because it sounds like "becoming rich," but for Liu fortune was not to last.

Another example of boldness is *Xinjing Bao*'s story of eighteen petitioners who were admitted to psychiatric hospitals and forced to take antipsychotic medication after they attempted to deliver their petitions to the government of Shandong province. This violation of civil rights was scandalous even in China.

The ownership structure of the newspapers explains how certain political stories make it into print. All Chinese media houses are owned by the government, but by government at different levels. Newspapers owned by the central government are not afraid to criticize anything or anyone below that level; newspapers owned by provincial authorities can dare to criticize circumstances up to the county level; and so on. Few, if any, dare to criticize the central government directly. It is also easier for newspapers to do investigative reporting elsewhere in the country—somewhere that will not affect their owners. Such cross-regional reporting is officially forbidden but done anyway.

A common method of describing sensitive issues is through an individual's story, as described by Elin Sæther in a PhD dissertation on the critical press in China.[5] Reporters use individuals and their difficult situations to reveal—more or less explicitly—underlying social problems. One of the best-known examples of reporting with political consequences is the case of twenty-seven-year-old Sun Zhigang, a migrant worker in Guangzhou in southern China. In March 2003 Sun was arrested for not carrying an ID and taken to a detention center to be sent to his home village. Soon after arriving at the center, he died from injuries sustained during a beating. The story was first reported in a local newspaper and then picked up by national ones. The case went straight to the top of the Communist Party. After three months of media brouhaha, then prime minister Wen Jiabao announced the abolition of detention centers.

One reason the authorities accept more real reporting today is that it is an important source of information for them. In the absence of political elections and credible polls, local investigative reporting provides useful insights. According to Sæther, the authorities systematically monitor local newspapers and Internet forums. This gives them a chance to handle problems before they cause social unrest. The authorities have in some cases become so "hyperresponsive" to the opinions of the population that they make decisions based more on emotion than professional acumen—in much the way Western politicians respond to news stories, perhaps.

Of course, when sensitive issues are made public on the Internet, official media houses are also forced to report them. When the senseless use of fireworks during the New Year's celebration in 2009 caused a fire in the main building of China Central Television (CCTV), known as "big underpants" (da kucha), information on the fire was conspicuously absent from CCTV's news broadcasts. The lack of reporting appeared increasingly ridiculous as more and more pictures and videos—taken on mobile phones—were posted online, and CCTV eventually reported the news with a video on its website.

The government risks losing all credibility if censorship becomes too obvious—if it covers up cases that become public regardless. The world's largest online population and its increasing contact with other countries will present the government with ballooning challenges.

Notes

1. Wu Yisan, "Internet Censorship in China," *Epoch Times*, 10 November 2006, http://www.theepochtimes.com/news/6-11-10/47995.html.

2. "World Report—China," Reporters without Borders, 29 August 2011, http://en.rsf.org/report-china,57.html.

3. "Liang hui qijian wangluo shencha zhiyi zhou zhiling" [Instructions for the Censorship during the First Week of the Two Sessions], *Boxun*, 7 March 2010, http://boxun.com/news/gb/china/2010/03/201003071605.shtml.

4. Qian Gang, "China's Reporters Push the Boundaries," *Wall Street Journal*, 3 August 2011, http://online.wsj.com/article/ SB10001424053111903520204576483811379409124.html.

5. Elin Sæther, "The Conditional Autonomy of the Critical Press in China" (PhD diss., University of Oslo, 2008).

Part II

The People

Myth 9

CHINESE CULTURE IS INCOMPATIBLE WITH DEMOCRACY

Both the Chinese government and some Western scholars argue that a Western-style democracy could not work in China. Democracy has never been part of Chinese culture, they say, further pointing out that the Chinese word for democracy, *minzhu*, which can be translated as "rule of the people," is not rooted in the country's political tradition and philosophy. Chinese history is full of revolutions, but these were often peasant rebellions that did not fundamentally change the style of government. One authoritarian dynasty replaced another.

Some submit that democracy is incompatible with Confucian teachings emphasizing harmony and submission. Competition between different political parties and broad political participation are completely alien concepts. "'Confucian democracy' is clearly a contradiction in terms," claimed the American political scientist Samuel P. Huntington.[1] In the West, thinkers who planted ideas about democracy, like François-Marie Arouet Voltaire and Jean-Jacques Rousseau, challenged old authoritarian and patriarchal dogmas. These ideas inspired both the American Revolutionary War and the French Revolution. But in China, Confucian philosophy was never challenged, and the Chinese remained trapped within an undemocratic political culture, according to Huntington.[2]

Others claim that the Chinese people are not sufficiently mature for democracy, a view advocated in the country's state-owned newspapers on a weekly basis. Vote buying is highlighted as a major problem. The poor Chinese are so poor that it would be too easy to buy their votes; the rich are so rich that they could easily buy votes and establish an oligarchy, argue proponents of the government. The popular blogger Han Han even claims that it is too soon to implement democracy in China because the

Chinese people's "quality" (*suzhi*)—taking into account everything from education to manners—has not attained the level at which democratic government can function.

Finally, there are those who think that Western democracy is unsuitable because it would create chaos (*luan*). There are elections at the local level. Since 1988, the party has conducted a vast experiment with "grassroots democracy," carrying out as many as 1 million elections in six hundred thousand villages; 3 million local representatives have been elected.[3] At the national level, however, the authorities keep holding back. "We have made a solemn declaration that we will not employ a system of multiple parties holding office in rotation," stated Wu Bangguo—at that time China's second most powerful man—during his speech to the National People's Congress in March 2011. He kept warning from the pulpit that with such a system, "it is possible that the state could sink into the abyss of internal disorder."[4] "If China imitates the West's multiparty parliamentary democratic system, it could repeat the chaotic and turbulent history of the 'Cultural Revolution' when factions sprang up everywhere," warned the state-controlled Xinhua news agency during the celebration of the Communist Party's ninetieth anniversary the same year.[5] Instead, the party calls for "democracy with Chinese characteristics," which is a "consultative democracy." In practice, this means continued authoritarian party leadership, with a smattering of elections within the party and more consultation with various interest groups on important matters.

Yet the claim that Chinese culture is incompatible with real democracy is highly questionable.

For one thing, China's democracy movement has been around for more than a century, surviving numerous setbacks. The author Liang Qichao was among the first to champion democracy in China. In 1895, he organized the first protest demanding that the Qing rulers give the people the right to political participation in Beijing. He translated the books of Rousseau, Thomas Hobbes, John Locke, David Hume, Jeremy Bentham, and other Western political philosophers into Chinese and published his own articles, which were eagerly read by Chinese intellectuals. In the wake of the Qing Dynasty's fall in 1911, several political parties were established. The first—and so far only—free parliamentary election in China's history took place between December 1912 and February 1913. As many as three hundred parties and organizations competed for votes. Less than 1 percent of the Chinese were entitled to vote, due to strict requirements related to gender, property, and literacy. Still, the election was an important democratic experience. The Nationalist Party (Guomindang) won the election. From the last years of the Qing Dynasty to the early days of the Communist era, elections were quite frequently held at the local, provincial, and national levels. In an excellent PhD study, Joshua Hill shows that these elections had a profound impact on the political consciousness of the Chinese.[6]

The call for democracy carried out by Liang Qichao and other intellectuals must also be seen in the light of the national liberation struggle at that time. Chen Duxiu and the students behind the May Fourth Movement, formed in 1919, demanded that "Mr. Confucius" give way to "Mr. Democracy" and "Mr. Science." Democracy was seen as a lifeline for China—a continuation of the "self-strengthening movement" of the late nineteenth century.

The idea of democracy survived even Mao Zedong, and from 1978 to 1979 the wall west of the Forbidden City became known as the "Democracy Wall." On this wall anyone could post ideas related to democracy and political liberalization. This was tolerated by the authorities, who experimented with various political reforms throughout the 1980s. In 1989, liberalization came to a sudden stop in Tiananmen Square, but not even this massacre crushed the democracy movement. Charter 08 was published on 10 December 2008, the sixtieth anniversary of the UN Declaration of Human Rights. At the outset, 303 Chinese intellectuals signed this petition, and many more followed suit. It demanded that the Chinese government improve the human rights situation and loosen the party's monopoly on power. Nobel Peace Prize laureate Liu Xiaobo, identified by the authorities as the troublemaker behind the petition, was arrested and sentenced to eleven years in prison for having "initiated subversion of state power."

Taiwan's population is Chinese, with the same Confucian heritage as people in mainland China, and it has experienced successful democratic development. It seems hard to argue, then, that democracy is fundamentally incompatible with Chinese culture. For a long time only one party was allowed: the Guomindang. Dissidents were suppressed, and Chiang Kai-shek and later his son, Chiang Ching-kuo, reigned as presidents for life. In 1986, however, the latter allowed the creation of several parties, and the first election was held—albeit within the framework of the Guomindang-dominated state. In 1996, Taiwan held its first free presidential election, and in 2000 the oppositional Democratic Progress Party took power.

There is reason to be optimistic about the spirit of democracy in mainland China too. The population has a strong awareness of justice, if not necessarily of democracy as such. The fact that China sees so many protests against corruption and other abuses of power every year—even in rural areas[7]—reflects a sort of natural democratic urge. In 2011, the villagers of Wukan in Guangdong province rebelled against corrupt local party officials who had confiscated land without offering proper compensation. The unpopular representatives of the Communist regime were literally thrown out of Wukan. The following year, more than 6,500 of its inhabitants—85 percent—voted in the election of a new village council. The voting was secret, and an independent council oversaw the election process. Despite government censorship, word got out. Several other villages have tried to follow Wukan's example.

China is a one-party state that has never been a democracy. Fear of chaos there is undoubtedly real, not only among the leaders but also among the people, who have experienced invasions, upheavals, wars, and extreme political campaigns between the mid-nineteenth century and the present day. Many even perceive the rapid developments in mainland China since 1978 as chaotic and unpredictable. But Chinese culture is not fundamentally incompatible with democracy. Early democratic movements, the example of Taiwan, and the ideas coming out of the mainland today demonstrate a vibrant democratic potential. It could be realized on the mainland within the framework of a controlled reform of the one-party system or in a way similar to the experience of Taiwan—or maybe there will be no real regime change in the near future.

Notes

1. Samuel P. Huntington, *The Third Wave* (Norman: University of Oklahoma Press, 1991), 307.

2. Ibid.

3. Kerry Brown, *Ballot Box China: Grassroots Democracy in the Final Major One-Party State* (London: Z Books, 2011).

4. "Chinese Leader Rules Out Democracy," BBC News, 11 March 2011, http://www.bbc.co.uk/news/world-asia-pacific-12697997.

5. "China Media: Multi-party System Would Bring Chaos," *Sino Daily*, 2 July 2011, http://www.sinodaily.com/reports/China_media_multi-party_system_would_bring_chaos_999.html.

6. Joshua Hill, "Voting as a Rite: A History of Elections in Twentieth Century China" (unpublished PhD diss., Harvard University, 2011).

7. Kevin J. O'Brien and Li Lianjiang, *Rightful Resistance in Rural China* (Cambridge: Cambridge University Press, 2006).

Myth 10

CHINESE HAVE NO MANNERS

We Westerners tend to be startled by the very direct questions we get from Chinese people. "How old are you?" "How much do you earn?" "How much money do your father and husband make?" "How much did you pay for your coat?" "Are you married?" And then, "What? You're actually married? You, with all those hideous freckles?" If you are married but childless, do not be surprised if an explanation is demanded. If you're wearing a new sweater, a Chinese acquaintance might exclaim, "Now, that's ugly!" If you meet her again, after spending a few weeks eating China's delicious food, the first thing she says might be, "Wow, you have put on some weight, haven't you!"

Visitors are often intimidated or offended by these personal and direct questions and comments, made just a few minutes into a first conversation.

Foreigners in China are stared and pointed at. One quickly discovers that the Chinese have few taboos about bodily noises. Air is discharged loudly through all channels. Phlegm is spat out, after much loud hawking and grunting, in crowded streets, in restaurants, in stores, and even on planes. "Thank you" and "excuse me" are rarely heard. Many Chinese approaching a line they think is too long in a shop or a ticket office will simply walk to the front. Boarding a crowded bus takes courage and alertness. Purse straps, cell phones, and glasses bounce off the walls, and bruises are common. Once on the packed bus, people shout at each other as if they were on a deserted mountaintop, with no regard for other passengers. Pregnant women and the elderly must fend for themselves.

Service in China is often lamentable, especially from public servants, police officers, bank employees, and the like. If you arrive at a post office fifteen minutes before the two-hour lunch break, you might be in for it: "Ah! Now I'll only have time for a forty-five minute nap!"

Chinese authorities know that Westerners are sometimes surprised by Chinese manners. In October 2013 China's National Tourism Administration issued a sixty-four-page book, complete with illustrations, advising Chinese how to behave when traveling outside China. The book advises Chinese travelers not to pick their noses in public, urinate or spit in swimming pools, ask people whether they have eaten, greet people by asking them where they are going, force people to take pictures of them, cut in lines, cheer or whistle if a performer in a show slips up onstage, or assume that steel cutlery, pillows, and airplane life vests are gifts.[1] The book was published shortly after a Chinese boy received international attention for inscribing "Ding Jinghao was here" on a 3,500-year-old temple in Egypt.

It is important to remember that these are simply cultural differences. There is no absolute standard of politeness better or worse met by this or that nation.

Indeed, a Chinese will react similarly to typical Western behavior.

Even before we sit down at a business meeting, we reveal a lack of manners according to Chinese standards. Our greeting is perceived as smug and disrespectful (the handshake is overly firm), cold and unfriendly (the handshake is too brief), and aggressive and challenging (direct eye contact is made). We often make mistakes when addressing our Chinese partners. We should choose a title a notch above the real one: a department head should be called director, and a PhD student should be called professor. We receive business cards, which are given to us with both hands, with just one hand and put them straight in our pocket after a quick glance. That is how little respect we have for the owner of the card. Once we sit down, we get straight to the point and start talking about the wording of a contract before we have shared a sufficient number of meals (with the alcohol and karaoke that go with them) and even before we have talked about personal things. We are dismissive and negative when we make it clear that items three and eight in the proposal are in fact unfeasible. We just want everyone to be familiar with the terms from the start, but for the Chinese, it is obvious that we do not "understand civility."

When it comes to hospitality, Westerners have nothing on the Chinese. Compliment an object in the home of a Chinese host, and it may be in your bag when you leave. Even the poorest families will treat you to so many dishes that you will feel embarrassed. It is not uncommon for guests at Chinese restaurants to tussle when the bill is delivered—everyone wants to pick it up. Chinese people on group tours abroad are often unhappy when they see "time at own disposal" in the program. The organizers obviously do not take their responsibility as hosts seriously!

Whereas we simply ask, "What's your name?" even in formal contexts, the Chinese will, out of respect for the family and ancestors, ask, "What is your precious family name?"

During a meal, we often help ourselves to food or tea without helping the person next to us first—thoughtless and crude, in the eyes of the Chinese around the table. The Chinese standing next to a Westerner who lights a cigarette without handing out cigarettes to everyone around feel the same way. If we are offered a gift, we usually accept it without much fanfare and open it immediately. Greedy and tactless, thinks the Chinese giver, who had assumed he would have to insist two or three times before we finally accepted and that we would wait until we got home to tear it open.

After humor, politeness is perhaps the hardest thing to translate between cultures. There are vast differences between Western and Chinese norms of behavior. In many cases, opposite norms apply. Westerners are annoyed by evasive answers from the Chinese, while the Chinese find Westerners unsophisticated, primitive, and aggressive when they cut to the chase and give a clear no. Chinese hospitality can be perceived as smothering; Western freedom looks like bad hosting. Whereas we think that Chinese people who probe about the most private things lack manners, the Chinese find the Westerner who fails to do so cold and uninterested, bordering on offensive. When a Chinese person is direct—uncomfortably direct—that confirms the closeness of the relationship. Being overly polite signals a distance. When Chinese people ask each other about their age, it is often because they wish to call each other "big brother" or "big sister" to establish ties and treat each other properly according to the age hierarchy.

Sometimes our priorities are simply different. The Chinese consider keeping air and mucus in the body unhealthy; after all, it is obvious that the body is trying to clear them. It is too easy—and in fact incorrect—to say that the Chinese in general are less polite than others.

Note

1. Karla Cripps, "China's First Tourism Law Comes into Effect, Tourists Issued Manners Guides," CNN, 4 October 2013, http://edition.cnn.com/2013/10/03/travel/new-china-tourism-law; Tom Phillips, "China's New Guide to 'Civilised Tourism,'" *Telegraph*, 2 October 2013, http://www.telegraph.co.uk/travel/travelnews/10348977/Chinas-new-guide-to-civilised-tourism.html.

Myth 11

CHINESE PEOPLE ARE NOT ALTRUISTIC

The tragic fate of two-year-old Wang Yue triggered a wave of self-examination among the Chinese. When she was run over by two vehicles and killed in October 2011, in Foshan in Guangdong province, none of the eighteen passersby stopped to help. Indeed, the incident was filmed and posted on the Internet, sparking a debate about selfishness in China.

Seen from the outside, Chinese do not appear to be particularly altruistic. Today it is every Chinese for him- or herself. Chinese society is characterized by fierce competition in education, in the job market, when it comes to wages, bonuses, and attention, and so on. And many believe that this results in selfishness. People care only for themselves and—at best—their families. Bertolt Brecht's *The Good Person of Szechuan*, written in 1943, makes altruism look impossible. The prostitute Shen Te tries hard to do right and live a moral life, but her goodwill is exploited by everyone around her. It is perhaps no coincidence that Brecht chose to locate this story in China.

There are indications that cultural differences exist when it comes to definitions and practices of altruism. The Chinese are less willing to give to charities than Americans but will provide much more than Americans to members of their family.[1] Altruism that benefits the family is important in China. Individuals are expected to be there for their extended families and to offer them their time and money, and doing so is considered impeccably moral. With such a large commitment to family and relatives, less is left over to give to strangers, for example, through anonymous organizations. Until quite recently such organizations did not even exist in China, so it is perhaps no wonder that the phenomenon of charitable giving has less of a foothold there than in the United States.

But we need not look far to find an ideal of altruism—good deeds that do not benefit oneself or one's immediate family—even in China. Confucianism emphasizes cardinal virtues such as generosity, charity, good morals, and obligations to others—even to those who are outside one's inner circle. One should not act for private profit.

The ancient altruistic ideals were reflected in practice during imperial times. Bridges, ferries, and schools—which we today regard as belonging to the public domain—were often built and run with the help of donations from affluent individuals. The well-to-do would also help the less fortunate by dispensing medicine and winter clothes to the poor and setting up free roadside tea stations for the benefit of weary travellers. They also sometimes provided substantial sums for disaster relief.[2]

During the Mao era, however, Chinese authorities frowned upon philanthropy, since it could be perceived as a sign that the Communist state was failing to provide people with everything they needed. The ideal of altruism was still promoted, however, through Lei Feng. Lei, if he indeed existed, was a selfless but by no means extraordinary soldier in the People's Liberation Army. Starting in 1963, he became the protagonist of national Learn from Lei Feng! campaigns. The authorities wanted to cultivate a collectivist, socialist spirit in the population by personifying the individual's sacrifice for the common good. The success of the Lei Feng campaigns owes much to Chinese traditions. Lei Feng would hardly have become a national hero if he had been imported from Russian or German communism. Today, young Chinese know Lei from the computer game *Learn from Lei Feng Online*, initiated by the government. It is interesting that the government has chosen to return to the models and instruments of the Mao era, perhaps fearing that the ideal of self-sacrifice has been weakened in the liberal China of the market.

Today, China gives aid to poor countries, albeit certainly not very much: about US$190 billion in 2011.[3] When considering China's assistance, we must keep some factors in mind. First, despite its fantastic economic growth, China is still home to the world's second-largest impoverished population, after India. China is in many ways still a developing country. A Chinese person on average earns a tenth of what an American does.[4] Second, the government's prioritizing of its own poor population is a form of domestic altruism. Third, the trend is positive: China's aid to poor countries, according to official figures, increased by 30 percent annually between 2004 and 2009.[5]

The Chinese state is not the only contributor; private companies are too. Haier, the giant manufacturer of electrical products, for example, provides money for charitable purposes, including child welfare and education. Wealthy villages provide money to poorer villages. Monasteries give to the poor in their areas. The monks usually live off donated food. It is not uncommon for wealthy Chinese to subsidize the education of poor students. Those who have no money to give offer their time, doing voluntary social work or guiding visitors around museums and religious or historical sites. Many are involved in causes related to the environment. More than 3,500 environmental nongovernmental organizations were registered with the Ministry of Civil Affairs in 2008. In addition there are possibly as many as two thousand organizations that choose not to register.[6] Another example is the "Brilliant China Study Aid" project at Qinghua University, which helps schools in the impoverished Gansu province. Qinghua students, alumni, and staff collect money and spend their time in Gansu to help local schools. If doing so pads their resumes as well, who are we to judge?

Altruism is an ideal, rather than a depiction of actual actions and motives, in all societies. For most of us, some form of egoism tends to underlie everything we do, even our charitable acts. Countries provide assistance as a strategy to improve their international reputation. Rich businesspeople donate to improve the reputations of their corporations, which is good for business. And people give money and time to good causes simply because it makes them feel better.

Notes

1. Charles Yuji Horioka, "An International Comparison of Altruism and Bequest Motives: The Case of China, India, Japan, and the United States," Institute of Economics, Academica Sinica, Taipei, 3 July 2010, www.econ.sinica.edu.tw/upload/file/0817.pdf.

2. Pierre Fuller, "China's Charitable Past," *New York Times*, 28 September 2010, http://www.nytimes.com/2010/09/29/opinion/29iht-edfuller.html.

3. Rand Corporation, "China's Foreign Aid and Government-Sponsored Investment Activities," Rand Corporation, 2013, http://www.rand.org/pubs/research_reports/RR118.html

4. "World Development Indicators," World Bank, http://databank.worldbank.org/ddp/home.do?Step=12&id=4&CNO=2.

5. "China's Foreign Aid," State Council Information Office, April 2011, http://english.gov.cn/official/2011-04/21/content_1849913_3.htm.

6. Numbers provided by the Ministry of Civil Affairs, quoted in Lei Xie, "China's Environmental Activism in the Age of Globalization" (Working Papers on Transnational Politics, City University, London, May 2009), https://www.city.ac.uk/__data/assets/pdf_file/0005/84056/CUWPTP006.pdf.

Myth 12

THE INDIVIDUAL HAS NO VALUE, ONLY THE COLLECTIVE DOES

> That Western starting point of the autonomous individual is alien to the Chinese consideration of human collectivity. . . . Chinese individuals see themselves as . . . bricks in a wall, one lends support to the other and they all hold up society.
>
> —Lam Ching Man, PhD [1]

The Chinese have no adequate word for "me," it is claimed; that is how collectivist they are. Chinese people see themselves first and foremost as part of a community, not as individuals. They do what is best for the collective and gladly sacrifice themselves for the common good. Chinese society is deeply characterized by the ideals of traditional Confucian morality: sacrificing the little me to complete the big me. Individuals hold value only inasmuch as they are parts of the community. It is a given that everyone follows the rules of society assiduously. A common assumption is that support for the death penalty and other harsh punishments demonstrates Chinese devaluation of the individual.

China is in fact a network-based society. Commitments and responsibilities to friends and family are significant, often more so than in the West. *Guanxi*, meaning "connections" or "network," is essential. As the services provided by the public sector have decreased during the reform era, the individual must take care of him- or herself, relying on the personal network. It is every man and woman—or at least every family—for themselves. What public goods do exist are not necessarily distributed according to objective criteria. The Chinese bureaucracy is characterized by discrimination. Laws and regulations are carried out on in an unpredictable and, for many, unfair manner. People are therefore more loyal to their own networks, which are more predictable and reliable than the impersonal public sector. Network-based societies tend to be more common in developing countries, where the public sector is inadequate. People depend on their networks for survival.

Yet it is not true that community means everything and the individual nothing in China. And it is doubtful that Chinese subordinate themselves to the community to a greater extent than other people do.

The importance of community wanes in network-based societies. According to Fei Xiaotong, China's most famous social anthropologist and sociologist, the need to develop a personal network contributes to a Chinese tendency toward egocentrism.[2] People are at the center of their own individual networks and therefore act first and foremost in their own behalf. As a Chinese proverb says, "Each person should sweep the snow from his own doorstep and should not fret about the frost on his neighbor's roof." We need look no farther than the nearest Chinese line if we want to study egocentrism. Everyone tries to make his or her way forward without a care for who has waited the longest. No one seems bothered about an abstract ideal of taking the community into account—to say nothing of sacrificing himself for the community. These line jumpers do not perceive themselves as subordinate or unimportant. The authorities in China want to improve the citizenry's poor queuing practices and have designated the eleventh of each month as the official countrywide day of the line. Everyone is supposed to line up properly on this day. The date was chosen because the number eleven resembles two people in a queue.

When one focuses intensely on one's own network, one has less attention to spare for strangers and outsiders. Chinese people distinguish sharply between "us" and "them"—those who are within their networks and those who are outside. The Chinese have greater obligations to everyone within their networks but fewer obligations to those outside. Automatic concern for strangers—based on our all being individuals in the same society—is less in China than in many countries in the West. Solidarity, care, and consideration are reserved for those within one's own network. Outside one's own network is the public, to which one has no obligations. Whatever is public is free for all to use, whether this manifests as throwing garbage anywhere or squeezing benefits from the public sector. Corruption and embezzlement demonstrate that people do not feel responsible for common property. The problem is widespread in China, at all levels of society. This does not merely have to do with the poor morality of the guilty. At least as important is the fact that the money belongs to strangers and often to the indefinite public.

In 2008 it became known that several infants had died and hundreds of thousands had become seriously ill after drinking poisoned milk and infant formula. This case shows that consideration for strangers is low. The toxic chemical melamine had, probably for several years, been added to milk products to make them appear to have a higher protein content. Manufacturers sold the products, knowing they were dangerous, and local authorities chose not to inform the public about the dangerous milk for fear of social unrest before the Olympics, which were held in Beijing later that year. Putting profits and stability ahead of children's lives is an extreme example of what happens when people feel no responsibility to strangers. The same people probably ensured that their family members and friends did not drink the tainted milk.

Individuals have value in China too, and the Chinese are no more willing to subordinate themselves to community interests than anyone else. But they do have greater obligations to the people closest to them—those inside their network—than we do in the West, generally speaking, and consequently they have less visible concern for everyone else—strangers. And in case anyone is in doubt: there are Chinese words for both "me" (*wo*) and "myself" (*ziwo*).

Notes

1. Lam Ching Man, *Not Grown Up Forever: A Chinese Conception of Adolescent Development* (New York: Nova Science Publishers, 1997).

2. Fei Xiaotong, *From the Soil: The Foundations of Chinese Society* (Berkeley: University of California Press, 1992).

Myth 13

ALL CHINESE ARE ONLY CHILDREN

> Not to mention words/concepts which are foreign to them: brother,
> sister, sibling rivalry.
> —Internet commenter[1]

Many in the West believe that Chinese families are allowed to have only one child. Consequently, all Chinese must be only children—and are therefore probably spoiled. In the economic boom of recent decades, parents have been able to give their children more things. Many people claim that as a result, Chinese children suffer from "little emperor" syndrome.[2] They ignore their parents and teachers, throw tantrums if they are not allowed to eat at McDonald's for the third time in one week, and flatly refuse to turn off their computer games to go to bed on school nights. Meanwhile, the pressure on these only children is significant. Two parents and four grandparents focus all their love on them—as well as all their expectations for the child's education and career, in the glory of which they will one day bask. One mother trailed her son at school every day in order to be absolutely on top of his education. These parents want something back for their efforts—at the very least full care during old age. The problem, called "4-2-1" (four grandparents and two parents all relying on one child), is being discussed extensively in China.

The legislation referred to as the "one-child policy" in the West is called "birth planning" (*jihua shengyu*) in Chinese. Its purpose—not surprisingly—is to limit the number of births. Soon after he came to power in 1949, Mao encouraged the Chinese to have numerous children. Mao believed that China was weak in a number of respects, including militarily, and hoped to remedy this with a large population. At that time, many people were experiencing relative stability and some prosperity. They were happy to jump into bed.

The result was a population explosion. The government realized that too-rapid population growth could impede China's development; in 1955, it launched campaigns for limiting births. The campaigns proved effective: the average family had three children in 1980, compared to six in 1970,[3] without any laws having been implemented. But the authorities thought the campaigns weren't effective enough and first stated that every family should only have one child at the National Party Congress in 1980. Since then, there have been severe restrictions on the number of children the Chinese can have.

During the Mao era, neighborhood committees or "menstrual police" in the work units often monitored women's menstrual cycles to ensure that they were not pregnant when they were not supposed to be. In some work units, IUDs were mandatory for female employees. It has also been well documented that many have been forced to have abortions and sterilizations. Chen Guangcheng, the blind lawyer granted asylum in the United States in 2012, is widely believed to have been prosecuted in part because he was involved in exposing such cases.

Today, families with more children than they are allowed are punished with fines and career setbacks. If, in order to avoid penalties, parents do not register their second child, the child risks losing his or her rights to education and health care. According to official government estimates, 400 million births have been "averted" nationwide as a result of the policy.[4] The government emphasizes the environmental benefits of limiting births; fewer people consume fewer resources. Authorities also say China would not be able to support an unconstrained population, pointing to poverty and population growth in India to prove this point. Many economists claim, however, that this argument does not hold water, because more people mean more production.

Many in the West think it is inhumane for the state to decide how many children people can have. And the "one-child policy" is often blamed for the shortage of girls in China: 118 boys are born for every 100 girls.[5] In 2020 there will be a surplus of 40 million men in China. But this phenomenon also exists in India, South Korea, and Taiwan, where people are allowed to have as many children as they want. The girl deficit in Asia has more to do with culture than with law. In the countryside, home to about half the population of China, a woman moves to her husband's house when she gets married. A female child must be provided for, and when she is of working age, she will move to her husband's home—requiring a dowry—instead of contributing to her birth family's household. Daughters entail real economic loss compared to sons in many Asian countries. What's more, sons carry on the family name.[6]

Limitations on childbirths reinforce the consequences of these gender differences but also provide some benefits to girls. Previously, it was common to give sons the best food in the house, the best education, and so forth, but a girl who is an only child will often be given opportunities she might not have had if she had had to compete with a brother.

Is it true then that no Chinese can have more than one child?

The legislation related to birth planning is complex. The population is divided into different categories according to a variety of criteria, including where they live and what ethnic group they belong to. The rules and limitations that apply to each category vary significantly. The law that is best known outside China—the one that states that a couple can only have one child—only applies to one in every three families: couples who live in urban areas and in which both partners have siblings. Around half of all Chinese couples are allowed to have a second child if the first is a girl or has a disability. One in ten families can have two children regardless of the gender of the firstborn, and some ethnic minority groups are allowed to have more than two children. One result of this is that ethnic minorities now make up about 9 percent of China's population,[7] compared to 6 percent in the 1950s.[8] And there are exceptions to the rules. After the earthquake in Sichuan province in May 2008, when many schoolchildren lost their lives, some of the grieving parents were allowed to have another child. In November 2013, during the third plenum of the Communist Party's Central Committee, the Chinese leadership decided to gradually loosen the birth-control policy. Couples in which one partner is an only child will now be allowed to have a second child, but many couples will still be prohibited from doing so.

It is not uncommon for Chinese families to bend these rules in different ways, having more children than they are allowed. Many families do not report the births of daughters, hoping to try again for a son. Others move when they become pregnant for the second time so that their employers or the local authorities will not find out that they are about to break the law. Moving away from where one has household registration (*hukou*) means moving out of the authorities' focus, and working for a private company often means that one's employer does not care how many children one has. Still others use their networks to obtain identity papers for the newborn baby, and wealthy Chinese can avail themselves of even more loopholes. They can go abroad, to Singapore or the United States, to give birth to the second or third child and will have little difficulty bringing the child back to China later.

Many Chinese can legally have more than one child, and many more have second children in secret. In addition, many are willing to pay the fine for a second baby. For many Chinese parents, having more children has become a status symbol—it shows that the family can afford to pay the fines. There is a big difference between ideals and practices when it comes to family planning—between what the law allows and what is actually possible.

Notes

1. See replies at Freerepublic.com, http://www.freerepublic.com/focus/f-news/2139507/replies?c=1.

2. Taylor Clark, "Plight of the Little Emperors," *Psychology Today*, 28 December 2011, http://www.psychologytoday.com/articles/200806/plight-the-little-emperors.

3. "A Discussion of China's Population Control Policy and Issues," Don Tow's Website, June 2009, http://www.dontow.com/2009/06/a-discussion-of-chinas-population-control-policy-and-issues.

4. "400 Million Births Prevented by One-Child policy," *People's Daily*, 28 October 2011, http://english.peopledaily.com.cn/90882/7629166.html.

5. "Gender Equality," UNICEF China, http://www.unicef.cn/en/index.php?m=content&c=index&a=lists&catid=135.

6. For more on the reasons for and consequences of gender-specific abortions, see Mara Hvistendahl, *Unnatural Selection: Choosing Boys over Girls and the Consequences of a World Full of Men* (New York: Public Affairs, 2011).

7. "Han Chinese Proportion in China's Population Drops: Census Data," Xinhua, 28 April 2011, http://news.xinhuanet.com/english2010/china/2011-04/28/c_13849933.htm.

8. Ma Rong, "Ethnic Relations in Contemporary China: Cultural Tradition and Ethnic Policies since 1949," *Policy and Society* 25, no. 1 (2006): 85–108.

Myth 14

THE CHINESE PEOPLE ARE HOMOGENEOUS

When god was creating the world he started getting tired when he reached China so he went make, copy, paste, copy, paste, copy, paste.
—Commenter on Yahoo! Answers[1]

It is remarkable how frequently one comes across depictions of the Chinese as being all the same. They all look alike, everyone eats rice, and everyone dresses (at least until very recently) in dark blue Mao suits. All Chinese are part of the same ethnic group and speak the same language. Chinese people have the same experiences and background, the same worldview, and the same values. They march in step. The Chinese are all so alike.

Although China has as many as 1.34 billion people—20 percent of the world's population—everyone in the country actually does have a number of things in common. The tradition of the Chinese state goes far back in time. The official language for the entire country is Mandarin (*Putonghua*), which is the mother tongue for approximately 900 million people. This is the largest language group in the world; in comparison, English and Spanish are the first language of approximately 300 million people each. Anyone who has attended school in China can speak and write Mandarin, at least to some extent, even if their first language is another dialect. Most Chinese television and radio broadcasts are in Mandarin. Unlike citizens of countries like Singapore and the United States, very few Chinese have roots outside China. The entire country is on Beijing time. Considering the size of the population, China is not particularly characterized by religious diversity. Most religious people are Buddhist,

Daoist, or a mixture of the two. There are also Muslims (Uyghur and Hui) and Christians.

But so many people in such a vast country naturally also have major differences.

The geographical differences between the different areas of China are significant. The country covers nearly 10 million square kilometers, which makes it about twice as large as the entire European Union and as large as the United States but smaller than Russia and Canada. China is so vast that it includes several climate zones: the southernmost provinces are tropical, whereas the north is subarctic. While snowstorms ravage the Liaoning province in the northeast during the month of January, farmers on the tropical island of Hainan are busy harvesting watermelons. The western parts of China are in fact four time zones away from Beijing. The whole country is supposed to follow Beijing time, and schools and government offices do. Other people often follow the unofficial local time and organize their daily lives according to the sun.

The economic development of the past thirty years has affected different parts of the country to varying degrees. In the prosperous city of Macao, residents are twenty-two times wealthier than residents of China's poorest province, Guizhou. Macao is at approximately the level of Qatar, measured in gross domestic product per capita, while Guizhou is at the level of India.[2] People thus live very different lives in different parts of the country. Nomads in Inner Mongolia, farmers in Sichuan province, Turkish Muslims in Xinjiang province, and wealthy businesswomen in Shanghai have very different values and lives.

China is a multiethnic state, even though more than 90 percent of the population is Han Chinese. The country has fifty-six official ethnic groups or nationalities. The fifty-five minority groups taken together include approximately 100 million people. The smallest group is the Lhoba, numbering about three thousand people, whereas the most populous group after the Han is the Zhuang, with about 16 million people.[3]

One should, however, be wary of the ethnic classification of the Chinese population, which was made after the Communists gained power in 1949. Thomas S. Mullaney has described this process on the basis of new historical material and interviews with ethnologists who participated.[4] More than four hundred groups applied for recognition as separate ethnicities. Ethnological experts considered that number too high, and so only fifty-five minority groups were granted separate ethnic group status. Some groups were merged; others were split up. The minorities' own ideas of identity and belonging are therefore not reflected in the official classification. The category Han Chinese is also a cultural construct. The name "Han" was first used for the Chinese people by the author Zhang Taiyan in the late nineteenth century, after the second dynasty of the unified China. At that point, the Chinese government was threatened by European powers, Japan, and civil unrest. Creating a strong sense of community among all Chinese was part of the government's strategy to strengthen the country. The category does in fact encompass many different groups of people.

China is a multilingual state. As mentioned, the vast country has one official language, Mandarin, but there are, unsurprisingly, great linguistic differences nonetheless. The claim that these differences merely constitute dialects of a single language reflects the political need for national unity. Linguistically the "dialects" are different languages, although most of them are written in the same characters.

In addition to Mandarin, six languages are regarded as Chinese: Wu (Jiangsu and Zhejiang provinces), Cantonese, Xiang (Hunan province), Hakka, Min (Fujian province and Taiwan), and Gan (Jiangxi province). Many Chinese also speak non-Chinese languages, such as Burmese, Thai, Tibetan, Uyghur, or Mongolian. Furthermore, hundreds of dialects within Mandarin are mutually unintelligible.

Considering the rapid development China has undergone since the People's Republic was established in 1949, it is not surprising that there are also major differences between generations. A sixty-year-old Chinese has lived all her life during the Communist period. She remembers the Great Leap Forward, and her adolescence was characterized by the values of the Cultural Revolution. Before she was thirty, she had never ridden in a car or made a private telephone call. She was assigned to a work unit in a state-owned enterprise, neither choosing the job nor lifting a finger to get it. Wages were paid in coupons for various consumable goods. She had almost no access to information about the world outside China. The twenty- and thirty-year-olds of today cannot remember the peak of communism during Mao. They are used to great social and economic freedom—and great social and economic inequalities. The urban youth have cell phones and consumer lifestyles to go with them. For many, going abroad is not just a dream but a real possibility. With the freedom the young enjoy comes much greater responsibility for their own careers and finances. Today it is every Chinese for herself.[5]

Given these geographic, linguistic, ethnic, and generational differences, it comes as no surprise that Chinese people do not think of themselves as "all alike"! There is also plenty of prejudice among Chinese people, giving rise to discrimination, which in turn causes real and alleged inequalities.

Those who live in the cities tend to view migrant workers as lazy fortune hunters who cannot be bothered to create a living where they are from. Han Chinese often perceive minorities as culturally and socially backward. Speaking Mandarin with a standardized pronunciation (similar to that of Beijing) is associated with education, ability, wealth, and success. Those who speak Mandarin with an accent, belong to ethnic minority groups, or come from rural areas are often assumed to be dimwitted, lazy, and uncivilized. They are even referred to as people of lower quality. In some cases these derogatory attitudes are clearly racist.

The government does its best to foster patriotism and national unity. It produces campaigns that promote national pride and Chinese unity, stresses Mandarin as the national language, and keeps the entire country on Beijing time. All this demonstrates that the government knows national unity—the idea of China as one state—is not necessarily a given. Keeping the country together has always taken a great effort. One country, one nation, one people, one language—this is wishful thinking, not reality.

Notes

1. "Why Do Chinese People All Look and Act the Same?" Yahoo! Answers, http://answers.yahoo.com/question/index?qid=20110612155829AAt667U.

2. "All the Parities in China: Which Countries Match the GDP, Population and Exports of Chinese Provinces?" *Economist*, http://www.economist.com/content/chinese_equivalents.

3. "The Zhuang Ethnic Minority," China.org.cn, http://www.china.org.cn/e-groups/shaoshu/shao-2-zhuang.htm; "The Lhoba Ethnic Minority," China.org.cn, http://www.china.org.cn/e-groups/shaoshu/shao-2-lhoba.htm.

4. Thomas Mullaney, *Coming to Terms with the Nation: Ethnic Classification in Modern China* (Berkeley: University of California Press, 2010).

5. For more on China's diversity, see Jeffrey N. Wasserstrom, *China in the 21st Century: What Everyone Needs to Know* (Oxford: Oxford University Press, 2010).

Myth 15

COMMUNISM HAS CREATED GENDER EQUALITY IN CHINA

Women hold up half the sky.

—Mao Zedong

On an altar in the living room of Mrs. Li, an old lady who lives in Nantong in Southeast China, is a statue of Mao among statues of Buddhist and Daoist gods. He holds this position of honor because his policies saved her life. When she was thirteen, she was married off to an old man, who soon died. As a widow, the young girl was rejected by both her own family and her in-laws; her future was most uncertain. When the Communists took over, Mao decided that all people, including girls, were to have opportunities for education. This saved the young widow Li, who received an education and consequently was later able to find work.

During the Mao era, Chinese authorities attempted to level their previously hierarchical society. The focus was on community; individualism and individual differences, whether between classes, generations, or genders, were suppressed and discouraged. Women were moved out of the home and into the community. Many of women's traditional functions, such as child care and cooking, became communal responsibilities, and the role of women was thus radically different, especially in urban work units. A woman's sacrifice was no longer to take place within her own four walls for her own husband and family. Now she was first and foremost to labor on behalf of the People's Republic. (For many women, however, the workload at home remained the same; working women throughout the world seem unable to avoid the dreaded second shift.)

Men and women were now supposed to be treated as equals in the workplace. Women were farmers, industrial workers, and political activists; they led militias and brigades of Red Guards. (The gender equality was, however, imperfect; women received fewer work points—which determined income—than men did for doing the same work.) The ideal for both genders was strength, health, and—most importantly—correct political attitudes. Women and men alike dressed in the shapeless dark blue, dark green, or gray outfits known as Mao suits. These clothes eliminated visible physical gender differences and individual characteristics— as uniforms are meant to do.

Government campaigns to promote gender equality and correct the unnatural deficit of girls continued in the reform period. One can still find posters all around China stubbornly maintaining that girls are equal to boys. Even slogans from the Mao era are still in use. The UN Fourth World Conference on Women, held in Beijing in 1995, for example, was called "Women Hold Up Half the Sky."

But China is still far from achieving full equality between women and men.

Discrimination begins at home. Widely different gender ideals exist in Chinese communities, but it is still common to consider family life more important than a career for women. Parents often encourage young girls to get some education but not too much—typically a bachelor's degree at most. They fear that too much education will limit their daughters' choice of husband. Some women lie, too, playing down their positions and salaries. In China, as elsewhere, more girls than boys study languages, which, in the big cities, provide the brightest opportunities for jobs in international companies. A woman with knowledge of Chinese culture, in addition to English, Mandarin, and the local dialect, can quickly become the boss's right hand. This frequently creates problems at home. For most Chinese men, it is unthinkable to marry a woman with a higher education level, position, or salary than himself. They also find it difficult to handle their wives surpassing them professionally.

In 2013, it was reported that 66 percent of female graduates agreed with the statement "It's better to marry a good man than find a good job."[1] Twenty-two-year-old Ma Nuo caused a ruckus when she stated on a dating show that she would "rather cry in a BMW car than laugh on the backseat of a bicycle."[2] Ma was widely criticized for her bald materialism, but her statement reflects the importance many Chinese women give to marrying an affluent man, even at the expense of their happiness. It also shows that for some in China, women's economic dependence on men is still taken for granted.

During the reform period, the habit of keeping concubines, or at least a variation of this practice, has been revived. Many rich and powerful men, married with children, keep one or more younger women on the side. Typically, a "second wife" receives an apartment and an allowance. In return, she is available to her provider whenever he likes. According to statistics cited by the state news agency Xinhua, 95 percent of the civil servants convicted of corruption kept such mistresses.[3]

Moreover, being a married woman in China is not without risk. One in three married women is subjected to domestic violence, according to surveys conducted in nine Chinese cities.[4] As long as the victim is in a relationship with the perpetrator, most people consider the violence to be an internal family problem that does not concern the police or the justice system. In the best-case scenario, police advise the man to stop beating his wife. An impressive grassroots effort is under way to change attitudes about violence against women; Beijing's Anti–Domestic Violence Network (Beijing Fanbao) is doing important work.[5]

Women are also discriminated against in the labor market. Chinese women make up 46 percent of the labor force and a quarter of the country's entrepreneurs.[6] But many job advertisements make it clear that the employer wants a man in the position, even in the public sector and state-owned enterprises. Advertisements specifically seeking women frequently have particular requirements for the successful candidate's appearance: she must be pretty or of a certain height. On the website www.zhaopin.com, a Chinese forum for finding jobs and employees, every fourth advertisement requires an attractive appearance, and every tenth specifies a minimum height for candidates. If we combine requirements for gender, age, appearance, and height (all of which fall into the category of unlawful discrimination in many countries), two out of three advertisements have at least one. Even office work in the public sector often entails such requirements. The People's Liberation Army is an example of an employer who knows to look for the important qualifications in women; it assesses female recruits according to their eloquence, artistic skills, and "appearance in sweeping moves"[7]—whatever that means. Many of these girls will never be near a weapon or a military operation. They are typically hired to join performance troupes, which might explain these requirements.

The fact that the position of women in the labor market is lower than men's is reflected in wage differentials—which are actually increasing. Women's average income was 67.3 percent of men's in 2012, a 10 percent drop from 1990. In rural areas, the differences are even greater. Female farmers in 2012 on average earned 56 percent of what male farmers earned, compared with 79 percent in 1990.[8]

The political arena can also be hostile to women. The leadership change in November 2012 represented a slight improvement but was no revolution for women's representation in Chinese politics. No woman has ever been deemed worthy of a seat on the Politburo Standing Committee, China's most powerful organ, not even in 2012. However, two women were elected to the Politburo, the second most powerful organ of the Communist Party, for the first time since the Cultural Revolution. On the party's Central Committee, which is the level below the Politburo, only 10 of the 205 newly elected representatives are women. Three of the twenty-seven ministers are women. In China's parliament only 21 percent are women. Those who had hoped that things were at least moving in the right direction will be disappointed to learn that male dominance is growing. In 1997 China was ranked number sixteen in the world in terms of female representation in parliament; in 2012 the country was ranked unimpressively at number fifty-three.[9] And the situation is even worse at the provincial level, where only 7 percent of the top political positions are held by women.

The Mao era did a lot for women in China. The reform period has seen the emergence of movements that question the prevailing gender ideals; among them are feminist movements and organizations for gay and lesbian rights. Nonetheless, the female ideal today is the opposite of what it was during the Mao era—submissive, soft, delicate, frail—and the position of women is far from equal with that of men.

Notes

1. "Money-Oriented Marriage Prevalent," *News China Magazine*, September 2013, http://www.newschinamag.com/magazine/money-oriented-marriage-prevalent.

2. "I'd Much Rather Weep in a BMW," Xinhua, 4 June 2010, http://news.xinhuanet.com/english2010/indepth/2010-06/04/c_13332993.htm.

3. "Anti-corruption Move Sparks Debate," Xinhua, 19 May 2005, http://news.xinhuanet.com/english/2005-05/19/content_2977889.htm.

4. Wang Yi, "Women's Situation in China during the Social Transition" (paper presented during the Nordic Association for China Studies' biannual conference, Oslo, Norway, 19 June 2011).

5. For more on Chinese women's position in the domestic arena, see Leta Hong Fincher, "Women's Rights at Risk," *Dissent* (spring 2013), http://www.dissentmagazine.org/article/womens-rights-at-risk.

6. Astrid S. Tuminez with Kerstin Duell and Haseena Abdul Majid, "Rising to the Top? A Report on Women's Leadership in Asia," Lee Kuan Yew School of Public Policy and Asia Society, April 2012, http://sites.asiasociety.org/womenleaders/wp-content/uploads/2012/04/Rising-to-the-Top-Final-PDF.pdf.

7. "PLA Raises Recruitment Standards for Women," *People's Daily*, 12 October 2009, http://english.peopledaily.com.cn/90001/90776/90882/6781438.html.

8. "China Faces Widening Gender Income Gap," *Women of China*, 6 April 2012, http://www.womenofchina.com.cn/html/report/4082-1.htm.

9. "Women Struggle for a Foothold in Chinese Politics," *New York Times*, 24 June 2010, http://www.nytimes.com/2010/06/25/world/asia/25iht-letter.html.

Myth 16

THE CHINESE ARE ATHEISTS

If you ask someone "what do you believe in?" the answer you get 99% of the time is "I believe in myself."

—Internet commenter[1]

China is a country without religion.

—Hu Shi[2]

"**R**eligion is the opium of the people," according to Karl Marx. In line with this, China's Communist Party is officially atheist, and religion has been controlled and regulated since 1949. During the most radical periods, like the Great Leap Forward and the Cultural Revolution, religious people were persecuted and religious sites were destroyed. Even today, the devotions of Tibetan Buddhists, Uyghur Muslims, Falun Gong adherents, and Christians are controlled and restricted. China's rich history of philosophy is well known, but whatever religious life existed in early China is often assumed to have been destroyed during the Communist era. If the Chinese believe in anything today, it must be hard work and money, right?

The short answer is no.

The Chinese are not restricted because the government in Beijing wants the people to be atheists. Rather, Tibetans and Uyghurs are constrained because their religion is tightly bound together with their struggle for autonomy. This is what scares pragmatic Beijing, not religion itself. In order to keep China together, Tibet and Xinjiang must join the ranks of the Chinese community. Religious movements whose leaders live abroad are also unacceptable. Christianity is accepted within the framework of state-approved churches, but Catholic churches with bonds to the pope in Rome are not accepted and are sometimes dissolved. The authorities fear movements whose members' loyalty lies outside China. Christianity is considered dangerous only inasmuch as it helps to undermine Chinese unity and has strong ties to foreign countries.

Tibetans, Uyghurs, Falun Gong adherents, and Catholics aside, the Chinese people have gained greater religious freedom during the reform period, both legally and in practice. The Constitution of 1982 guarantees freedom of religion, but that applies only to the five approved religions: Daoism (Taoism), Buddhism, Islam, Catholicism, and Protestantism (within the limitations described above). The result of this new freedom has been a boom in religious life. Of Chinese people over age sixteen, 31.4 percent (or 300 million) claim to be religious. This is the conclusion of a survey conducted in 2007, the first of its kind, carried out by a university in Shanghai.[3] State media have reported the survey, correcting the official estimate of 100 million believers, which had been in place for years.

Even members of the Communist Party, who are formally not allowed to participate in religious life, now openly attend local religious ceremonies, particularly in the countryside.

The flourishing religious life we see today is not newborn; rather, it has been awakened from a dormancy enforced by periods of oppression. Buddhist and Daoist monasteries and temples that had fallen into decay have been repaired and reopened, as have mosques and churches. People once again set up altars in their homes and in their shops, placing fruit and incense on them. Religion seems to fill the void left by the ebbing of Communist ideology and values.[4]

Not surprisingly, religious life has been influenced by neoliberalism. This is obvious when one visits temples and monasteries, which today tend to be tourist sights as much as places of religious worship. It is obvious during the so-called tomb-sweeping festival (*Qingming jie*), during which people honor their ancestors. People gather around family graves and burn paper printed with tokens of wealth for their ancestors to use in the afterlife. People once burned beautifully colored and patterned paper to represent precious silk fabrics; today they burn pictures of Mercedes sedans, credit cards, iPhones, and other luxury goods the ancestors might need in the hereafter. Kits with pictures of such luxury goods are sold at cemeteries. Religion has also made its mark on industry. The world's largest Bible-printing factory is located in Nanjing, in the south of China. One in four of the world's new Bibles is printed here—in eighty different languages, including eight Chinese minority languages.

The Chinese authorities are pragmatic when it comes to religious life, as they are with many social questions. As long as religion is not destabilizing society or threatening those in power, people are mostly allowed to believe and do what they want.

Notes

1. "Why Is China Mostly Atheist?" Yahoo! Answers, http://answers.yahoo.com/question/index?qid=20100517184543AA7YS0m.

2. Hu Shi, "Ming Jiao" [The Doctrine of Names], quoted in C. K. Yang, *Religion in Chinese Society* (Berkeley: University of California Press, 1961), 5.

3. Fan Xiujuan, "Shehui zhuanxingqi zongjiao jiazhiguan yanjiu" [A Study of Religious Values during the Period of Social Change], *Jiangxi Kexue Xueyuan Xuebao* [*Journal of Jiangxi Technological University*], 12 August 2011.

4. For more on religion in historical and contemporary China, see Ian Johnson, "China Gets Religion!" *New York Review of Books*, 22 December 2011, http://www.nybooks.com/articles/archives/2011/dec/22/china-gets-religion.

Myth 17

SHANGHAI IS MORE LIBERAL
THAN BEIJING

"**H**eaven is high and the emperor is far away," according to a proverb from the imperial era. In China there is a long tradition of places located far from the capital having greater freedom to ignore the central government's guidelines. There is a widespread idea that it is easier for the government to maintain control near the center, where the incentive to do so is greater: unrest there impacts policy makers directly. The greater the proximity to the power center, Beijing, the stricter the government control.

Many visitors to China also believe that the inhabitants of Shanghai enjoy the greatest freedom. The city has a tradition of openness and extensive, long-standing contact with foreigners. Large-scale European immigration to Shanghai began in the nineteenth century, and the international environment naturally influenced the city's residents, culturally and socially. Western men patronized the city's many brothels—Shanghai was known as the "Whore of the Orient." Literature flourished. In the foreign concessions, Chinese law did not apply, and much of the city was thus exempt from political censorship. Another reason Shanghai is perceived as more liberal is its booming economy. Europe's historical experience gave rise to a widespread idea that economic growth begets political deregulation. Moreover, Shanghai is perceived as standing in political opposition to Beijing. Shanghai has even lent its name to a faction within the Communist Party—the Shanghai clique—which is associated with economic liberalization. Many thus suppose that Shanghai is much more liberal than Beijing.

However, it is not necessarily so.

There is virtually no critical news coverage in the Shanghai media, even less than in other parts of the country. During the World Expo in Shanghai in 2010, the coverage in local newspapers was entirely positive, despite the fact that the exhibition brought scores of negative consequences for the local population. For example, as many as eighteen thousand people were forced to move to provide land for the exhibition. News stories that mentioned problems, such as noise from construction work, focused on residents' being only too happy to make sacrifices for such a grand event.

The contrast to the preparations for the Asian Games in Guangzhou the same year is striking. Critical articles appeared in local newspapers on a daily basis, covering topics such as traffic congestion, noise, and heavy expenses. The local authorities on several occasions showed up to meet the complainers and respond to the criticism in public.

There are many indications that Beijing enjoys a greater freedom of expression than Shanghai. The capital is home to several newspapers and journalists engaged in critical investigative journalism. One of these is Wang Keqin with the *China Economic Journal* (*Zhongguo Jingji Shibao*), which has gained a reputation for conducting serious investigative journalism and exposing corruption and abuses of power. It is also far easier to come across critical literature in the capital than in bookstores in Shanghai.

Shanghai's tolerance of modern art is lower than Beijing's. Shanghai's artists used to enjoy great freedom, and in the first decades of the twentieth century, the city's art scene flourished.[1] But during the first decades of the twenty-first century, the art displayed in public has been subject to very strict censorship. Shanghai's art scene today is a shadow of its former self. Innovative, experimental, and politically challenging art is difficult or impossible to find. There are several examples of exhibitions being shut down because authorities found their content unacceptable, for either political or aesthetic reasons. An example is the exhibition *Reinterpretation of History*, which opened in Shanghai during the spring of 2010. The pictures displayed depicted controversial versions of Chinese history, especially related to the Cultural Revolution. The municipal authorities ended up closing not only the exhibition but also the gallery that had dared to host it.

Art exhibitions that have gone up without problems in Beijing have been denied the right to open—or have been closed quickly—in Shanghai. A series of pictures called *I Fuck Me*, showing the artist Chi Peng in various sexual situations, met the same fate as the historical exhibition mentioned above. The pictures were displayed in Beijing in 2006 without problems but were removed from an exhibition in Shanghai later the same year. While *Reinterpretation of History* was probably closed because it touched on a sensitive period in the history of the People's Republic—that is, for political reasons—Chi Peng's photos were in all probability considered pornographic and thus unwanted.

In January 2011, the Shanghai studio of the outspoken artist Ai Weiwei was torn down. Ai responded to the announcement of the demolition in his trademark style. He went out with a bang, throwing a party at which he served river crabs. The message could not have been clearer: "river crabs" (*héxiè*) is pronounced almost the same as the Communist Party expression "harmonious society" (*héxié*). Ai got the last word.

Ai still has a studio in Beijing, however. In the capital one comes across exhibitions that push political and sexual limits much more often, especially in the popular art district "798," which consists of old factories that have been turned into galleries. There are many indications that the authorities in Beijing see a vibrant arts scene as a status symbol. When showcasing the modern cities of China to visiting foreigners, it is a great advantage to be able to offer contemporary and experimental art, in addition to skyscrapers and huge intersection layouts. Because Beijing is the capital and thus a showcase for the entire country, a perception that the city is truly modern lends the whole nation a certain glamour.

There are large regional differences in the degree of freedom and control within China. Many believe that the Communist Party governs censorship through detailed directives. But censorship is decentralized, implemented differently in different parts of the country. This creates diverging local cultures of self-censorship. Shanghai's culture fosters self-censorship in its major newsrooms and among its artists.

Beijing is home to several political groups—some conservative, others liberal—competing among themselves for power. The existence and tacit acceptance of different political groups provides security for advocates of a wider range of political views. In Shanghai, by contrast, all political power is monopolized by one political group. Political diversity has been absent in Shanghai since the Qing Dynasty (1644–1911), when the governor held all political power. Since the 1990s, former president Jiang Zemin's group has dominated Shanghai. This group has chosen a safe path in the Chinese political landscape: conservatism. There is hardly any debate or innovation within the political realm; nor is there a civil society to speak of. Shanghai's scholars play a role in this. Or rather, they don't. The network between academic institutions is generally not an active one; scholars tend to have more contact with their colleagues in Beijing than with each other. They thus fail to drive political debate. The political monotony among the leadership is reflected in the city's media and art scenes.

Note

1. Lynn Pan, *Shanghai Style: Art and Design between the Wars* (San Francisco: Long River Press, 2008).

Part III

Business and the Economy

Myth 18

"CHINA INC." IS BUYING UP THE WORLD

The last decade could be characterized by the three words "made in China." In this next decade, it will be "owned by China."
—Gerard Lyons, financial analyst [1]

"Goodbye U.S. Bacon?" was the alarming headline of an article published by *Agriculture* on 10 July 2013. [2] Chinese buyers are aggressively picking off American icons—from the nation's favorite breakfast meat to the AMC movie theater chain—and are eager to invest in the booming US oil and shale gas industries. Chinese direct investments in US companies are skyrocketing; they shot up 42.5 percent in 2012, to $6.7 billion, according to Rhodium Group, a New York–based research firm. [3] China's creep into the American market is raising worries related to food safety, espionage, and increased access to sensitive US technology.

Chinese companies are very active in the international market, not just the American one. The iconic Swedish Volvo is owned by a Chinese company. China has made significant acquisitions in European countries going through financial difficulties. The Chinese businessman Huang Nubo attempted to buy a three-hundred-square-kilometer area of Iceland to develop tourism. But the politicians in Reykjavík refused and banned him from purchasing land on Saga Island as well. Later, he applied to rent the same area for forty years. The Chinese have signed billion-dollar contracts with other crisis-ridden countries, such as Greece, Ireland, and Spain. The Chinese state-owned company Cosco is to operate the Greek port of Piraeus for thirty-five years. China has also made lucrative trade deals in Africa, in exchange for building roads and other infrastructure, and invested heavily in the extraction of natural resources from South America.

Chinese total foreign acquisitions exceeded $77.2 billion in 2012—an increase of 28.6 percent over the previous year and a new record.[4] State-owned enterprises spearhead China's expansionary foreign investments. It is estimated that they alone are responsible for fully two-thirds of all Chinese investments in Europe. Such enterprises used to be behind nearly all Chinese activities in Africa. The close connection between the Chinese government and business sets off alarms all over the world.[5] Journalists seem to jump every time a new Chinese restaurant opens in the Western Hemisphere. In June 2011 the *Wall Street Journal* warned that naive Europeans were less prepared than Americans to protect their national economic security when China was shopping around.[6] The fear is that these investments stem from political considerations as well as the profit motive.

The fear is, however, exaggerated.

China has a trade surplus. This surplus has been accumulated as foreign currency reserves in state-owned institutions such as the People's Bank of China, China's central bank. For China, using a portion of these funds to purchase real capital abroad—be it businesses, real estate, oil, or other commodities—is beneficial. But other countries invest in China as well: in 2009, China made foreign direct investments worth around $250 billion, while other countries made direct investments in China worth about $1 trillion, according to figures from the Chinese Ministry of Commerce.[7] There is, however, often a big difference between Western investments in China and Chinese investments in the West. Western investors tend to buy liquid securities—they are easy to sell. Chinese companies buy factories and real capital that are highly illiquid and thus difficult to sell.

Moreover, the popular belief that Chinese state-owned enterprises are "foot soldiers" for the government in Beijing is false. These companies are largely commercial firms, and most of them are listed on various stock exchanges. In China, these state enterprises are in intense competition with each other, as well as with private and foreign companies. This competition extends to the companies' overseas investments. Chinese authorities often struggle to control the state-owned enterprises. Officials complain that leaders of state-owned companies have been given too much power and that their decisions at times run counter to the wishes of political authorities. In order to regain influence, Beijing has formulated a "grab the large, release the small" policy, which prioritizes state ownership and gives the government control of the major companies in six strategic sectors: finance, defense, energy, telecommunications, railways, and ports.

At the same time, there is a tendency to exaggerate Chinese state-owned enterprises' capacity to operate abroad. Most of these companies operate at the local or regional level in China—not at the national level. It is hard to see how these companies could establish themselves globally. Their lack of knowledge about language and other conditions of commercial importance in other countries is a major obstacle. Having said that, more and more Chinese companies are in the process of overcoming this limitation. The Chinese are already among the largest groups of foreign students in Western countries, and a growing number of students are learning foreign languages at Chinese universities.

The notion that "China Inc." is buying up the world at Beijing's command is therefore incorrect. It is not a stretch to call it a modernization of "yellow peril" fearmongering. We saw these same concerns in the 1980s and 1990s about Japanese acquisitions in the West, particularly in the United States. Japanese companies were also often state owned and were thus considered tools of "Japan Inc." in that country's quest for world domination. Chinese companies are becoming formidable competitors, but their goals are largely commercial. They strive to gain market share at home and abroad—like every multinational company in the world.

Notes

1. Cited in Tom Bawden and Kevin Shalvey, "The Era of 'Owned by China,'" *Guardian*, 12 January 2011, http://www.guardian.co.uk/business/2011/jan/12/era-of-owned-by-china.

2. Daniel Looker, "Goodbye U.S. Bacon? Smithfield Buyout Debate Continues," *Agriculture*, 10 July 2013, http://www.agriculture.com/news/policy/goodbye-us-bacon-smithfield-buyout_4-ar32437.

3. "China Investment Monitor," Rhodium Group, http://rhg.com/interactive/china-investment-monitor.

4. Jamil Anderlini, "Foreign Direct Investment in China Falls," *Financial Times*, 16 January 2013, http://www.ft.com/cms/s/0/5537736c-5fc8-11e2-8d8d-00144feab49a.html#axzz2J4fIEIDn.

5. John W. Miller, "Chinese Companies Embark on Shopping Spree in Europe," *Wall Street Journal*, 6 June 2011, http://online.wsj.com/article/SB10001424052748704355304576214683640225122.html.

6. Ibid.

7. "China Cumulatively Attracted More than USD 1 Trillion," Ministry of Commerce of the People's Republic of China, 10 November 2010, http://www.ciipp.com/en/index/view-236206.html.

Myth 19

CHINA HAS THE UNITED STATES OVER A BARREL

China is bilking us for hundreds of billions of dollars by manipulating and devaluing its currency. Despite all the happy talk in Washington, the Chinese leaders are not our friends. I've been criticized for calling them our enemy. But what else do you call the people who are destroying your children's and grandchildren's future? What name would you prefer me to use for the people who are hell bent on bankrupting our nation, stealing our jobs, who spy on us to steal our technology, who are undermining our currency, and who are ruining our way of life? To my mind, that's an enemy.

—Donald Trump[1]

China is both factory and bank for the United States—or so it is commonly assumed. Americans buy cheap Chinese products with money they borrow from China. By keeping their currency, the renminbi (RMB), artificially low, the Chinese grow their own export industry to the detriment of American industry and jobs. As a result, China has had a substantial trade surplus with the United States every year for the last twenty years, while the United States has never had a larger trade deficit with any country. The trade imbalance between the two economic giants in 2011 was $295 billion—in China's favor.[2] With that, the country has accumulated vast foreign exchange reserves. At the end of 2012, its dollar reserve held $3.3 trillion,[3] making it the largest foreign exchange reserve in the world. The composition of foreign exchange reserves is a state secret in the People's Republic of China, but it is commonly assumed that about two-thirds of China's assets are denominated in dollars.[4] American politicians and businesses dislike this deficit, to say the least. In April 2009, President Barack Obama said during his first meeting with his

Chinese counterpart, Hu Jintao, that he aimed to halve the trade deficit with China. Since then, the deficit has increased.

In addition to stockpiling dollars accumulated through trade with the United States, the Chinese have bought large amounts of government bonds, which, in practice, means American debt. Traditionally, these bonds have been considered ultrasafe: the Americans will always be able to pay their bills because they can print more dollars, In August 2011, China owned American debt in the amount of $1.137 trillion, according to official American statistics.[5] It is claimed that the United States has come to depend on the Chinese buying its bonds to finance its large budget deficit. In February 2009, then secretary of state Hillary Clinton publicly encouraged China to continue investing in government bonds to help the American economy: "We are truly going to rise or fall together."[6]

On the basis of these figures, it would be natural to think that the Chinese have the upper hand with America, but this is far from true. Rather, the two countries are highly dependent on each other.

Americans have long benefited from China-as-factory. Without China the prices of consumer goods would be higher in the United States. Today, however, other low-cost countries, such as Vietnam, Thailand, and Indonesia, are about to take on this role. China, for its part, has benefited from the international financial system with all its institutions and rules, all of which are products of the United States. As a result of vast Chinese investments, in many sectors the country produces more than it can consume. Thanks to the free trade system, which is protected by the United States both politically and militarily, Chinese industry can export this surplus to other countries, not least the United States. China depends on the Americans to maintain free trade, and American protectionism would be very harmful to Chinese industry. In addition, the US Navy ensures that Chinese goods can be transported safely across the seas.

China's purchases of government bonds have helped the American economy. But the Americans do not depend on the Chinese to finance their budget deficits, contrary to what many people argue. The government bonds that the Chinese have bought make up less than 10 percent of America's total national debt. Overall, the American government has far more outstanding to private creditors (individuals, banks, insurance companies, and corporations), its own federal government (the central bank and federal funds), and other countries than to the Chinese. China is dependent on the financial system in which the US dollar is the world reserve currency and on the American bond market, long seen as a safe haven. The Chinese own significant amounts of dollars and treasury bonds, and if the value of these drops, as the Chinese are well aware, they will lose a lot of money.

Therefore, even if they wish it were otherwise, it is important for the Chinese to help maintain trust in the US dollar and government bonds by not selling their shares—at least not too quickly. The market is hypersensitive. In 2009, then premier Wen Jiabao said that he was "a little concerned" about the safety of Chinese investments in American government debt.[7] This statement was enough to affect the dollar negatively. To quote the great British political economist John Keynes, "If you owe your bank a hundred pounds, you have a problem. But if you owe a million, it has."

In the words of Chinese vice premier Wang Yang, "The economic relationship between China and the U.S. is like that of a romantic couple. A divorce, like [that of] Wendi Deng and Rupert Murdoch, would cost far too much."[8]

Notes

1. Donald Trump, *Time to Get Tough: Making America #1 Again* (Washington, DC: Regnery Publishing, 2011), 2.

2. "2011: U.S. Trade in Goods with China," US Census Bureau, http://www.census.gov/foreign-trade/balance/c5700.html#2011.

3. "China Reserves Ample to Buy World's Gold Twice," *Bloomberg*, 3 March 2013, http://www.bloomberg.com/news/2013-03-03/china-reserves-ample-to-buy-world-s-gold-twice-chart-of-the-day.html.

4. Ibid.

5. "Major Foreign Holders of Treasury Securities (in Billions of Dollars)," US Department of the Treasury, http://www.treasury.gov/resource-center/data-chart-center/tic/Documents/mfh.txt.

6. Indira A. R. Lakshmanan, "Clinton Urges China to Keep Buying U.S. Treasury Securities," *Bloomberg*, 22 February 2009, http://www.bloomberg.com/apps/news?pid=newsarchive&sid=apSqGtcNsqSY.

7. Michael Wines, "China's Leader Says He Is 'Worried' over U.S. Treasuries," *New York Times*, 13 March 2009, http://www.nytimes.com/2009/03/14/business/worldbusiness/14china.html.

8. *News China Magazine*, 1 September 2013, 5.

Myth 20

CHINA'S ECONOMY IS EXPORT DRIVEN

Undoubtedly the most important impact of the global financial crisis (GFC) on the Chinese economy came from the fall in global demand, reflecting China's extremely high export dependency.
—Yu Yongding, professor and past director of the Institute of World Economics and Politics, Chinese Academy of Social Sciences [1]

China is sometimes described as "the world's factory." In 2009 China surpassed Germany as the world's largest exporting country. The Chinese held 10 percent of world exports, that year exporting goods worth US$1.214 trillion. [2] By 2013, the number had risen to US$2.21 trillion. [3] Over the past twenty-five years, exports have almost doubled as a share of gross domestic product (GDP), from 14.8 in 1987 to 27.3 percent in 2012. [4] China's main export articles are electronics and clothing, and the major buyers of Chinese products are the European Union and the United States. Given these numbers, it is no wonder that many people believe the country's rapid economic growth has been driven exclusively by exports of cheap mass-produced goods to the rich Western world. Often this is seen as a weakness of the Chinese economy, since dependency on exports leaves it vulnerable to global recessions. A downturn means lower demand for Chinese goods—and lower revenues.

But the perception that China's economy is export driven is in fact the biggest myth about it.

Since the late 1970s, growth in the Chinese economy has been remarkably stable. China fared well in the 1997–1998 Asian crisis, the Internet bubble of 2000, and the 2008–2009 financial crisis. In 2009, the country's exports dropped 20 percent, but the economy grew 8 percent, indicating that there are other growth drivers besides exports. Growth remained so high largely thanks to the Chinese government's focus on domestic real investments in 2009 and 2010, funded for the most part by state-owned banks.

The official figures, which show that gross exports account for 40 percent of GDP, are highly misleading. They exaggerate how much the country actually makes on goods that are "made in China." Companies established with foreign capital—taking advantage of the cheap Chinese labor force—are responsible for many of the high-tech exports. Chinese companies typically assemble components made in more technologically advanced countries like Japan and South Korea, as well as in Taiwan, and then export the finished products to the West. Take, for example, an iPod, which retails for $299 in the United States. Of the $150 that the Chinese manufacturer receives for each sold item, 95 percent goes to different companies abroad that made the components. Only about 5 percent, or $7.50, of the wholesale price comes from Chinese parts and labor and stays in China.[5] Thus a $150 export might actually contribute only $7.50 to GDP.

Exactly how much of the Chinese economy export makes up is difficult to calculate. McKinsey has estimated that China's real export is only about half of what official figures stated between 2001 and 2008.[6] To arrive at this estimate, the consulting firm subtracted components and services purchased from abroad to produce goods for export. These goods and services accounted for between 40 and 55 percent of the value of China's total exports. Jonathan Anderson, an economist at Union Bank of Switzerland, subtracted imported components and services and concluded that exports accounted for as little as 10 percent of China's GDP in 2007.[7]

China's fantastic growth can be traced to real investments rather than exports. Such investments represent more than 40 percent of the country's GDP. The Chinese government has invested enormously in infrastructure and heavy industry as the private sector has invested in light industry.[8]

Private households' consumption still represents a relatively small share of the Chinese economy, despite Beijing's goal of increasing domestic consumption. In an early phase of industrialization, it is common for growth in real investments to be a much bigger part of the economy than consumption. This was the case for Japan and Taiwan. China's leaders see both economic and political gains in a gradual increase in private households' consumption. This will help keep the wheels of the Chinese economy spinning; it is also reasonable to suppose that the government thinks material wealth will make the Chinese less likely to challenge political stability. Consumption will likely gradually account for a larger part of the Chinese economy. Indeed, China is expected to overtake the United States as the world's biggest retail market by 2016.[9]

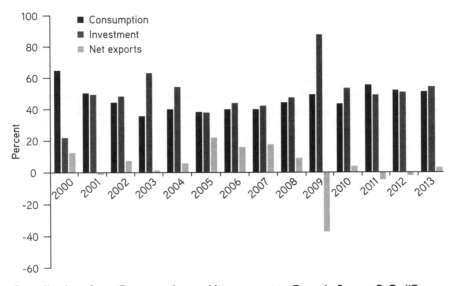

Contributions from Consumption and Investment to Growth. *Source:* **S. C., "Rebalancing China: China's Consumer-Led Growth,"** *Economist,* **20 October 2012, http://www.economist.com/blogs/freeexchange/2012/10/rebalancing-china.**

The financial crisis confirmed that real investments drive the Chinese economy more than exports do, discrediting predictions that trouble in the world economy would lead to collapse in China. Aided by a stimulus package, the economy managed to grow even when the major Western import markets stumbled.

Notes

1. Yu Yongding, "China's Response to the Global Financial Crisis," East Asia Institute, 24 January 2010, http://www.eastasiaforum.org/2010/01/24/chinas-response-to-the-global-financial-crisis.

2. "Trade to Expand by 9.5% in 2010 after a Dismal 2009, WTO Reports," press release, World Trade Organization, 26 March 2013, http://www.wto.org/english/news_e/pres10_e/pr598_e.htm.

3. "China's Foreign Trade Up 7.6 Pct in 2013," *Global Times,* 10 January 2014, http://www.globaltimes.cn/content/836785.shtml#.UwC6bVLKxjo.

4. "Exports of Goods and Services (% of GDP)," World Bank, http://data.worldbank.org/indicator/NE.EXP.GNFS.ZS.

5. Rana Foroohar, "Everything You Know about China Is Wrong," *Newsweek,* 17 October 2009, http://www.newsweek.com/id/21890/output/print.

6. John Horn, Vivien Singer, and Jonathan Woetzel, "A Truer Picture of China's Export Machine," *McKinsey Quarterly,* September 2010, http://www.mckinseyquarterly.com/Strategy/Globalization/A_truer_picture_of_Chinas_export_machine_2676.

7. "An Old Chinese Myth," *Economist*, 3 January 2008, http://www.economist.com/node/10429271?story_id=10429271.

8. Ibid.

9. Moran Zhang, "As China Rebalances Its Economy, Western Companies Rethink Their Business Strategy," *International Business Times*, 3 April 2013, http://www.ibtimes.com/china-rebalances-its-economy-western-companies-rethink-their-business-strategy-1167985.

Myth 21

CHINESE PEOPLE ARE BORN MONEYMAKERS

The almost perfect correlation between Chinese heritage and economic success could hardly be due to chance.

—G. L. Hick and S. G. Redding[1]

King Vajiravudh of Thailand described the Chinese as "the Jews of the East" in 1914. One hundred years later, the Chinese still dominate the economies of many Southeast Asian countries. In Malaysia the Chinese control 70 percent of the national economy despite constituting only one-third of the population. In the Philippines Chinese stockbrokers dominate the stock exchange. They also control much of the shipping and construction industries and the property market. Chinese tycoons own sixty-three of the seventy largest companies in Thailand.[2] Eight of the ten richest people in both Malaysia and Singapore are of Chinese origin.[3] Andrew Tan is a typical Chinese moneybags. Tan came from underprivileged circumstances in China and moved to Manila, where he started off selling kitchen appliances. He went on to produce his own brandy label, Emperador, which became the world's best seller; Tan is now a billionaire. Lee Shin Cheng is another example. He went from selling ice cream from his bicycle to owning the IOI Group, the world's largest producer of palm oil, with thirty thousand employees worldwide.[4] Chinese corporate forays into Europe and Africa contribute to the image of all Chinese—or at least the vast majority—as having an exceptional instinct for making money. The Chinese in Southeast Asia are doing so well that it can hardly be due to chance. Some claim that financial success is deeply rooted in Chinese culture; others even say it is in their genes.

But this kind of speculation ignores a number of important factors.

First, there are historical and legal reasons why there are so many successful Chinese businesspeople in China's neighboring countries. The colonial era laid the foundation for Chinese business empires. When European colonizers arrived in Southeast Asia in the early seventeenth century, the Chinese traders, who had already established networks, gained access to new markets. The Europeans preferred using established and experienced Chinese as middlemen. Moreover, this provided Chinese traders with new markets in Europe, in addition to the markets they already had in China, Taiwan, Hong Kong, and Singapore. With the exception of the trading business, options were limited for Chinese living outside China. Chinese immigrants were banned from a number of jobs for long periods, including in the public sector—even the educational system. They were frequently banned from owning land. In addition, in Vietnam, the Chinese in the early twentieth century enjoyed advantages in the business world relative to both Vietnamese and other foreigners. Because Chinese men were exempt from military service and forced labor, they had an advantage over the Vietnamese. French colonial rulers gave them great freedom and a uniquely advantageous status compared to other foreigners. They could set up shops and other businesses almost as freely as the French themselves.[5]

It is reasonable to assume, too, that those who chose to leave their homes did not represent a cross section of the Chinese population. Like emigrants all over the world, they had a strong entrepreneurial mentality—more pep and a greater willingness to take risks—than those who remained at home. Many left China not knowing what awaited them and without a guarantee that they would find a way to make a livelihood. Few are willing to take such a risk. Indian contract laborers who came to Southeast Asia, on the other hand, were chosen by white farm owners. They were thus more passive in the process of leaving their country, and jobs were waiting for them. This is not to romanticize the slave-like conditions in which they lived but rather to point out that they were not necessarily entrepreneurs the way Chinese immigrants were.

In the end, the idea that all Chinese in Southeast Asia are wealthy—run business empires, lunch on thousand-dollar fish stomach soup, and live in palaces—is a far cry from reality. Most linger on the lower rungs of the social ladder, and many work for a pittance. While the urban Chinese population in Southeast Asia often does well financially, rural areas in Malaysia, Thailand, and Java are home to Chinese who have lived in poverty for generations. But we hear very little about them.

It is a myth that all Chinese are clever businesspeople. Those who have done well in Southeast Asia have often benefited from favorable historic conditions. Although China's growth is fantastic, there are many Chinese struggling to make ends meet, both in China and elsewhere in the world. They just don't make good copy—which is why wealthy Chinese businesspeople, preferably cunning and ruthless ones, get all the attention.

Notes

1. G. L. Hochs and S. C. Redding, "The Story of the East Asian 'Economic Miracle': Part Two: The Cultural Connection," *Euro-Asia Business Review* 2, no. 4 (1983): 22.

2. All figures obtained from Amy Chua, *World on Fire: How Exporting Free Market Democracy Breeds Ethnic Hatred and Global Instability* (New York: Doubleday, 2003), 35–38.

3. See, e.g., Faizul Azri, "Top 10 Richest People in Malaysia 2012," *Malaysian Digest*, 16 July 2012, http://www.malaysiandigest.com/archived/index.php/15-features/personality/9267-top-10-richest-people-in-malaysia-2012.html; Naazneen Karmali, "21 Billionaires among Singapore's Richest," *Forbes Magazine*, 25 July 2012, http://www.forbes.com/singapore-billionaires.

4. "The World's Billionaires," *Forbes Magazine*, 19 September 2012, http://www.forbes.com/billionaires/list.

5. Peter Brush, "Vietnam, China and the Boat People," Jean and Alexander Heard Library, 2007, http://www.library.vanderbilt.edu/206central/Brush/BoatPeople.htm#_edn4; E. S. Ungar, "The Struggle over the Chinese Community in Vietnam, 1946–1986," *Pacific Affairs* 60, no. 4 (winter 1987–1988): 596–614.

Myth 22

CHINESE DON'T TAKE RISKS

Chinese managers with high uncertainty-avoidance lack adventurous spirit and the sense of risks.

—Cisse Daouda[1]

There is a widespread belief that Chinese people are reluctant to take risks—especially in business. Chinese culture is often perceived as cautious, conservative, and collectivist. Western—and particularly American—culture is viewed as the opposite. Many have blamed the financial crisis on American investment banks' irresponsibility and willingness to take foolish risks. "The early bird gets the worm," American children are taught. Chinese children learn instead that "the first bird out will be shot."

The importance of being cautious is also emphasized by the ancient Chinese concept of "hiding one's capabilities." Deng Xiaoping made this ideal real when he famously exhorted the Chinese to hide their capability and bide their time in relations with the outside world. Chinese companies make secrecy their mantra. The idea is to reveal as little as possible about yourself in order to protect valuable business secrets.

Many refer to Chinese carefulness as a barrier to innovation. No one dares to try new things and run the risk of failure. The Chinese savings rate is high, another sign of caution, and an obstacle to the development of a consumer-based economy. China saves about half of its GDP; in 2010, the share was 53 percent.[2]

But Chinese are not entirely sober.

The Chinese are gamblers. Elderly Chinese women swarm the casinos in Macao and Singapore. They love gambling, and stock market speculation has become a national pastime. It is not uncommon for Chinese couples to split up because they disagree about the share of the household budget to be used for gambling and speculation in the stock market.

Moreover, the economic growth of recent decades has shifted attitudes in the business community: young industry leaders, particularly investors, increasingly believe it necessary and right to take risks. Henning Kristoffersen and Gao Jinsong describe the Chinese entrepreneurial spirit as "extreme," characterized by "boundless ambition, great willingness to take risks, and high flexibility."[3] The high number of Chinese private businesses that go bankrupt—an estimated eight hundred thousand companies went bankrupt in 2008—reflects a risk tolerance that at times may be too high.[4] However, this is positive for the Chinese business community when it comes to innovation. "We don't want to lose a single minute. We have a lot of confidence, and we are very comfortable with risk," declares the Chinese businessman Wei Chen.[5]

Americans underestimate the Chinese people's willingness to take risks, and Chinese correspondingly exaggerate the American appetite for it. This is the conclusion of Christopher K. Hsee and Elke U. Weber,[6] who compared the risk readiness of Americans and Chinese and found that the former were more risk averse than the latter. Chinese and American university students were given a choice: take US$400 or flip a coin to determine whether they received US$2,000 or nothing. The guinea pigs were also asked to choose between a safe investment where the return was 4 percent and a less safe investment where the return could be anything between 0 and 8 percent. In both cases, the Chinese students were far more willing to take risks than the Americans.

The researchers explained the findings by pointing out that China today is a land of opportunity. "Today's China is very similar to America during the Gold Rush,"[7] note Hsee and Weber. The Chinese economy is developing at a rapid pace, and many people make huge fortunes by taking big risks. Such opportunities are far rarer in a country with a more developed economy, such as the United States. Today running economic risks seems much less potentially profitable to Americans than it does to the Chinese. According to Hsee and Weber, the Chinese appetite for risk might also be explained by the sense that they have a cushion. In individualistic societies, such as the United States, personal freedom and independence are emphasized, while the Chinese embrace social relationships and interdependence in the context of family and community. Unlike people who live in an individualistic society, the researchers conclude, those who live in a network society are more likely get help if they find themselves in a difficult situation. Accordingly, risks seem less scary.

The notion that Chinese people suffer from risk aversion is as untrue as the idea that Americans have an insatiable appetite for risk.

Notes

1. Cisse Daouda, "Cultural Differences in Business Relations: The Case of China and Africa," Chinainvests.org, 30 December 2010, http://chinainvests.org/2010/12/30/cultural-differences-in-business-relations-the-case-of-china-and-africa.

2. See, e.g., "China (People's Republic of China) Gross National Savings (% of GDP) Statistics," Economy Watch, http://www.economywatch.com/economic-statistics/China/Gross_National_Savings_Percentage_of_GDP.

3. The authors' translation from Norwegian is taken from Henning Kristoffersen and Gao Jinsong, "Kinas nye entreprenører" [China's New Entrepreneurs], in *Kinas økonomi*, ed. Jo Inge Bekkevold and Henning Kristoffersen (Oslo: Gyldendal akademiske forlag, 2012), 158.

4. "China's Hidden Bankruptcy," *Economic Observer Online*, 5 May 2009, http://www.eeo.com.cn/ens/finance_investment/2009/06/05/139307.shtml.

5. Erin Meyer and Elisabeth Yi Shen, "China Myths, China Facts," *Harvard Business Review*, 2010, http://hbr.org/2010/01/china-myths-china-facts/ar/pr.

6. Christopher K. Hsee and Elke U. Weber, "Researching Risk Preference," *Capital Ideas* 1, no. 3 (1998), http://www.chicagobooth.edu/capideas/sum98/hsee.htm.

7. Ibid.

Myth 23

THE CHINESE ARE JUST COPYCATS

The Chinese are like vampires. They come and suck up our technology
to take it back to China.
   —Jean Granjon, Bluestar Silicones in France (authors' translation)[1]

Everything between heaven and earth is, they say, copied by unscrupulous Chinese pirates: Norwegian smoked salmon, Japanese cars, Russian
weapons, Finnish Nokia phones, and Swedish IKEA furniture, for start-
ers. There is an entire fake Apple Store in Kunming in Southwest China.
The scenic Austrian mountain town of Hallstätt has been replicated to the
smallest detail by a Chinese real estate developer, half an hour's drive
from the less appealing city of Huizhou. Even the flowers (which are
fake) are the same. The Hallstätters think it is partly flattering, partly
bizarre.

In fact, the copying industry is called *shanzhai*, or "mountain village,"
in Chinese. The term is meant to indicate that the business is far from
official control, since villages in the mountains were historically often
governed by bandits and warlords.

The Chinese have a long tradition of copying, which is itself an esteemed art form. Painters often copied the works of earlier masters. An
accurate copy is esteemed almost as much as the original. Many ancient
Chinese paintings no longer exist, but copies of them painted centuries
later are kept and admired. Addressing post-1989 China, the writer Yu
Hua argues that "the force and scale of copycatting demonstrate that the
whole nation has taken to it as a form of performance art."[2]

Clearly, there are also legal reasons for all this copying. Pirates are
often protected by local officials and police, who share in their profits: a
trinity that makes criminal prosecution very unlikely. The nature of the

Chinese market also feeds piracy: it is characterized by low average purchasing power, and many consumers have a limited ability to assess quality, especially of the more technically advanced products. Nevertheless, consumer culture is on the rise, and therefore so is demand for pirated products. It is easy to understand why Westerners associate China with copying and the production of cheap products rather than with innovation and quality.

In the West, there is a deep belief that political freedom is a fundamental precondition for innovation. Historical evidence, however, hardly supports this view. Few of the most creative societies of the ancient world were free, including China, which invented paper, the compass, gunpowder, and the printing press. About two hundred years ago, the Industrial Revolution began and flourished in a Europe of limited political freedom. More recently, both Nazi Germany and the Soviet Union punched well above their weight in innovation despite having highly authoritarian governments.

It is important, too, not to ignore trends toward greater innovation in contemporary China.

China has made great progress in research. The traditionally dominant research powers—the United States, Europe, and Japan—face serious competition, according to the Royal Society Science Academy in a report published in 2011.[3] The report predicted that China would surpass the United States in the number of scientific papers published in international journals within a few years. Chinese scientists are still cited less frequently—citation is a commonly used measure of academic quality—but there is progress even on that front.

These findings are hardly surprising. The Chinese are investing heavily in innovation. China's funding for research and development has increased by 20 percent annually since 1999. In 2012, the budget was US$198.9 billion, higher than Japan's budget, which was US$157.6 billion the same year, and half of the European Union's, which was US$338.1 billion. Comparing country by country, only the United States' budget was larger, at US$436 billion.[4] If Chinese authorities allow the budget to continue growing at this pace, the country's investments in research and development could in a few years exceed the budget of the European Union and approach that of the United States. Between 2006 and 2010, the number of Chinese international patent applications tripled, according to the UN's World Intellectual Property Organization.[5] Although most of these applications are adjustments of existing products, the development clearly indicates increased innovation. And in 2009 as many as ten thousand Chinese students defended dissertations in science and engineering.[6] This provides the basis for innovation in the future.

Trends in Global R&D Spending

	2010		2011		2012	
	(Billion US $)	as % of GDP	(Billion US $)	as % of GDP	(Billion US $)	as % of GDP
United States	415.1	2.8	427.2	2.8	436.0	2.8
Japan	148.3	3.4	152.1	3.5	157.6	3.5
China	149.3	1.5	174.9	1.6	198.9	1.6
Europe	310.5	1.9	326.7	1.9	338.1	2.0

It is no longer difficult to find innovative Chinese companies. *Forbes* rated Chinese search engine Baidu as the world's sixth most innovative company in 2013, ahead of, among others, Amazon.[7] Further down in *Forbes* top fifty, we find Henan Shuanghui Investment, Tencent Holdings, Kweichow Moutai, and China Oilfield Services. Chinese innovation will continue to grow in international prominence. As many as 88 percent of Chinese business leaders say they plan to increase their innovation budgets, while only 48 percent of their American colleagues say the same.[8]

The *Fast Company* website has also found room for several Chinese enterprises in its ranking of the world's most innovative companies.[9] Electronics company Xiaomi ends up in third place, surpassed only by giants Google and Bloomberg Philanthropies. Also on the top fifty list are Chinese fashion houses Mary Ching, NSISS, and Rose Studio, along with tourism company WildChina, etiquette school Institute Sarita, and research institute BGI.

Still, most Westerners are unable to name a single famous Chinese brand. Several Chinese companies want to change that situation. These include sports equipment manufacturer Li-Ning, telecom companies China Mobile and Huawei, computer manufacturer Lenovo, and renewable energy companies such as Suntech Power Holdings. In 2008, thirty-four Chinese companies ranked among the Fortune 500. Five years later, the number had increased to eighty-nine,[10] ninety-five when including Taiwan.[11]

But this is not fast enough for Beijing. Chinese authorities fear that local companies are not able to grow large enough on their own. Besides, they compete too much with each other. In January 2013, the Ministry of Industry presented a new plan with the goal of creating global giant corporations by merging Chinese companies. The hope, for example, is to reduce the number of Chinese car manufacturers to a maximum of five—down from today's sixty-five—which will compete with South Korean and Japanese companies internationally.[12]

China increasingly benefits from a large and well-educated diaspora. In the United States, one of the largest groups of foreign students is Chinese. Nearly one hundred thousand Chinese students were enrolled in American institutions of higher education in 2009, many of them at top universities.[13] A previous trend was for graduates to seek lucrative jobs in the United States; one of three experts in Silicon Valley is Chinese. But more and more graduates are tempted by well-paid jobs in their home country, and today about 20 percent of all Chinese educated abroad return home.[14] They bring with them valuable expertise: as many as 81 percent of the scientists at China's prestigious Academy of Sciences and 54 percent of the employees at the Chinese Academy of Engineering are returnees.[15]

The notion that the Chinese are copycats rather than innovators might soon belong to the past. China follows the same innovation strategy used with great success by other Asian countries. At the beginning of the 1980s, Japan, miraculously rebuilt after World War II, had become an economic superpower. Nonetheless, we remember from childhood how "made in Japan" was a joke. For most people this label meant that the product was cheap, low in quality, and most likely copied. Our fathers nicknamed Japanese cars "rice burners" and bought Saabs or Volvos instead. Today, Japanese industry is associated with innovation and quality, and Japan is a world leader in the production of automobiles, household appliances, and all kinds of high-tech products. South Korea and Taiwan underwent similar development. Half of this book, for example, was written on a Taiwanese Acer.

In the future, "made in China" could also be associated with innovation and quality if investments in research and development continue—and bear fruit. In this arena the Chinese have a proud, ancient tradition to uphold.

1. Cited in "Kineserne er som vampyrer" [The Chinese Are like Vampires], *Dagens Næringsliv*, 12 January 2011, http://www.dn.no/nyheter/naringsliv/2011/01/12/-kineserne-er-som-vampyrer.

2. Yu Hua, *China in Ten Words* (New York: Anchor Books, 2011), 189.

3. "Knowledge, Networks and Nations: Global Scientific Collaboration in the 21st Century," Royal Society Science Academy, 27 March 2011, http://royalsociety.org/uploadedFiles/Royal_Society_Content/Influencing_Policy/Reports/2011-03-28-Knowledge-networks-nations.pdf.

4. For comparative research and development figures, see "2012 Global R & D Funding Forecast: R & D Spending Growth Continues While Globalization Accelerates," *R&D Magazine*, 16 December 2011, http://www.rdmag.com/articles/2011/12/2012-global-r-d-funding-forecast-r-d-spending-growth-continues-while-globalization-accelerates.

5. Joseph Calamia, "China Rising: International Patent Applications," *IEEE Spectrum* 48, no. 7 (2011): 68.

6. Geoff Colvin, "Desperately Seeking Math and Science Majors," *CNN Money*, 29 July 2010, http://money.cnn.com/2010/07/29/news/international/china_engineering_grads.fortune/index.htm.

7. "The World's Most Innovative Companies," *Forbes*, August 2013, http://www.forbes.com/innovative-companies/list/#page:1_sort:0_direction:asc_search:_filter:All%20regions_filter:All%20industries.

8. *Businessweek*, 15 April 2010, http://www.businessweek.com/magazine/content/10_17/b4175034779697.htm?chan=magazine+channel_special+report.

9. "The World's Most Innovative Companies 2014," *Fast Company*, http://www.fastcompany.com/section/most-innovative-companies-2014.

10. "World's 500 Largest Corporations in 2013: The Chinese Are Rising," *Forbes*, 7 July 2013, http://www.forbes.com/sites/panosmourdoukoutas/2013/07/17/worlds-500-largest-corporations-in-2013-the-chinese-are-rising.

11. "95 Chinese Companies Make Fortune Global 500," *Global Times*, 8 July 2013, http://www.globaltimes.cn/content/794696.shtml.

12. *Dagens Næringsliv*, 24 January 2013, 36.

13. "China Is Sending More Students to U.S.," *New York Times*, 16 November 2009, http://www.nytimes.com/2009/11/16/education/16international-.html.

14. James Wilsdon and James Keeley, "China: The Next Science Superpower?" Naider, 2007, http://www.naider.com/upload/82_China_Final.pdf, 30–31.

15. Ping Zhou and Loet Leydesdorff, "The Emergence of China as a Leading Nation in Science," Cornell University Library, 2009, http://arxiv.org/ftp/arxiv/papers/0911/0911.3421.pdf, 84.

Myth 24

THE STATE HINDERS ECONOMIC DEVELOPMENT IN CHINA

First, implement structural reforms to strengthen the foundations for a market-based economy.
—The World Bank's number one message to China[1]

Western neoliberals—Americans more than Europeans—highlight post-1978 China as a success story for the "Washington Consensus": less government, privatization, and trade liberalization.

And the country's growth is truly impressive.

"China's growth record since 1978 is nearly unparalleled in human history," according to Joseph E. Stiglitz, Nobel laureate in economics.[2] Improvements in the Chinese people's standard of living are impressive. In the period from 1978 to 2012, the GDP per capita grew close to 10 percent annually.[3]

Many neoliberals believe the Chinese economy would have done even better if all state-owned enterprises were privatized and the country had become a fully capitalist society. For example, the *Economist* states, "State-owned enterprises are much more concerned to maintain patronage and employment than to generate profits, and even the best are not globally competitive. China's fledgling private businesses, by contrast, have shown astounding growth and produced the country's first crop of wealthy entrepreneurs."[4] Despite liberalization, the economy is still dominated by the state. Using state-owned banks, the state budget, and five-year plans, the Chinese government controls the direction of the economy. The state maintains tight control of land, labor, and capital. China still does not have private ownership of land. Free labor unions do not exist, which keeps wages down. Large state-owned banks dominate the capital market. China's stock market is dominated by state enterprises. The large private companies are dependent on good relations with the government and state-owned banks.

The neoliberals now see obstacles to China's continued economic growth. An entire choir sings that the country must disempower state-owned enterprises and open up to the free flow of capital in order to maintain economic growth and prevent lurking crises. China's leadership faces major management challenges, and the Chinese government is neither very efficient nor corruption-free.

That said, it is important to assess critically whether the state hinders economic growth in China.

China's economic policy to date can be defined as a success—and the Chinese government must be commended for its past and present growth-promoting role. Moreover, state ownership and influence should not be seen as evils just because the state has objectives besides pure value maximization. The state also works toward goals such as low unemployment, equitable distribution, and political stability—which may be just as important to a state's development as profit.

Several factors clearly indicate that an active government has facilitated and still contributes to economic growth in China.

First, it was the state that laid the foundation for the astonishing economic growth that began in 1978.[5] The state provided basic social infrastructure in terms of education and health care for workers. The government built power grids in the Chinese countryside, which facilitated industrialization later on. The state secured egalitarian land distribution, which came to be a social safety net in the disruptive time that followed market reforms. The state created a decentralized economic system in which, for example, local authorities controlled manufacturing enterprises. The regional and local expertise thus built up aided later economic processes. For example, such expertise was used in the development and management of the rural enterprises and the rural industrialization they represented. The government set up a national system of scientific research and innovation; as early as 1980 China spent more on research and development as a share of GDP than most other poor countries. It is rarely noted that China's success in the international market is not restricted to labor-intensive sectors such as toys, clothing, and shoes. China has also succeeded in making and exporting products far more sophisticated than is expected of countries with a similar GDP per capita—such as telecom equipment, computer networking devices, and mobile phones. In addition, the state facilitated high female education and labor participation, increasing women's contribution to economic growth.

Furthermore, the post-1978 prosperity cannot be attributed to economic opening alone, as the neoliberals tend to argue. Much of the growth in the first half of the 1980s was due to internal factors, not globalization. Foreign investments and trade with other countries increased in earnest in the 1990s and beyond. But already between 1978 and 1993, China had an annual average growth rate of almost 10 percent. The internal factors for growth included changes in agricultural organization, regional experimentation, and a policy whereby local achievements were rewarded with promotion within the Communist Party. Even in the period after the mid-1980s, much suggests that domestic investments in education, agricultural research, and infrastructure have been the major engine behind poverty reduction, especially in rural areas.

The very different experiences of China and Russia illustrate the advantages of a state-led economic restructuring and the disadvantages of a neoliberal strategy. Russia's reforms after the Soviet Union's collapse were designed by Western economists who argued for minimal government intervention in the economy. The neoliberal strategy implemented in Russia had three components: liberalization (the abolition of government restrictions on pricing and trading); stabilization (keeping government spending down); and privatization (transferring state-owned enterprises to the private sector). For example, Russia moved quickly to guarantee relatively free import, free capital movements, and a freely convertible currency. When China initiated its economic reforms in 1978, Western experts tried to persuade the Chinese leadership to choose a similar strategy. Their advice fell on deaf ears. When China began its period of economic reforms, the government assumed a leading role in the restructuring of the economy. With regard to economic performance, there is no doubt that China beats Russia: China's GDP was 60 percent of Russia's in 1991; a decade later Russia's GDP was 60 percent of China's.

Many state-owned companies are actually profitable. There are now fewer state-owned companies than there were in the late 1990s, but the ones that remain are larger, more capital and knowledge intensive, and more profitable. They are not necessarily less efficient or less profitable than private companies. The private sector has seen remarkable growth since 1978, but so have state-owned companies.[6] The 121 largest Chinese state-owned enterprises, all of which are subject to the authority of the State-Owned Assets Supervision and Administration Commission, represent an important part of Chinese industry. Many have global ambitions and are among the world's largest and most competitive companies. Three state-owned Chinese companies rank among the ten most profitable companies in the world: Sinopec, China National Petroleum Company, and State Grid. All of Europe, by comparison, has only two companies on this list: Shell and BP.[7] Companies in which the state is a dominant but not the only owner play a particularly important role in the Chinese economy. These mixed enterprises make up only 2.7 percent of all industrial enterprises, but they employ 9 percent of the labor force, account for 16 percent of industrial output, and generate 25 percent of the profits from the industrial sector.[8] This particular type of company is more profitable than any other public or private industrial undertaking. Furthermore, state-owned enterprises are behind much of China's research and development activity.[9]

Finally, an active state has been able to mitigate the effects of economic crisis. Just six weeks after Lehman Brothers collapsed on Wall Street in 2008—and brought the international financial markets to their knees— Chinese authorities issued a massive package to stimulate the economy. In the United States, on the other hand, the government argued for ten months before agreeing on similar action—by which time the stimulus was less effective than it might have been. The Chinese stimulus package was complemented by cuts in interest rates and a strong increase in loans granted. The results were impressive, and China's economy continued to grow significantly. Much criticism was leveled at the stimulus package. Critics argued that it led to unsustainable growth that would make China even more dependent on exports and investments and would fail to do anything to drive consumption. Although there might be some truth to this, even the critics must acknowledge that the alternative to the package would have been a marked decline in economic growth.

In China's case, one should be careful not to underestimate the importance of an active state.

Notes

1. "China 2030: Building a Modern, Harmonious, and Creative High-Income Society," World Bank, 27 February 2012, http://www.worldbank.org/en/news/2012/02/27/china-2030-executive-summary, xv.

2. Joseph E. Stiglitz, "China: Forging a Third Generation of Reforms," World Bank, Beijing, China, 23 July 1999, http://unpan1.un.org/intradoc/groups/public/documents/APCITY/UNPAN004886.pdf, 1.

3. "5. Report for Selected Countries and Subjects," International Monetary Fund, http://www.imf.org/external/pubs/ft/weo/2011/02/weodata/weorept.aspx.

4. "Behind the Mask," *Economist*, 18 March 2004, http://www.economist.com/node/2495113.

5. Pranab Bardhan, *Awakening Giants, Feet of Clay: Assessing the Economic Rise of China and India* (Princeton, NJ: Princeton University Press, 2012).

6. Alberto Gabriele, "The Role of the State in China's Industrial Development: A Reassessment," *Munich Personal RePEc Archive*, 5 April 2009, http://mpra.ub.uni-muenchen.de/14551/1/MPRA_paper_14551.pdf, 2.

7. *Economist*, 21 January 2012, 4.

8. Gabriele, "The Role of the State in China's Industrial Development," 11.

9. Ibid., 13–16.

Myth 25

UNEQUAL DISTRIBUTION OF WEALTH IS A SOURCE OF SOCIAL AND POLITICAL UNREST

"Let some people get rich first," Deng famously declared in 1983.[1] Since these winged words were spoken, the Chinese have gotten richer and richer—but to varying degrees. The gap between rich and poor is now enormous. China has gone from being an egalitarian society, under Mao Zedong, to a country where wealth is unevenly distributed as a result of the transition to a market economy. According to a report commissioned by the Chinese government, 0.4 percent of the population owns some 70 percent of China's wealth.[2] Hordes of wealthy Chinese go on holidays abroad and enjoy all sorts of luxuries. The country's army of millionaires notwithstanding, as recently as 2009 it was estimated that nearly 500 million Chinese—more than one in three—had to survive on less than US$2 per day.[3] Income differences are large not just between the rural and urban areas but also within cities and between people in the countryside.

The Gini coefficient is used to measure a society's economic inequality. Zero describes a society where everyone earns the same amount; in a society at level 1, one person has all the income. The point above which there is a severe risk of social unrest due to inequality is 0.4. In China, the coefficient has increased significantly since market reforms were introduced in 1978. China stopped publishing its Gini results in 2000, and the World Bank stopped in 2005, when China's coefficient was estimated to be 0.42. The Chinese Academy of Social Sciences, whose economists enjoy a reputation for academic excellence, calculated the coefficient to be 0.54 in 2008.[4] In December 2012, China's central bank, in partnership with a Chinese university, published the results of a study showing that the coefficient had increased further, to as high as 0.61 in 2010.[5] This means that over the past three decades, China has become more unequal than other large countries, such as the United States, Japan, India, Russia, and Brazil.[6]

A common belief is that unequal distribution of wealth creates dissatisfaction and consequently social and political unrest.

Karl Marx believed that it did not matter to people whether they lived in small or large houses. As long as all the houses in the neighborhood were small, there was a good chance residents would be satisfied with their own small house. As soon as one mansion was built, however, discontent would spread throughout the neighborhood. In the same vein, Western observers often declare that unequal growth will cause social unrest that will challenge the legitimacy and power of the Chinese Communist Party.

The economist Albert O. Hirschman uses traffic to explain why economic disparity is a source of dissatisfaction. When we are stuck in a traffic jam, we feel frustrated and powerless. As soon as another lane starts moving, we are filled with joy and optimism, thinking it will soon be our turn to move. However, according to Hirschman, our optimism quickly becomes redoubled frustration if our lane remains still. The effect of lasting large—and growing—disparities cannot be ignored when considering long-term stability.[7]

Nonetheless, it is not a given that income inequality creates envy and anger in the case of China.

So argues Martin King Whyte, professor of sociology at Harvard University, in *Myth of the Social Volcano*.[8] On the basis of a nationwide survey, Whyte shows that the vast majority of the Chinese actually accepts the differences that come with a market economy, and they welcome the opportunity to improve their standard of living through talent and hard work. Whyte believes many Chinese tolerate economic inequality because they see the current system as fairer than the rigid socialist system under Mao. Before the reform period it did not matter much if you were a lazy piggybacker or well educated, hardworking, and innovative. In the spirit of socialism, workers, bureaucrats, and soldiers were all supposed to earn the same amount, and peasants on collective farms had little to gain by working themselves to death in the rice fields. In light of this experience, it is not surprising that the Chinese largely accept the income inequalities created by three decades of market reforms. Despite these differences, the Chinese see that they have opportunities for social mobility through education and hard work. Their belief that hard work creates wealth is almost American, concludes Whyte.[9]

Acceptance of social inequality has been one of the strengths of the Chinese system—so far.

The leadership in Beijing has wisely defined more equal and inclusive growth as a key aim in the economic five-year plan for 2011 to 2016. But just as important as inclusive growth is taming corruption. Chinese find personal enrichment through political contacts and positions hard to swallow.

Notes

1. Quoted in Duncan Hewitt, *China: Getting Rich First: A Modern Social History* (New York: Pegasus, 2009), xix.

2. Cited in Qian Gang, "A Few More Facts about China's 'Fake News' Purge," *China Media Project*, 30 November 2009, http://cmp.hku.hk/2009/11/30/3226.

3. "UNICEF and U.N. Human Development Report," UNDP, http://hdrstats.undp.org/en/indicators/103.html.

4. For references to these figures, see, e.g., James Parker, "Inharmonious Society? China's Rising Income Inequality," *Diplomat*, 15 December 2012, http://thediplomat.com/pacific-money/2012/12/15/inharmonious-society-chinas-rising-income-inequality.

5. Ibid.

6. For a comparison, see, e.g., "GINI Index," World Bank, http://data.worldbank.org/indicator/SI.POV.GINI; "The United Nations Human Development Report, 2007–08," UNDP, http://www.hdr.undp.org/en/statistics.

7. Albert O. Hirschman and Michael Rothschild, "The Changing Tolerance for Income Inequality in the Course of Economic Development; with a Mathematical Appendix," *Quarterly Journal of Economics* 87, no. 4 (1973): 544–66.

8. Martin King Whyte, *Myth of the Social Volcano: Perceptions of Inequality and Distributive Injustice in Contemporary China* (Stanford, CA: Stanford University Press, 2010); see also Martin King Whyte, "Do Chinese Citizens Want the Government to Do More to Promote Equality?" in *Chinese Politics: State, Society, and the Market*, ed. Peter Hays Gries and Stanley Rosen (New York: Routledge, 2010), 129–59.

9. Whyte, *Myth of the Social Volcano*, 71.

Myth 26

ALL ECONOMIC DEVELOPMENT IS HAPPENING IN THE BIG CITIES ON THE EAST COAST

China's coastal areas have led the rest of China in economic development and low fertility rates.

—R. Song[1]

Most people associate the rapid development and growth in China with cities on the east coast—Shanghai, Hong Kong, and Xiamen—where you will find a millionaire or billionaire on every corner. No wonder, as all the major international companies have set up offices there. The cities look like sets for a futuristic science fiction movie. They develop so rapidly that if you leave for a few months, you may no longer be able to find your way around when you return. Western China—the inland and the rural areas—is envisaged as the cities' antithesis, anachronistic in the extreme. Everybody does things exactly as they have been done since the Tang Dynasty. It has not occurred to anyone to change anything. Farmers pull their own plows. It isn't just foreigners who imagine China this way. When talking to Chinese city people, one is left with the impression that dwellers in the rural parts of the country hardly produce anything and live off financial support from the cities. Cities and coastal areas pull all the weight, and the inland is merely static deadweight.

The idea that development takes place only in the cities along the east coast ignores two basic conditions.

First, the provinces with the fastest growth are in fact inland. Out of a total of thirteen provinces with an economic growth of more than 12 percent in 2012, Tanjin is the only coastal province. China's richest city is neither Hong Kong nor Shanghai and is situated far away from the east coast: Erdos, with 1.5 million inhabitants, is located in Inner Mongolia. The density of Jaguars, Ferraris, and Rolls-Royces in Erdos is larger than anywhere else in China. The source of the city's wealth is its large coal deposits—a quarter of the world's total reserves.[2] Erdos is not a unique example; Inner Mongolia as a whole has had an average annual economic growth of 17 percent since 2001.[3]

Chongqing is another example of an inland city pulling its weight for the economic development of the country. This rural city's economic growth is around 14 percent—the fastest in China.[4] The city was separated from Sichuan in 1997 and granted autonomy as a province in order to stimulate economic growth inland—a strategy that has proved effective. The city's revenues come not from exports—its location in the middle of the country is unsuitable for that—but from a diverse industry that produces various goods for domestic customers: prepared meals, chemicals, and textiles, to name a few.

Chongqing owes much to one of the major campaigns of the twenty-first century: "Developing Western China" (*Xibu da kaifa*). A total of 1 trillion RMB (about US$160 billion) has been spent on building infrastructure, attracting foreign investment, and improving education in western China. The strategy has so far proved successful. Chongqing is not the only western city to experience growth; in the first six years of the campaign, the western regions reported an annual average economic

Provinces or Province-Level Cities with Economic Growth Greater than 12 Percent in 2012

Province or Province-Level City	Percentage Growth
Guizhou	14.0
Tianjin	13.8
Chongqing	13.6
Gansu	13.0
Yunnan	13.0
Shaanxi	12.9
Sichuan	12.6
Qinghai	12.3
Anhui	12.1
Heilongjian	12.0
Jilin	12.0
Tibet	12.0
Xinjiang	12.0

growth of 10.6 percent.[5] The trend is clear: the differences between the east coast and inland are evening out. Investments from home and abroad are now increasing faster inland than along the east coast.[6]

Second, economic development does not take place only in cities. The cities have certainly seen more of the country's economic growth than have rural areas, and rural people on average still make only a third of what city dwellers do. But average income for farmers nearly tripled between 2000 and 2010, according to official statistics. And the economy is now growing faster in the countryside than in the cities.[7]

One major reason farmers now make more money is that market reforms have reached the Chinese countryside. As early as the late 1970s, the financial responsibility for production was transferred from the collective—where hard work brought little profit for the individual—to individual households. The farmers were given greater freedom to choose what to grow, and they were allowed to sell their goods on the private market. As a result they produced more. In addition to the increase in agricultural production, more and more villagers make a living in other ways. From the early 1980s, the government encouraged everyone with a mind for entrepreneurship to start up his or her own business through the campaign "Town and Village Enterprises" (*Xiangzhen qiye*). A brand-new livelihood emerged: the service industry. Local entrepreneurs opened their own noodle shops or small stalls where they repaired bicycles and sewing machines. Quite a few people gave it a go: in 1985 there were 15 million such businesses in the Chinese countryside; in the 1990s they employed more people than the state-owned enterprises did. At the campaign's peak these private companies provided one-third of China's gross national product.[8] Although the campaign has run its course, it sparked the development we see in the countryside today.

An example of this development is Huaxi village in Jiangsu province. Every one of the thirty thousand inhabitants is good for at least US$250,000. With a unique mix of communism and market liberalism—all villagers are shareholders in Huaxi Group, managed by the local party secretary and listed on the Shenzhen Stock Exchange—the village has managed to flourish in several sectors: shipping, steel, tobacco, and textiles. And 2 million tourists visit the miraculous Huaxi every year. The fifteenth tallest building in the world is located in Huaxi, and a future skyscraper will be the world's second highest at 128 floors. The village has its own aviation company and will have twenty aircraft by 2015. If you get hungry while visiting Huaxi, the restaurants Triumphal Arch and The White House are among your options.[9]

The Chinese countryside also contributes to the national treasury. Western and Chinese research alike shows that, despite earning less on average, farmers pay more in taxes than do city dwellers.[10] An increasingly large proportion of the farmers' taxes goes to Beijing, and less is transferred to local authorities for local purposes. Many welfare benefits that are free or highly subsidized for urban dwellers require full pay from farmers. Some researchers therefore hold that Chinese farmers subsidize those who live in cities and that this is an important reason for the persistent economic gap between urban and rural areas in China.[11]

Notes

1. R. Song, "China's Coastal Population and Economic Development: Summary of the Symposium," *China Journal of Popular Science* 4, no. 2 (1992): 197–202, http://www.ncbi.nlm.nih.gov/pubmed/12317925.

2. Zhang Zhiming, "Inside the Growth Engine: A Guide to China's Regions, Provinces and Cities," *HSBC Global Research*, December 2010, http://www.research.hsbc.com/midas/Res/RDV?p=pdf&key=nmMuQ3lvVa&n=284797.PDF.

3. "Little Hu and the Mining of the Grasslands," *Economist*, 14 July 2012, http://www.economist.com/node/21558605.

4. "Chongqing's Economic Growth Rebounds," *China Daily*, 14 July 2012, http://www.chinadaily.com.cn/bizchina/2012-07/14/content_15580385.htm.

5. Silviu Petre, "Returning to West: China's Long Road Developmental Domestic Policy," Scribd.com, http://www.scribd.com/doc/44846441/Returning-to-West-de-Silviu-Petre.

6. Daniel Rosen, Rhodium Group, quoted in "China's Rural Growth Spurs Copper Demand," *Businessweek*, 2 November 2010, http://www.businessweek.com/globalbiz/content/nov2010/gb2010112_326953.htm.

7. "China Rural Incomes Rising Most since '84 Show Lure for Job-Seeking Obama," *Bloomberg*, 20 January 2011, http://www.bloomberg.com/news/2011-01-20/china-rural-incomes-rising-mostsince-84-show-lure-for-job-seeking-obama.html.

8. Sanjeev Kumar, "Rural Development through Rural Industrialization: Exploring the Chinese Experience," *Asian Scholarship*, http://www.asianscholarship.org/asf/ejourn/articles/Sanjeev%20Kumar2.pdf.

9. Zhiming, "Inside the Growth Engine"; "China's 'Richest Village' Takes Tourism to the Skies," CNN, 10 August 2012, http://travel.cnn.com/shanghai/life/chinas-richest-village-takes-tourism-skies-258582.

10. Wang Xiaobing and Jenifer Piesse, "Inequality and the Urban-Rural Divide in China: Effects of Regressive Taxation," *China and World Economy* 18, no. 6 (November–December 2010): 36–55; Justin Yifu Lin et al., "Urban and Rural Household Taxation in China: Measurement and Stylized Facts," Chinese University of Hong Kong Paper Collection, July 2002, http://www.usc.cuhk.edu.hk/PaperCollection/webmanager/wkfiles/1722_1_paper.pdf.

11. See, e.g., Wang and Piesse, "Inequality and the Urban-Rural Divide in China."

Part IV

China and the World

Myth 27

THE CHINESE ARE RACIST

Many Chinese are too brainwashed to overcome their racist attitudes towards blacks.

—Internet commenter[1]

In China taxi drivers sometimes refuse to pick up black passengers. Those who have dark skin tend to sit alone on the bus because no one wants to get too close to them. For fear of contracting HIV, hotel and restaurant workers allegedly burn bedding and chopsticks used by foreigners. In the summer of 2007, in Beijing's popular bar area Sanlitun police rounded up and brutalized all black people—including students, tourists, established businessmen, women, and the children of diplomats—as part of a drug raid aimed at young African dealers. Two years later, twenty-year-old Lou Jing made it far in the competition *Go, Oriental Angel!*—a program with a strong resemblance to *American Idol*—causing great uproar in the real world and online. Why? Lou has an African American father and a Chinese mother. "Ugh, it's really disgusting when black and yellow people mix," posted one angry commenter.[2]

We come across racist statements from Chinese people quite frequently, particularly against blacks. But this truth must be examined for nuance as well.

Racism in China today might seem more apparent than in the West, but this does not necessarily mean that it is stronger or more widespread. The Chinese tend to have a different standard of political correctness and permissible speech. In China, race-related statements are less shocking than in the West, largely because the Chinese lack the West's historic legacy of slavery and colonization. In addition, it is generally more acceptable to comment on people's appearance in China than it is in the

West. If you are fat, thin, freckled, tall, or have a visible disability—well, it is all up for discussion. A Chinese who comments on the skin color of a dark-complexioned person is often simply stating that he or she is dark, nothing more. Frank Dikötter, who has made a study of Chinese attitudes toward race throughout history, argues that while China is definitely no stranger to racism, "[racism] was certainly more virulent and widespread in the West."[3]

In order to understand racism in China today, a look at Nigerians living in the metropolis of Guangzhou is particularly enlightening. This is the largest group of Africans in Asia, numbering several hundred thousand. The markets they have established in the city are booming, and relations between them and the Chinese are for the most part friendly.[4] In fact, some of the African young men have Chinese girlfriends and wives, and the girls' parents often do not disapprove. A very young generation of African Chinese is growing up now, speaking at least two languages.[5] The hottest clubs hire African DJs.[6] African clothing and music are beginning to spread among the Chinese in Guangzhou.

Singer Lou Jing (of *Go, Oriental Angel!*) is not from Guangzhou but claims that she had never experienced racism in her native Shanghai until she became a television celebrity. And many Chinese expressed strong disappointment in the negative feedback she received.

Chinese people have a long tradition of marrying foreigners—the highest form of acceptance of someone perceived as different. During the Tang Dynasty, immigrants from Central Asia and the Middle East were encouraged to take Chinese wives in order to help integration. The encouragement hardened into a decree during the Ming Dynasty. Several emperors took Persian wives themselves. Today marriage between Chinese and foreigners is not unusual. In Shanghai about three thousand interracial couples get married annually, making up about 3 percent of all weddings in the city.[7]

Similarly, studies of Chinese behavior in Africa do not report widespread racism. On the contrary, there are strong indications that the Chinese are often more likely than Westerners to treat locals as equals. The biggest development project in China's history was the construction of the TAZARA railway from Zambia to Tanzania in the 1970s. For five years tens of thousands of African and Chinese workers worked and lived together. Jamie Monson, president of the Tanzania Studies Association, interviewed Zambian and Tanzanian workers about their relationship to the Chinese.[8] Many contrasted the Chinese people's behavior with that of European colonizers. Educated Africans in particular tended to become friends with their Chinese counterparts. To their amazement, their Chinese colleagues would invite them home for dinner or various festivals. Sitting at the same table as a white person at the time would have been unthinkable. "It was true friendship; it was so good that you just can't understand it," recalls foreman John Gilbert.[9]

Even today Africans tend to hold a more positive image of Chinese immigrants than one would think. This is the conclusion of a study performed by Barry Sautman in 2009. He found that Africans believe Chinese immigrants adapt well to local conditions, far better than Westerners do. About half of the respondents in the survey—which included nine African countries—replied that Chinese are the best at adapting, while only 22 percent found that Westerners adapt best. Only 2 percent thought the Chinese were racist.[10]

Finally, it is important to point out that Chinese people, generally speaking, have little knowledge of and experience with foreigners. Many have never met one. China's contact with the outside world is relatively new. The number of foreigners in China is increasing, and Chinese people travel overseas more. More contact will probably lead to more nuanced attitudes toward foreigners, for better or for worse.

Notes

1. About.com, 1 June 2000, http://veritas-lux.blogspot.no/2013/05/research-shown-that-indians-are.html.

2. For a firsthand account of being black in China, see Marketus Presswood, "A Minority in the Middle Kingdom: My Experience Being Black in China," *Tea Leaf Nation*, July 17, 2013, http://www.tealeafnation.com/2013/07/chinese-raciality-and-black-reality-in-china/#sthash.hHVRg6iG.dpuf.

3. Frank Dikötter, *The Discourse of Race in Modern China* (London: Hurst and Company 1992), 195.

4. "The Promised Land: Guangzhou's Canaan Market and the Rise of an African Merchant Class," *New Yorker*, 9 February 2009, http://archives.newyorker.com/?i=2009-02-09#folio=050.

5. Heidi Østbø Haugen, "Afrikanere redder Kinas handel" [Africans Come to the Rescue of Chinese Trade], *Ny Tid*, 24 July 2009.

6. Heidi Østbø Haugen, "Globaliseringens fotsoldater" [The Footsloggers of Globalization], *Aftenposten Innsikt*, October 2009.

7. James Farrer, "From 'Passports' to 'Joint Ventures': Intermarriage between Chinese Nationals and Western Expatriates Residing in Shanghai," *Asian Studies Review,* March 2008, http://sophia.academia.edu/JamesFarrer/Papers/590164/From_Passports_to_Joint_Ventures_Intermarriage_between_Chinese_Nationals_and_Western_Expatriates_Residing_in_Shanghai.

8. Jamie Monson, *Africa's Freedom Railway* (Bloomington: Indiana University Press, 2011).

9. Ibid., 61.

10. Barry Sautmann, "African Perspectives on China-Africa Links," Center on China's Transnational Relations, 14 May 2009, https://www.google.com/url?

q=http://www.cctr.ust.hk/materials/conference/workshop/18/20090514-
bsautman.ppt&sa=U&ei=M5W0U8bIGbSksQTAn4DoBQ&ved=
0CAYQFjAB&client=internal-uds-cse&usg=
AFQjCNEJTJH0555IxAMozVL8pT1eurhZOw.

Myth 28

THE COMMUNIST PARTY IS KINDLING NATIONALISM

Now that communism is dead, the Communist Party sees its legitimacy as linked to its role in promoting and defending Chinese nationalism.

—Fareed Zakaria[1]

Nationalism is on the rise in China. The slightest provocation from abroad causes people to protest at full volume as furious postings explode with statements like "All citizens must stand together and fight against the anti-Chinese forces and their traitorous lackeys!"[2] You don't have to ask a Chinese twice to join anti-Japanese demonstrations. "What you must understand is we Chinese all hate Japanese": an American guest lecturer heard this sentence so frequently while in China that he wondered if it might be a typical practice phrase in English conversation classes.[3] "Taiwan is ours. Tibet is ours. Compromising with the U.S. and Japan is shameful!" declares a Beijing rock band in one of its songs. Xi Jinping, the new party leader, is no stranger to nationalist proclamations himself. While serving as vice president, he asserted that there are "foreigners who have had enough to eat, and who have nothing better to do than to vociferously criticize [China's] affairs."[4]

Many believe the authorities foster nationalism to strengthen their own legitimacy. "Appealing to nationalism is an easy way to score points with the public," says Yun Sun at the Brookings Institution.[5] If we look at China's recent history, the authorities have indeed encouraged Chinese nationalism. The country is—officially—home to fifty-six ethnic groups, whose affinities to the Chinese state vary. Keeping the country together is a never-ending job—hence all the patriotic campaigns, particularly in schools. After the massacre around Tiananmen Square in 1989, the party had to work to win back the people's trust. The result was a record number of patriotic campaigns—in which the party was the protagonist.[6]

But today the notion that the government is feeding Chinese nationalism is a truth that must be qualified. Nationalism is largely spontaneous and genuine and has been around much longer than the Communist Party, since as far back as the mid-nineteenth century.[7]

In fact, today the authorities must actually attempt to limit the nationalists' utterances and actions. They tried, for example, to restrain Chinese nationalists when the conflict with Japan over the Diaoyu Islands erupted in August 2012. The Diaoyu Islands are located just north of Taiwan, and Taiwan, China, and Japan all claim sovereignty. In several Chinese cities demonstrations degenerated into violence and destruction. The authorities used state media to halt the protests, fearing further mayhem. Nor was this the first time the government sought to curb nationalist mobilization. An anti-Japanese group with as many as seventy thousand registered supporters on the Internet attempted to organize a demonstration in 2009. The government gave a clear no. In 2005, large and aggressive anti-Japanese demonstrations erupted in more than forty cities across the country—and were stopped after only a few days. Many people received texts from the government urging them to stay away from the demonstrations.[8]

The government closely monitors online forums to learn about the nationalists' complaints and wishes. The nationalists can largely do as they please online, as long as they do not accuse the party of failing the nation or betraying national interests. In general the government is reluctant to oppose these powerful forces, but it does occasionally put its foot down. The Communist Party newspaper *People's Daily* has repeatedly printed articles telling aggressive nationalist bloggers to tone down their rhetoric. The nationalist song quoted above has been banned.

Nationalism is in fact a double-edged sword.

The Chinese leaders fear that demonstrations aimed at other countries might eventually turn against them, if the protesters feel that they do not safeguard national interests. Looking at China's recent history, it is easy to understand such anxieties. In 1919 the May Fourth Movement, disappointed by the Treaty of Versailles, protested against what it deemed an unpatriotic government. The movement was a precursor to the Communist Party and contributed to the fall of the government. Nationalist bloggers' calling the Ministry of Foreign Affairs the "Ministry of Traitors" sends shivers down leaders' spines.[9]

Another reason the leadership restricts nationalist utterances is that they undermine the government's tireless efforts to reassure the world about China's "peaceful rise." Those sitting in Tokyo or Washington and reading tough attacks on Japan and the United States on Chinese websites naturally question the peacefulness of Chinese intentions. Such uneasiness is not in Beijing's interest.

Nationalism in China thrives—all on its own. The Communist Party occasionally rides the nationalist wave to win popularity and placate the nationalists. However, it is simultaneously careful not to stoke these passions too much, lest they burn out of control.

Notes

1. Fareed Zakaria, "Don't Feed China's Nationalism," *Daily Beast*, 12 April 2008, http://www.thedailybeast.com/newsweek/2008/04/12/don-t-feed-china-s-nationalism.html.

2. Quoted in Simon Shen and Shaun Breslin, eds., *Online Chinese Nationalism and China's Bilateral Relations* (Lanham, MD: Rowman & Littlefield, 2010), 212.

3. Jeff Kingston, "What You Must Understand Is We Chinese All Hate Japanese," *Japan Times*, 27 February 2011, http://www.japantimes.co.jp/text/fl20110227x1.html.

4. "Xi Jinping tongpi shaoshu waiguoren dui Zhongguo zhishou huajiao" [Xi Jinping Criticizes a Small Number of Foreigners Who Loudly Pass Judgment on China's Affairs], *QQ News*, 12 February 2009, http://news.qq.com/a/20090212/001882.htm.

5. Yun Sun, "Chinese Public Opinion: Shaping China's Foreign Policy, or Shaped by It?" Brookings Institution, 13 December 2011, http://www.brookings.edu/research/opinions/2011/12/13-china-public-opinion-sun.

6. Zhao Suisheng, "China's Pragmatic Nationalism: Is It Manageable?" *Washington Quarterly* 29, no. 1 (winter 2005): 131–44.

7. See, e.g., Peter Hays Gries, *China's New Nationalism: Pride, Politics and Diplomacy* (Berkeley: University of California Press, 2004).

8. Interview with professor Lowell Dittmer, Singapore, October 2011.

9. More on the Chinese government's relationship to nationalist protests in Jeffrey N. Wasserstrom, "Student Protests in Fin-de-Siècle China," *New Left Review*, September–October 1999, https://newleftreview.org/I/237/jeffrey-wasserstrom-student-protests-in-fin-de-siecle-china.

Myth 29

CHINA WILL ONCE AGAIN DOMINATE EAST ASIA

> The role of the Hegemon is deeply embedded in China's national dreamwork, intrinsic to its national identity, and profoundly implicated in its sense of national destiny.
>
> —Steven W. Mosher[1]

The phrase *Pax Sinica*, Latin for "Chinese peace," is used to describe periods of peace in East Asia overseen by a hegemonic China. Extended periods of peace occurred during the Han, Tang, early Song, Yuan, and Ming dynasties, as well as during the first phase of the Qing. These periods were characterized by Chinese dominance in East Asia, based on undisputed political, economic, cultural, and military power.

Many observers envision today's rising China once again assuming the role of regional hegemon. If we are to believe Steven W. Mosher, author of the rather alarmist book *Hegemon*, the Chinese believe they are engaged in "a worldwide contest with the U.S. to replace the current *Pax Americana* with a *Pax Sinica*."[2] The Chinese want to organize the world exactly as they have for two thousand years: with China at the center, surrounded by kowtowing tributary states. This world order is reflected in the country's name in Chinese, *Zhongguo* (Middle Kingdom), according to Mosher. But he also tells us that the Chinese have another name, even more revealing, for their country: *Tianxia*, meaning "all under heaven," a suitable name for the world's future ruler. The prospects for peace in East Asia and the rest of the world are grim, according to Mosher.

In many ways China is about to become East Asia's strongest power. The country surpassed Japan as the region's largest—and the world's second-largest—economy in 2010. The People's Republic has become the regional economy's center of gravity and has taken the lead in regional economic integration. Beijing is also strengthening political ties with neighboring states through a variety of partnerships.

The United States, however, will be a major obstacle to Chinese dominance in East Asia as long as the Americans have the will and ability to contain China in Asia. And the Obama administration has made it very clear that it does. "The future of politics will be decided in Asia, not Afghanistan or Iraq, and the United States will be right at the center of the action," Hillary Clinton declared in *Foreign Policy* in the autumn of 2011.[3] She stressed that the United States will, over the next decade, bring together its political, military, and economic powers in Asia. "The region is eager for our leadership and our business," the then secretary of state confidently stated.[4] Beijing choked on its green tea.

These were not empty words. Washington has strengthened relations with India, Indonesia, Singapore, New Zealand, Malaysia, Mongolia, Vietnam, Brunei, and the small states of the Pacific. Joint military exercises have been conducted, which Beijing interprets as the Americans trying to build an anti-China alliance. The United States has had formal alliances with Japan, South Korea, Australia, Philippines, and Thailand for many years. America is Taiwan's most important backer. In January 2012, President Obama announced a new American military strategy that shifts the focus from Afghanistan and Iraq to Asia and the Pacific.[5] That June, Defense Secretary Leon Panetta announced that 60 percent of the US Navy will be operating in the Pacific by 2020.[6]

At the same time Chinese influence is constrained by its twenty-four neighbors, including populous and strong military powers such as India, Vietnam, Japan, and Russia. There is skepticism toward China in all these countries. The Indians suspect the Chinese of engaging in strategic encirclement, the Japanese fear a military conflict triggered by territorial disputes with an increasingly assertive neighbor, and the Russians worry about an eventual invasion of eastern Siberia. The backdrop for the Russian fear is the fact that 6 million Russians live east of the Urals, whereas Northeast China's population is 130 million. Illegal Chinese immigration to resource-rich Siberia concerns Russia, as does military balance. Only one-fifth of Russia's army is deployed to the Far East; the three northern Chinese military districts alone have more troops than the entire Russian army. Moscow is painfully aware of the fact that Russia is unlikely to win a conventional war against China.[7]

East Asians are not generally enthusiastic about the People's Republic. In 2013, the Pew Research Center published a survey revealing that many held a more positive view of the United States than of China. The Japanese expressed by far the worst view of China: only 5 percent of the Japanese held a favorable view of their traditional archrival.[8] There is even considerable skepticism about China in Singapore, where 75 percent of the population is ethnically Chinese. "Rich people from China, with suitcases full of cash, are driving up the housing prices!" "Poor laborers are flowing in from China, and forcing down wages!" "Cheap Chinese women are pulling the plug out of the market!" lament local prostitutes. Lee Kuan Yew, Singapore's ethnic Chinese founding father, recently publicly urged America not to pull out of Asia.

Given these strong opposing forces, China's path to a new era of hegemony in East Asia is far from unobstructed.

Notes

1. Steven W. Mosher, *Hegemon: China's Plan to Dominate Asia and the World* (New York: Encounter Books, 2000), 1.

2. Ibid., 99.

3. Hillary R. Clinton, "America's Pacific Century," *Foreign Policy*, 11 October 2011, http://www.foreignpolicy.com/articles/2011/10/11/americas_pacific_century.

4. Ibid.

5. For the strategy, see "Sustaining U.S. Global Leadership: Priorities for 21st Century Defense," *New York Times*, January 2012, http://graphics8.nytimes.com/packages/pdf/us/20120106-PENTAGON.PDF.

6. See, e.g., "Leon Panetta: US to Deploy 60% of Navy Fleet to Pacific," BBC News, 2 June 2012, http://www.bbc.co.uk/news/world-us-canada-18305750.

7. For regional constrains on Chinese power, see, e.g., Andrew J. Nathan and Andrew Scobell, *China's Search for Security* (New York: Columbia University Press, 2012); Edward N. Luttwak, *The Rise of China vs. the Logic of Strategy* (Cambridge, MA: Belknap Press of Harvard University Press, 2012).

8. "America's Global Image Remains More Positive than China's," Pew Research Council, 18 July 2013, http://www.pewglobal.org/2013/07/18/americas-global-image-remains-more-positive-than-chinas.

Myth 30

CHINA IS COLONIZING AFRICA

China takes our primary goods and sells us manufactured ones. This
was also the essence of colonialism. Africa is now willingly opening
itself up to a new form of imperialism.
    —Sanusi Lamido Sanusi, Nigeria's central bank governor[1]

Africa is full of Chinese people. Western aid workers in the Ethiopian
countryside are asked, "Are you Chinese?" Apparently in the eyes of
some African people, all outsiders are Chinese. Along the roads built by
Chinese labor, there are supposedly no snakes or dogs left—the Chinese
have eaten every last one. Chinese companies, urged on by their government, recklessly swarm African countries in their rush for natural resources. China drains poor countries of their raw materials and treats the
African workers as slaves. The local authorities are forced to accept whatever the Chinese do. But calling Chinese activities in Africa colonization
is an exaggeration.[2]

Those who believe that China is literally colonizing the African continent the way European powers did in the nineteenth century are probably
very few and far between. More often the word is used by people who
wish to harness the power of its negative connotations, both in the former
colonies and with the former colonizers, in order to criticize what they see
as ugly Chinese behavior in Africa.

Is China plundering the African continent's raw materials? Many people seem to forget that Chinese investments in resource extraction also
benefit Africans. In many cases it is not an option for Africans to extract
their own resources by themselves. Ethiopia, for example, has significant
mineral resources, in addition to gold and marble, but would hardly be
able to afford to extract them without Chinese investment in mining and
infrastructure. The prices of raw materials go up as a result of the large

Chinese market opening, a development that also benefits Africans. It is worth noting, too, that China provides development assistance to many countries in Africa—not just the ones rich in natural resources.

Another oft-heard criticism is that the Chinese neglect environmental and social conditions in host countries in their quest for business opportunities and profits.[3] This is largely true—as it is for many Chinese companies in China.[4] Working in a Chinese mine, for example, is not something we would recommend in Africa or in China, where it is the most dangerous type of work. In Angola, Zambia, and Congo, local workers have demonstrated against Chinese companies with poor working conditions. But in most cases, these companies have simply brought their habits and norms with them from China; they have not imposed or allowed worse working conditions in their African operations.

Chinese companies in Africa are also criticized for their failure to hire local African workers, denying communities the jobs they feel they are entitled to. Some critics have taken the accusations farther, alleging that China sends its convicts to Africa as cheap or free labor.

The assertion that there are Chinese chain gangs in Africa is highly questionable. No one has been able to document their existence—and not for lack of trying.[5] Why would the Chinese government send convicts to Africa when they could get more out of them by making them build roads in remote areas of China? As for the claim that Chinese enterprises do not employ local workers, this varies by country and type of project. It often depends on the ease with which companies can find the type of labor they need. For an oil company, it is often easier to find a local receptionist than a local engineer. The number of local employees also varies depending on how long the company has been established in Africa. During the initial setup, companies often bring with them most of the personnel they require. Finally, Chinese labor practices in Africa vary depending upon local authorities and laws. Host countries can require that a certain proportion of employees in a firm be local, as the authorities in Angola and the Democratic Republic of Congo have done. In Zambia, Chinese enterprises have thirteen Zambian employees for every Chinese, according to Zambian economist Dambisia Moyo.[6] If Chinese companies in Africa do in fact employ more of their own countrymen than do, say, Western multinational companies, one reason is wage differentials. Sending a Western engineer to an African land is expensive. She often requires supplementary compensation for working abroad in a difficult and sometimes inhospitable environment, as well special allowances for her family. Therefore a Western multinational company would be likely to employ a local engineer instead. Chinese workers, however, usually do not expect or get the same increases in salary and benefits when sent overseas. A Chinese company has little to gain economically from hiring local staff instead of sending its own people.

Self-interest and profit undoubtedly account for most Chinese business practices in Africa—as they account for the practices of most businesses operating overseas (or, indeed, anywhere). China benefits from Africa's natural resources. And, in many ways, African countries benefit from their relationship with Chinese companies. If Chinese firms are as rapacious abroad as they are at home, this has more to do with Chinese business culture than colonialism.

Notes

1. Samuel Burke, "Is China Buying Up Africa?" CNN, 29 March 2013, http://amanpour.blogs.cnn.com/2013/03/29/is-china-buying-up-africa.

2. For a discussion of the Chinese presence in Africa, see Howard W. French, "The Next Empire," *Atlantic*, May 2010, http://www.theatlantic.com/magazine/archive/2010/05/the-next-empire/308018.

3. See, e.g., "Has China Been a Friend in Africa?" *South China Morning Post*, 2 April 2013, http://www.scmp.com/comment/insight-opinion/article/1204853/has-china-been-friend-africa.

4. For more on the situation of workers in Chinese mines in Zambia, see "You'll Be Fired If You Refuse," Human Rights Watch, 3 November 2011, http://www.hrw.org/reports/2011/11/03/you-ll-be-fired-if-you-refuse-0.

5. For a discussion of the origin and validity of such claims, see Yan Hairong and Barry Sautman, "Chasing Ghosts: Rumours and Representations of the Exports of Chinese Convict Labour to Developing Countries," *China Quarterly* 210 (June 2012): 398–418.

6. Dambisa Moyo, "Beijing, a Boon for Africa," *New York Times*, 27 June 2012, http://www.nytimes.com/2012/06/28/opinion/beijing-a-boon-for-africa.html.

Myth 31

CHINA IS AN ENVIRONMENTAL BADDIE

How do I know China wrecked the Copenhagen deal? I was in the room.

—Mark Lynas[1]

Beijing is perceived as passive and unhelpful in international joint efforts to meet the threat of climate change. The Chinese government has, for example, been reluctant to commit to cutting the country's carbon dioxide emissions—the world's largest since 2007. Many say China is the biggest problem at UN climate conferences, labeling itself a developing country and refusing to commit to emissions cuts. This is a pure derogation of responsibility, it is claimed—considering that China is the world's largest emitter of climate gases and the second-largest economy.

At the same time, China is among the countries that will be hit hardest by a global rise in temperature. Himalayan glaciers are sources for the Yangtze and Yellow rivers, and if the glaciers melt, China risks flooding. If the climate gets warmer, the water will evaporate faster, and for China—already struggling with a precarious water shortage—this could be serious. Natural disasters, a high number of deaths due to air pollution, water shortages, and demonstrations about local environmental problems are realities in today's China. And yet Chinese authorities—deaf, dumb, and blind—ignore their country's huge environmental problems, right?

Indeed they do not.

During the reigns of Deng Xiaoping and Jiang Zemin, economic growth was all that mattered, and the authorities did not pay much attention to social conditions or environmental problems. But the situation is different today. In 2008, the Communist Party established "scientific development" (*kexue fazhan guan*) as the guiding socioeconomic ideology for China. Sustainability is an important part of this new trend, reflecting the priorities of the leadership.

The Chinese government is investing heavily in environmental protection at home. In August 2012, the government announced plans for environment-related measures worth 2.366 trillion RMB (US$380 billion).[2] China focuses particularly on saving energy and developing renewable energy sources, a sector in which China leads the world. In 2012, US$65.1 billion worth of investments were placed in clean energy in China. This was the highest number in the world and roughly one-quarter of total global investments in clean energy. China is thus well ahead of the second-highest investor, the United States, with $35.6 billion.[3] China's increase goes against the global trend; worldwide total investments in clean energy are decreasing. The government plans to invest an additional 5 trillion RMB (about US$800 billion) before 2020,[4] as it aims for renewable energy sources to make up 15 percent of the country's total energy consumption by that date.[5] China already has the world's largest capacity for renewable energy—that capacity having increased by 92 percent between 2006 and 2011.[6] China has become the world's biggest producer of solar panels, and 30 percent of global solar panel production takes place in China—40 percent if Taiwan is included. Four of the world's five largest producers of solar panels are Chinese.[7] Many of the solar panels are exported, but generous subsidies for installing solar panels keep many at home. China also invests heavily in wind energy; two of the world's top three producers of wind turbines are Chinese.[8] China's total capacity to produce renewable energy is the world's largest, even though it still has a long way to go in connecting all the windmills, solar panels, and water turbines to its power grid.

There have also been organizational changes favoring environmental responsibility.[9] In 2008, the State Environmental Protection Agency was upgraded to the Ministry of Environmental Protection. This means that the State Council, China's government, now takes direct responsibility for environmental problems. Thus, China is an organizational step ahead of the United States, which does not have a cabinet-level department of environmental protection. In 2007, the national leading group to work on issues related to climate change was moved up directly under the State Council and headed by then prime minister Wen Jiabao.[10] The party traditionally creates leading groups on issues it considers to be particularly important and complex, requiring the involvement of several parts of the government as well as national experts. The powerful National Development and Reform Commission and the Ministries of Environmental Protection, Foreign Affairs, Finance, and Science and Technology are all represented in the group.[11]

Recent years have seen a marked growth in Chinese research on environmental and climate issues. Chinese scientists now publish eight times as many papers on climate change as they did just a few years ago. [12] What's more, policy makers, newly interested in this subject, now actually listen to researchers. Climate experts have direct access to the Chinese leadership through meetings in the Politburo. [13]

Given these efforts at home, the notion of China being a hindrance in international contexts also needs to be nuanced. Chinese authorities have undoubtedly been skeptical of supranational mechanisms in the area of climate change, but this attitude has changed in recent years.

China is a relatively active participant in UN climate negotiations. It signed the Kyoto Protocol in 1998 and ratified it in 2002; the United States signed but did not ratify it. The vice chairman of one of the three working groups of the UN Intergovernmental Panel on Climate Change is Chinese, and twenty-eight Chinese experts helped draft the panel's fourth assessment report in 2007. The country has also acceded to the target of limiting global temperature rise to two degrees Celsius. During the UN climate negotiations in Cancun in December 2010, the Chinese delegation played a more positive and constructive role than it did in Copenhagen the year before. Not only did China sign the agreement negotiated during the meeting, but the Chinese representatives also tried to expand the agreement in some areas. In Durban in 2011, the Chinese went even further, signing the Durban platform—the first legally binding agreement on emissions cuts that included all countries, even China, India, and the United States. This platform states that industrialized countries and developing countries alike contribute to emissions reductions, a point that has previously been a deal breaker for Beijing. This was also the first time that the Chinese set up a pavilion during the conference. The pavilion housed a host of experts and interest groups championing their own agendas—which were often quite different from the official one. [14] Most recently, in Warsaw in 2013, China and India initially held the conference hostage by disapproving of the idea that all nations should "commit" to greenhouse gas emission cuts, arguing that developed economies should carry a greater burden than developing countries. Later, the two giant nations succeeded in brokering a compromise: all nations would "contribute" to emission cuts. [15] The Chinese pavilion in Warsaw hosted even more—and a broader scope of—participants and activities than during the two previous years.

Moreover, China is the biggest participant in the international trade in carbon emissions quotas—the so-called Clean Development Mechanism (CDM). Almost half of all allowances released worldwide come from China. The country also has a representative on the United Nation's CDM Executive Board.

The Chinese government is indeed concerned with issues related to the environment and climate change. The most significant efforts are made domestically, but China is also becoming a more active international participant. The government realizes the need for international cooperation to address the threat of climate change. Since it doesn't have to worry about reelection, it has more room for making unpopular decisions—perhaps precisely what is needed to handle environmental challenges.

Notes

1. Mark Lynas, "How Do I Know China Wrecked the Copenhagen Deal? I Was in the Room," *Guardian*, 22 December 2009, http:// www.guardian.co.uk/environment/2009/dec/22/copenhagen-climate-change-mark-lynas.

2. "Guowuyuan guanyu yinfa jieneng jianpai 'shier wu' jihui de tongzhi" [The State Council's Announcement on the Twelfth Five-Year-Plan for Emission Reductions], Central People's Government of the People's Republic of China, 6 August 2012, http://www.gov.cn/zwgk/2012-08/21/content_2207867.htm.

3. "Who's Winning the Clean Energy Race? 2012 Edition," Pew Charitable Trusts, 2013, http://www.pewtrusts.org/uploadedFiles/wwwpewtrustsorg/News/Press_Releases/Clean_Energy/clen-G20-report-2012-FINAL.pdf.

4. "China Develops 5-Trillion-Yuan Alternative Energy Plan," *People's Daily*, 22 October 2010, http://english.peopledaily.com.cn/90001/90778/90862/7076933.html.

5. "From Copenhagen Accord to Climate Action: Tracking National Commitments to Curb Global Warming," Natural Resources Defense Council, http://www.nrdc.org/international/copenhagenaccords.

6. "The New Global Energy Landscape," Milken Institute, 1 May 2012, http://www.milkeninstitute.org/presentations/slides/GC12-3170.pdf.

7. "Suntech Tops 2011 PV Module Rankings as Chinese Dominance Continues," *IMS Research*, 27 February 2012, http://imsresearch.com/news-events/press-template.php?pr_id=2649.

8. "Changing Competitive Landscape in Wind Turbine Manufacturing— Can the Chinese Conquer the Global Wind?" Frost & Sullivan, 3 January 2012, http://www.frost.com/sublib/display-market-insight-top.do?id=250453052.

9. For more on the development of China's climate change policy, see Iselin Stensdal, "Chinese Climate-Change Policy, 1988–2013: Moving On Up," *Asian Perspective* 38, no. 1 (2014): 111–36.

10. Gørild Heggelund, Steinar Andresen, and Inga Fritzen Buan, "Chinese Climate Policy: Domestic Priorities, Foreign Policy, and Emerging Implementation," in *Global Commons, Domestic Decisions*, ed. Kathryn Harrison and Lisa McIntosh Sundstrom (Cambridge, MA: MIT Press, 2010), 239–61.

11. Zhu Xufeng, "China's National Leading Group to Address Climate Change: Mechanism and Structure," EAI Background Brief 572, East Asian

Institute, National University of Singapore, 22 October 2010, http://www.eai.nus.edu.sg/BB572.pdf.

12. Jost Wübbeke, "China's Climate Change Expert Community—Principles, Mechanisms and Influence," *Journal of Contemporary China* 22, no. 82 (2013): 712–31.

13. Heggelund, Andresen, and Buan, "Chinese Climate Policy."

14. Deborah Seligsohn, "China at Durban: First Steps toward a New Climate Agreement," *WRI Insights*, 16 December 2011, http://insights.wri.org/news/2011/12/china-durban-first-steps-toward-new-climate-agreement.

15. For more on China's environmental problems and efforts, see China Dialogue, https://www.chinadialogue.net.

Myth 32

THE CHINESE COULD TAME NORTH KOREA—IF THEY WANTED TO

China has always been key to resolving the North Korean nuclear problem, but now it is absolutely essential that Beijing lives up to its commitments or faces being held accountable for a lost opportunity that could result in a permanent nuclear North Korea.
—Jack Pritchard, president of the Korea Economic Institute in Washington, DC, and former special envoy for negotiations with North Korea[1]

If only China would exert pressure on North Korea, Pyongyang would immediately give up its nuclear weapons and missile programs. China and North Korea have been blood brothers since the 1950–1953 Korean War, during which about 170,000 Chinese died. In 1961, the countries signed a friendship treaty, which meant that China would help its neighbor economically and militarily. Today North Korea survives on food, fuel, energy, and fertilizer from China. All the Chinese have to do is threaten to cut off supplies, and Pyongyang will obey Beijing's every word.

Many in the West see the situation this way. According to this view, the Chinese government does not want to push the North Koreans.

This is true to a certain extent, because North Korea presents China and the United States with very different threats. The Chinese government fears the collapse of North Korea more than anything. If the current regime should fall, China would be directly affected by waves of North Korean refugees, cross-border smuggling and crime, likely interference from the United States, and perhaps a reunited, US-friendly Korea. Beijing is unwilling to exert an amount of pressure that might threaten the stability of North Korea. If the Kim regime needs nuclear weapons in order to be safe—so be it. China is more likely to be hit by the collapse of North Korea than by North Korean nuclear weapons, in Beijing's opinion.

China's ability to influence North Korea is also limited—just as Washington has very limited ability to dictate the actions of allies such as Israel and Saudi Arabia. The leaders in Pyongyang constantly act contrary to China's wishes, in many cases without informing Beijing or despite Chinese protests. Before North Korea launched a rocket over the Pacific in 2009, Wu Dawei, then China's vice foreign minister and special representative for the Korean Peninsula, visited Pyongyang to convey Chinese authorities' concerns about North Korean armament. The Chinese also sent a delegation to Seoul to discuss aggressive North Korean behavior. Neither mission was of any use. The North Koreans fired the rocket on 5 April and—making things even worse—conducted a nuclear test the same year.

Actions that escalate tensions between North and South Korea are clearly not in China's interest. Yet we have seen examples of aggressive North Korean behavior that obviously was not cleared with Beijing. North Korea conducted a nuclear test on 12 February 2013 despite dissuasive efforts from Chinese media and diplomats. The test was just the latest in a host of North Korean aggressive actions that China could have done without. When the ballistic Taepodong-2 missile was launched in July 2006, the Chinese authorities claimed that they had been given no notice and called it "regrettable." In March 2010, the South Korean navy ship *Cheonan* was sunk—by North Korea, according to the International Commission of Inquiry. In April 2012, North Korea tried and failed to send a satellite into space.

The Six Party Talks on North Korea's nuclear program include South Korea, the United States, Russia, and Japan, in addition to North Korea and China. The Chinese government has made it very clear that it wants to resume negotiations, but there have been no meetings since September 2007, mainly because Pyongyang objects to this format.

These are the limits of Chinese influence over Pyongyang. It is unlikely that the leadership in North Korea informs—let alone asks permission from—Beijing before it fires rockets and missiles, conducts nuclear tests, or sinks vessels. What's more, when China does protest, Pyongyang does not give China's views any consideration worth mentioning. China is like a mother who has limited control over the actions of her disobedient son.

For the Chinese, the North Koreans offer little but frustration and headaches. In the words of a Chinese officer, "Here's to the death of Kim Jong-il. Cheers!"[2]

Notes

1. Jack Pritchard, "China Is Key to N. Korea," *Choson Ilbo*, 6 February 2010, http://english.chosun.com/site/data/html_dir/2010/02/06/2010020600241.html.

2. Interview with Bonji Ohara, Iida Masafumi, Masayuki Masuda, and Saito Makoto, National Institute for Defense Studies, Tokyo, May 2010.

Myth 33

CHINA DOES NOT INTERFERE IN OTHER STATES' INTERNAL AFFAIRS

China adheres to an independent foreign policy as well as to the five principles of mutual respect for sovereignty and territorial integrity, mutual non-aggression, non-interference in each other's internal affairs, equality and mutual benefit, and peaceful coexistence in developing diplomatic relations and economic and cultural exchanges with other countries.

—Constitution of the People's Republic of China [1]

The principle of mutual noninterference in internal affairs (*hu bu ganshe neizheng*) is one of the so-called five principles of peaceful coexistence that the Chinese government established in 1954 when it came to an agreement with India over Tibet. Formulated against the backdrop of the Cold War and superpower rivalry, the principles must be understood as a friendly gesture to Asia's non-Communist countries. The five principles were later enshrined in the preamble to the Constitution of 1982 and have formally been pillars of Chinese foreign policy ever since.

The principle of noninterference does not reflect China's actual foreign policy and probably never has. China does indeed influence—or attempt to influence—the internal affairs of other countries. Such influence is exerted in several ways.

One common method is trying to convince the other party, as when China urged the government of Sudan to accept a UN peacekeeping force in Darfur in 2007. Chinese authorities have even boasted that they were the ones who persuaded the Sudanese authorities in this matter—despite the fact that they rarely admit to pressuring other states. [2]

Beijing also uses rewards to make other states do what it wants. Previously there were financial rewards for states that cut diplomatic ties with Taiwan and instead established diplomatic relations with the People's Republic. Taiwan, in turn, financially rewarded states that cut diplomatic ties with the People's Republic and instead established ties with Taiwan. China agreed to buy Costa Rican government bonds worth US$300 million ahead of Costa Rica's decision to no longer recognize Taiwan as an independent state and to establish diplomatic relations with Beijing in 2007.[3] The Chinese and Taiwanese policy is known as "checkbook diplomacy."

When the carrot is not an option, the Chinese government uses the stick (or threat thereof). We do not even have to leave our native Norway to find an example. Prior to the announcement of the Nobel Peace Prize each year, Chinese authorities try to make the Norwegian government prevent the Nobel Committee from awarding the prize to a Chinese dissident, which Beijing has repeatedly warned would seriously damage relations between China and Norway. Immediately following the announcement that the 2010 laureate was the Chinese dissident Liu Xiaobo, Chinese authorities severed political contact with Norway. All high-level visits to and from Norway were cancelled or postponed indefinitely. Several Norwegian cultural events, academic joint projects, and business meetings in China met with the same fate. Another example relates to North Korea. Following Pyongyang's nuclear test in 2009, China supported UN Resolution 1874, which led the way for strong economic sanctions against North Korea. China simultaneously cut aid and energy supplies to its neighbor to the north. The same happened after the nuclear test in 2006, at which point China also stopped bank transfers to and investments in North Korea.

There is obviously a disparity between the principle of noninterference and China's actual foreign policy. The main goal of the rhetoric of noninterference is not to describe Chinese foreign policy accurately but to keep the West out of China's internal affairs. The doctrine is also used to defend China from outside criticism, especially when China fails to join international sanctions. A final goal of this rhetoric is to reassure those who fear China as a great power.

Yet the gap between rhetoric and practice poses problems for the Chinese government. Chinese academics openly debate the principle and different ways of rephrasing it. Academics especially discuss two issues related to the noninterference principle. The first is that the doctrine is in conflict with the need to secure Chinese interests abroad for citizens and businesses—interests that have soared as a result of China's economic growth. Debaters are particularly concerned about the security of raw material supplies and Chinese citizens who live in unstable parts of the world. The second problem of noninterference being discussed in China is the burden of being perceived as an actor that shrugs off international responsibility.

The authorities in Beijing have probably initiated this debate themselves, with the goal of redefining the noninterference principle in order to make it more consistent with actual policies. The debate among Chinese scholars allows authorities to collect and test different proposals and opinions.

The principle of noninterference is exercised in a flexible manner, a point made by Gao Zugui, senior researcher at China's Institutes of Contemporary International Relations.[4] China needs a new doctrine, according to Gao. Several others similarly point to the existence of both good and bad forms of interference. Authors describe positive or necessary interference as "constructive intervention" (*jianshi xing jieru*), "creative intervention" (*chuangzao xing jieru*), and "positive intervention" (*jiji jieru*). Chinese involvement in Sudan and North Korea are mentioned as examples.[5]

The Chinese government's interventions in other countries' internal affairs will have to increase in the future. China is becoming more and more dependent on developments in other countries and must protect its growing interests abroad—both its investments and expatriate Chinese nationals. Simultaneously, the demand for China to be a responsible international actor will grow with the country's economy and international role.

In other words, we will see more and more "interference with Chinese characteristics" in the future.

Notes

1. The English version of the Constitution of the People's Republic of China is available at http://english.people.com.cn/constitution/constitution.html.

2. See, e.g., "China's Position on the Issue of Darfur, Sudan," Ministry of Foreign Affairs of the People's Republic of China, March 2008, http://www.fmprc.gov.cn/ce/ceun/eng/xw/t415999.htm.

3. "Cash Helped China Win Costa Rica's Recognition," *New York Times*, 12 September 2008, http://www.nytimes.com/2008/09/13/world/asia/13costa.html.

4. Gao Zugui, "Constructive Involvement and Harmonious World: China's Evolving Outlook on Sovereignty in the Twenty-First Century," Friedrich Ebert Stiftung, Briefing Paper 13, October 2008, http://library.fes.de/pdf-files/iez/05923.pdf.

5. Wang Yizhou, "Guanjian reng zai neizheng" [Domestic Policy Is Still the Crucial Point], 360doc.com, 25 June 2010, http://www.360doc.com/content/12/0104/20/322140_177285699.shtml; interviews with Professor Zhu Liqun, Pro-

fessor Wang Fan, and Lecturer Gao Wanglai at China Foreign Affairs University and Professor Wang Yizhou at Peking University, Beijing, May 2010.

Part V

The Past

Myth 34

CHINA'S HISTORY SPANS FIVE MILLENNIA

China is world famous for its 5,000-year history as a civilized nation. Unfortunately, a 2,000-year gap in China's development has concealed the country's true age.
—Li Xueqin, manager of the Xia-Shang-Zhou Chronology Project[1]

In 1996, the Communist Party's Central Committee decided that China had a continuous five-thousand-year history. The Xia-Shang-Zhou Chronology Project was launched that year in order to prove the claim. But after five years of hard work—the equivalent of one thousand working years—the project's two hundred multidisciplinary scientists and scholars and their leader, noted historian and paleographist Professor Li Xueqin, had still not managed to find evidence of Chinese history from earlier than 1300 BCE. The project was thus 1,700 years off.[2]

Most Chinese still maintain that the country has five thousand years of continuous history. We come across this claim in many contexts—in nationalist statements, in response to criticism of the current political system, and in speeches. During a party conference in 2002, China's former president Jiang Zemin said, "For more than 5,000 years, the Chinese nation has evolved a great national spirit centering on patriotism and featuring unity and solidarity, love of peace, industry, courage and ceaseless self-improvement."[3]

But how long is China's history really?

By history, we mean periods documented in written sources. The time before this is called prehistoric. So how far back do the written sources go?

Until around 1910 Chinese history books stated that Chinese history began with the Yellow Emperor. According to legend, he ruled a kingdom around the Yellow River—the cradle of Chinese civilization—almost five thousand years ago. Some believe that he is the ancestor of all Chinese people. This mythical figure appears for the first time in the *Records of the Historian* (*Shiji*), written by historian Sima Qian between 109 and 91 BCE. Sima defined the Yellow Emperor's reign as the beginning of China's history, and the idea stuck for some time. In the late nineteenth century, however, toward the end of the imperial era, the myth of the Yellow Emperor began to unravel. The trend among Chinese historians was to dismiss anything undocumented.

Another year said to mark the start of Chinese history is 841 BCE. In the *Records of the Historian*, we find credible annual accounts from this year. The chapters dealing with the times before that are not annual and are considered less reliable. If credible written sources constitute history, it is reasonable to date Chinese history from 841 BCE. This leaves more than two thousand years unaccounted for.

A number of historians call the Shang Dynasty, from 1600 to 1045 BCE, the start of China's historical period. Around 1900, it was discovered that certain cattle bones and pieces of tortoiseshell imprinted with Chinese characters were of historical significance; people had been finding and using them in medicine for hundreds of years. They were "oracle bones" from the Shang Dynasty: in those days, people's questions were carved into bones, which were then heated until they cracked. The patterns of cracks were interpreted to answer the questions. These are the first known, recognizable writings in Chinese characters. We thus have writing from well before 1000 BCE. But even if we accept Shang as the beginning of China's history—and many hold that the sources are inadequate—there still remain 1,400 undocumented years to get to five thousand.

Those who go even further back believe there is evidence that the Shang Dynasty was preceded by the Xia Dynasty, from 2200 to 1600 BCE. The city assumed to have been the capital during the Xia Dynasty was excavated in 1959 in today's Henan province. Carbon dating of the findings suggests that our dates for the Xia are correct, but as long as there are only archaeological discoveries and no written sources, it is difficult to call this historic time. And there are still eight hundred years for which we lack evidence.

It is therefore not possible to prove that China has five thousand years of history, although politicians, scholars, and scientists have tried hard.

Nonetheless, the idea is widespread, thanks in large part to the Communist Party. China's leaders do not hesitate to speak of the Yellow Emperor as the nation's ancestor. Government representatives frequently

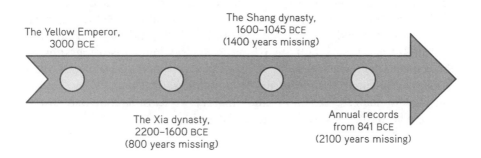

The Yellow Emperor, 3000 BCE

The Shang dynasty, 1600–1045 BCE (1400 years missing)

The Xia dynasty, 2200–1600 BCE (800 years missing)

Annual records from 841 BCE (2100 years missing)

China's History: You Do the Math

participate in celebrations of this mythical figure; they fund statues of him and often mention him in speeches.

The government emphasizes this notion of five thousand years of continuous history for two reasons.

The first is internal and relates to efforts to generate popular support for the party. As revolutionary and ideological messages have been toned down during the thirty-year reform period, the party has had to search for other ways to justify its monopoly on power—something larger and more worthy than economic growth. One solution is to portray the People's Republic as a natural continuation of China's proud five-thousand-year-old tradition. The myth also fits well with China's growing nationalism. A long history separates China from the rest of the world—especially the United States—and this uniqueness is important for China's national pride. The government hopes, too, that a very long historical perspective can make current problems—pollution, a weak welfare system, and increasingly uneven distribution—seem insignificant.

The second reason concerns China's relationship to the world. When people point a critical finger at China's lack of democracy, it is useful to be able to say that five thousand years of continuous history make dramatic overnight changes impossible. Such a long history would make China fundamentally different from other countries, and therefore the experiences and standards of other countries could not be transferred to China. *We have been cultivating our own principles of governance for five thousand years, so who are you to tell us what to do?* Moreover, it is convenient to point out to those who fear China's rise that over those five thousand years China has valued peace and solidarity and has not behaved aggressively toward other states (although not everyone agrees with this statement).

The Chinese are not the only ones who favor nice round numbers. In 1950, Oslo, the capital of Norway, celebrated its nine hundredth anniversary, and in 2000—only fifty years later—the city celebrated one thousand years. Skien—the birthplace of Norway's national author, Henrik Ibsen—was a proud six-hundred-year-old in 1958 and an even prouder thousand-year-old in 2000. In China and elsewhere, historiography is about the present. Current self-image, challenges, wishes, and needs often influence the interpretation of history as well as the sources and events that get emphasized. When we study history we learn as much about the people who wrote it as we learn about the past.

Notes

1. *China Daily*, 16 December 1998.
2. Yun Kuen Lee, "Building the Chronology of Early Chinese History," *Asian Perspective* 41, no. 1 (2002): 15–42.
3. "16th Party Congress Report," *China Daily*, 7 October 2010, http://www.chinadaily.com.cn/china/2007-07/10/content_5424948_6.htm.

Myth 35

CHINA IS CALLED THE MIDDLE KINGDOM BECAUSE CHINESE PEOPLE BELIEVE THEIR COUNTRY IS THE CENTER OF THE WORLD

The oral short version of the Chinese name for China is *Zhongguo* (中国), and the two characters directly translated mean "Middle Country," a fact that has not gone unnoticed in the West. Many believe the name reflects an arrogant belief that China is the center of the universe. This is often used as an example of Chinese arrogance, and China's behavior in the international arena has long been seen as self-satisfied. In 1793, Emperor Qianlong returned gifts to King George III of England, explaining that "strange and costly objects do not interest me. . . . [W]e possess all things. I set no value on objects strange or ingenious, and have no use for your country's manufactures."[1] Please do not send more weird stuff from England. Thanks anyway.

Today this supposed self-satisfaction usually takes a different form: failure to participate in international joint efforts. Examples include Chinese vetoes on the UN Security Council, which effectively block UN resolutions on Syria, and perceived obstruction of international climate negotiations. In such cases people are quick to argue that the Chinese see their country as the center of the world, relegating everything else to the status of inconsequential hinterlands; then the name "Middle Kingdom" is given as proof.

Yet it is worth looking into the validity of this translation.[2]

The characters that we interpret as meaning "Middle Kingdom" bear further analysis. The character 中 (*zhong*) means "middle" or "center," and 国 (*guo*), an abbreviation of 国家 (*guojia*), means "country" or "state" in modern Chinese. But the original meaning of *guo* was "city" or "province," not "state" the way we conceive of it today.

Throughout history, the "Middle Kingdom" has been used for several different territories within the area we now call China. The term *Zhongguo* first appeared around 900 BCE in China's oldest book, *The Book of Songs*; it was used to denote the capital, where the emperor lived.

During the Spring and Autumn period (722–481 BCE), the term "Middle Kingdom" was used for a larger territory, namely "the central states"—the ones near the capital, Luoyang, in today's Henan province—as opposed to the states farther away, where the emperor had only indirect control. The Middle Kingdom represented civilization, whereas the periphery was seen as barbaric.

The term was used in this way even after China was united into one great kingdom with vast cultural differences in 221 BCE. Until then, warlords had controlled their own separate areas. The area closest to the capital was perceived as the most civilized and progressive.

After the Han Dynasty was established in 206 BCE,[3] the imperial court actually began to view the empire as the center of the world, and "Middle Kingdom" acquired a new meaning. China had been united for only fifteen years but did not lack self-confidence. The empire was stable, and the imperial administration could focus on social progress. Philosophy and literature flourished. China's first educational institutions were established, and Chinese inventors produced the first paper, the first steel, and the first compass. Trade with Western countries was blooming, and Chinese traders made fortunes selling silk to the Roman Empire. (The Roman Senate eventually banned Chinese silk because too much gold made its way east to pay for the comfortable fabric.) This was the backdrop to the idea of China as the center of the world. China is far from the only country in history to hold such a worldview, of course. In many ancient kingdoms, people believed that their king was actually king of the world.

The "Middle Kingdom" was never the name of the whole country during imperial times, although the emperor was considered the son of heaven and ruler of all under heaven. Old maps show that at any given time the empire was named after the dynasty in power. The empire was, for instance, called *Mingguo* during the Ming Dynasty (1368–1644). Chinatowns around the world are often called *Tangren jie* (Tang people's street), inspired by the proud Tang Dynasty (618–907).

The character for "center" (中, *zhong*) has been part of the Chinese name for China since the Republic of China was established in 1912. In this case the character is part of the word *zhonghua*, which means China or Chinese, not "center." However, people frequently abbreviate "People's Republic of China" in informal settings; *Zhonghua renmin gonghe-*

guo thus becomes *Zhongguo*, meaning the central country. You might, for example, see *Zhongguo* on the national football team's shirts.

These colloquial, informal references to the "Middle Kingdom" are not the result of a huge Chinese ego. Ordinary Chinese people probably give as little consideration to the fact that the name means "Middle Kingdom" as Americans give to the fact that their continent is named for the Italian explorer Amerigo Vespucci. Nevertheless, this abbreviation pleases Chinese nationalists—especially when the national football team is doing well and their shirts announce in yellow and red that they represent the Middle Kingdom.

Notes

1. Paul Halsall, "Qian Long: Letter to George III, 1793," *Internet Modern History Sourcebook*, August 1997, http://www.fordham.edu/halsall/mod/1793qianlong.asp.

2. For more on earlier use of *Zhongguo*, see Joseph Esherick, "How the Qing Became China," in *Empire to Nation: Historical Perspectives on the Making of the Modern World*, ed. Joseph Esherick, Hasan Kayalı, and Eric Van Young (Lanham, MD: Rowman & Littlefield, 2006).

3. Michael Loewe and Edward L. Shaughnessy, *The Cambridge History of Ancient China: From the Origins of Civilization to 221 BC* (New York: Cambridge University Press, 1999).

Myth 36

CHINA DISCOVERED THE WORLD IN 1421

In 1421, Chinese sailors navigated around most of the world, writes retired British naval officer and amateur scholar Gavin Menzies.[1] They crossed the Pacific and the Atlantic and mapped the shores of the Americas, Greenland, Antarctica, and Australia. Zheng He—government official, eunuch, Muslim, and discoverer—led these Chinese expeditions, which took place more than three centuries before those of British explorer Captain James Cook (and a few decades before Christopher Columbus "discovered" America). Those who are currently trying out shipping routes from Asia to Europe through the Northeast and Northwest Passages (as ice decreases) will be interested to hear that the Chinese succeeded in this eight hundred years ago, according to Menzies—who has sold stacks of books and established a small business on his website (www.gavinmenzies.net). He also claims that European explorers like Columbus, Vasco da Gama, and Ferdinand Magellan had a far easier task than previously thought—they simply followed Chinese maps. Nothing to it.

World history must be rewritten, concludes Menzies.

Chinese shipping during the early part of the Ming Dynasty (1368–1644) was impressive, and Zheng He was undoubtedly a skilled explorer. Under his leadership seven expeditions were completed between 1405 and 1433. These expeditions lasted about two years each and involved up to thirty thousand participants—sailors, technicians, interpreters, and soldiers. During the second-to-last expedition, from 1421 to 1423, Zheng reached Aden in Yemen and Mogadishu on the east coast of Africa. During the last expedition, between 1431 and 1433, Zheng and his men arrived in Islam's holiest city, Mecca. The expeditions intended neither to discover new territory nor to collect taxes or colonize. Their main goal was probably to show off the mightiness of Ming China's shipping prowess. This was important, not least because the Ming was the first Chinese dynasty after about a hundred years of Mongolian rule. Emperor Yongle, who ruled China from 1402 to 1424, hoped to increase China's prestige through tribute relations, compelling leaders of other countries to acknowledge the supremacy of the Chinese emperor. We should not underestimate the court's desire for exotic objects such as herbs, plants, and giraffes. As the expeditions reached places farther from China, the importance of such items increased, and the importance of tribute relationships decreased. The Chinese did not establish permanent colonies, as the Europeans were beginning to do at this time.

But not all of Menzies's so-called evidence holds water, and Western experts on Chinese history are competing among themselves to tear his work to pieces.

One of Menzies's main arguments is about Chinese maps from this period. The famous European explorers, he alleges, used Chinese maps, which they got hold of through the Italian cartographer Niccolo da Conti, who acquired them while spending several years aboard a Chinese junk. Da Conti is said to have handed the maps on to Christopher Columbus, who thus easily found his way to America. But da Conti never mentioned Zheng He in his personal travel stories, although they are quite detailed. And there is no trace of Chinese cartography in European maps from this period.

Moreover, the maps made by the Chinese at this time hardly covered anything beyond East Asia and the Indian Ocean. It has been argued that some Chinese world maps from as early as 1418 show much more, but these are of disputed authenticity. Chinese cartography—of the territory that the Chinese had actually mapped—was indeed advanced. Chinese maps from as early as 1320 correctly showed the southern tip of Africa pointing straight south, more than a hundred years before European maps corrected their misrepresentation of the continent, in which the tip bent east. These maps were also probably the first to include geographic symbols for important landmarks and points such as cities, main roads, and military bases. You could probably find your way around the southern coast of Africa with the help of Chinese maps from this time, but not across the Atlantic Ocean.

Menzies also claims that there are DNA traces of Chinese heritage in Europe, America, the Pacific, and Africa. Among other things, he states that there is evidence that the gene for breaking down alcohol in New Zealand's Maori population matches Taiwanese genetic material[2] and that Chinese DNA is found among the population of northern Norway.[3] Stephen O'Brien at the US National Cancer Institute has characterized the genetic tests Menzies refers to as a "scam."[4] Only an eye clouded by preconceived notions would take them as evidence that the Chinese reached all the continents during the Ming Dynasty.

It is also doubtful whether Chinese shipping during the Ming Dynasty was advanced enough to complete the expeditions Menzies describes. Chinese shipbuilding technology and seamanship were far advanced. The Chinese explorers started using the compass for navigation sometime between the ninth and eleventh centuries, having invented the magnetic compass as a device for divination as early as 200 to 300 BCE.[5] Later, Chinese scientists discovered they could stabilize the magnetic tongue of the compass by placing it in water. This made it possible to use the compass on ships, opening up new possibilities for long-distance sea travel. The so-called treasure ships (*baochuan*) were reportedly more than 120 meters long and had masts that were 50 meters high. By comparison, the flagship of Columbus's first expedition in 1480, the *Santa Maria*, was only twenty meters long. Other estimates suggest that Zheng He's ship might have been as small as just above sixty meters, but even so it was much larger than anything Europeans would be able to build for centuries to come. But although Chinese ships at this time were advanced and sailed steadily during the monsoon winds in the Indian Ocean, they were hardly able to handle the weather in the Atlantic.

The Chinese government today makes a great effort to publicize Zheng He's achievements through English-language media and exhibitions around the world. The aim is to promote a picture of China's grand history and especially to substantiate the claim that the country has long been an international actor. For example, Zheng He's voyage to Africa has been used to show that Chinese investment in Africa is no recent phenomenon. But even Chinese presentations are usually soberer than Menzies's, and many reputable Chinese scholars are trying to set his claims straight.

Western historiography has traditionally given little attention to developments in Asia and China—including shipping—and it is high time to correct this imbalance. China during the Ming Dynasty was the world's leading maritime state. The voyages that the Chinese embarked on were unequalled, surpassing Western, Arab, and Indian expeditions in size and complexity. Although the West should indeed give more attention to Chinese history, it should not overcompensate for past nearsightedness by wildly claiming that "China discovered the world in 1421."

Notes

1. Gavin Menzies, *1421: The Year China Discovered the World* (London: Bantam Press, 2002).

2. "1421 Extract," Gavin Menzies, http://www.gavinmenzies.net/china/book-1421/1421-extract.

3. "31 Annexes 30, 31, 32—Evidence of Chinese Fleets to Northern Europe—Vice Admiral Chou Wen," Gavin Menzies, http://www.gavinmenzies.net/Evidence/31-annexes-30-31-32-evidence-of-chinese-fleets-to-northern-europe-%E2%80%93-vice-admiral-chou-wen.

4. Quoted in Geoff Wade, "Most Outrageous Claims by Mr. Menzies in *1421*," 1421 Myth Exposed, http://www.1421exposed.com/html/most_outrageous_claims.html.

5. William Lowrie, *Fundamentals of Geophysics* (Cambridge: Cambridge University Press, 2007), 281.

Myth 37

ALL WOMEN WERE OPPRESSED IN ANCIENT CHINA

"**W**oman's greatest duty is to produce a son." "Women's nature is passive." "Disorder is not sent from Heaven, it is produced by women." "Those who cannot be taught cannot be instructed. These are women and eunuchs." "Women are to be led and to follow others." "A woman should see her husband as if he were Heaven itself, and never grow weary of thinking how she may yield to him." There are many such teachings associated with Confucianism, which was the dominant way of thinking about life during imperial times. According to this mind-set, the woman was to obey her man. She was bound by the "three ties of obedience": obedience to her father while young, obedience to her husband once married, and obedience to her eldest son when widowed. "Women always have been fighting for a way out of the Confucian shadows," writes the Chinese gender researcher Xiao Ma.[1]

Confucianism was a reflection of the society's patriarchal organization. A woman's place was in the "inner chambers," and her feet were bound to ensure that she remained there. Protecting women's chastity—and thereby the honor of men—was of the utmost importance. In ancient, or imperial, China, women had no legal rights, no right to own property, and no rights within the family.

Nor did the cosmological system of imperial China serve women's cause. All things feminine were referred to as *yin*, and the masculine was known as *yang*. Although *yin* and *yang* were complementary and mutually dependent, *yang* was preferable.

So what we know about Confucianism, patriarchy, and Chinese cosmology supports the notion that imperial women were oppressed, each and every one powerless, passive, and silent. This picture has been politically convenient for some, and so they have glossed over historical facts.

The May Fourth Movement, for instance, turned women into symbols of imperial repression, contrasting past injustices with its own progressive gender policy in order to gain legitimacy. The movement, founded by students on 4 May 1919, sought a radical break with the past and called the recently fallen Qing Dynasty feudal, static, and rotten. A new, modern China was to be built. The May Fourth Movement linked women's liberation to Marxist and Leninist theories of class revolution. Women were to be freed from feudal social structures—just like peasants and workers. Not surprisingly, there were close ties between the May Fourth Movement and China's Communist Party, which was established in 1921. With slogans about liberation, the party mobilized women in the fight against Japanese aggressors and the enemies of the Communist revolution.

After the Communists established the People's Republic in 1949, the May Fourth Movement's radical views were enshrined as the official version of Chinese women's history. Henrik Ibsen's strong and rebellious female characters appealed to Chinese Communists. *A Doll's House* was the only Western drama tolerated during the Cultural Revolution, in large part because Mao's wife, Jiang Qing, herself had played the role of Nora ("Nala" in Chinese).

Western historiography also did its best to portray the lives of Chinese women as a living hell. The women of the "Orient"—including the Chinese—were assumed to be passive victims of men's sexual abuse and violence. In this way, "Oriental" women were portrayed as Western women's negative opposite. This flattered Western civilization, happy to believe itself superior, and established the idea that Western women were the leaders of global feminism. Such notions tell us as much about Western self-perceptions as about the historical conditions of Chinese women.

In any event, recent research has begun to challenge these generalizations.[2]

The Confucian tradition was not a monolithic, static set of thoughts dominating the lives of all women who were unfortunate enough to be born in China for more than 2,500 years. Although the official teachings in general remained unchanged, Confucianism in practice was far more flexible. It has survived so long precisely because individual scholars have interpreted and adjusted it in light of continually changing social realities, including the roles of men and women.[3]

Furthermore, Chinese women have never been one group. In dynastic China, women's positions varied by age, region, and social status. Not all women were hapless victims in the male-dominated society.

In Chinese history many prominent women have made their mark. Female scholars, ministers, and generals were praised by contemporaries for their wisdom, strategic skills, and talent as administrators. They have been regarded as the glue that held dynasties together and as threats to dynastic continuation.[4] Female scholars contributed to the development of the Confucian tradition,[5] while other women willingly carried on traditions that have subsequently been interpreted as purely oppressive. Most people, for instance, associate foot binding with male desire for control and sexual perversity. But this tradition was for many women also a source of identity, pride, and influence. Women who could afford to bound their own and their daughters' feet to signal their prominent social status and self-respect.[6]

Ancient China was even de facto ruled by three women: Wu Zetian, China's only female emperor, during the Tang Dynasty from 690 to 705, as well as Lü Zhi and Cixi, who ruled as empress dowagers during the Han Dynasty from 195 to 180 BCE and at the end of the Qing Dynasty from 1861 to 1908, respectively.

Being a woman in ancient China was not necessarily that bad.

Notes

1. Cited in Lyn Reese, "Gender Equity and Texts," *Social Studies Review* 33, no. 2 (1994): 12.

2. See, e.g., Dorothy Ko, *Teachers of the Inner Chambers: Women and Culture in Seventeenth Century China* (Stanford, CA: Stanford University Press, 1994); Rey Chow, *Women and Chinese Modernity: The Politics of Reading between West and East* (Minneapolis: University of Minnesota Press, 1991); Lisa Raphals, *Sharing the Light: Representations of Women and Virtue in Early China* (Albany: State University of New York Press, 1998); Susan Mann and Yu-Yin Cheng, eds., *Under Confucian Eyes: Writings on Gender in Chinese History* (Berkeley: University of California Press, 2001).

3. Ko, *Teachers of the Inner Chambers*, 17.

4. Raphals, *Sharing the Light*.

5. See, e.g., Mann and Cheng, *Under Confucian Eyes*; Joseph A. Adler, "Daughter/Wife/Mother or Sage/Immortal/Bodhisattva? Women in the Teaching of Chinese Religions," *ASIANetwork Exchange* 14, no. 2 (winter 2006), http://www2.kenyon.edu/Depts/Religion/Fac/Adler/Writings/Women.htm.

6. Dorothy Ko, *Cinderella's Sisters: A Revisionist History of Footbinding* (Berkeley: University of California Press, 2005).

Myth 38

CHINA HAS NO WARRIOR CULTURE

The defensive nature of China's national defense policy also springs from the country's historical and cultural traditions. China is a country with 5,000 years of civilization, and a peace-loving tradition. Ancient Chinese thinkers advocated "associating with benevolent gentlemen and befriending good neighbors," which shows that throughout history the Chinese people have longed for peace in the world and for relations of friendship with the people of other countries.

—White paper on China's national defense, 2004 [1]

In the year 850, an unnamed Chinese alchemist was searching for an elixir that would give eternal life. Instead he (or she) accidentally invented gunpowder. Instead of conferring immortality, the mixture of saltpeter, charcoal, and sulfur blew up the alchemist's house. Although historians debate whether gunpowder really came into the world in such an innocent manner, [2] the official Chinese story is that gunpowder was long used only in fireworks to scare away evil spirits during New Year celebrations. Moreover, the Chinese like to point out, as soon as gunpowder spread to Europe in the late thirteenth century, the Europeans developed guns and firearms to conquer foreign countries, including, eventually, China—yet another plank in the idea of China's "peaceful rise," later modified to "peaceful development." The latter term was introduced to the public by the former leader duo Hu Jintao and Wen Jiabao in 2003, and according to former prime minister Wen, it means that China will never threaten any other nation, even when it becomes a superpower.

It is not in China's nature to threaten anyone, if we are to believe Beijing.

Even the White Book of the Chinese military, which elaborates on its status and ambitions, emphasized in 2008 that China will seek to resolve all conflicts with nonmilitary means, certainly never attacking first.

Western sinologists, too, long held that China lacked a warrior culture, in stark contrast to Japan. Sinologists were therefore less concerned about China's military heritage and claimed that Chinese culture advocated nonviolent solutions to national challenges. Instead of subjugating neighboring peoples, the Chinese built protective fortifications such as the almost nine-thousand-kilometer Great Wall. Moreover, the Chinese have never celebrated warrior heroes, unlike the ancient Greeks and Romans. Instead, said Western sinologists, they tended to admire people who lived according to the strict Confucian codes of ethics.

John K. Fairbank—who in 1936 started teaching at Harvard University and in 1955 established its center for Chinese studies, which was later given his name—turned to geography to explain China's defensive strategic culture.[3] The Chinese civilization emerged as an "island" surrounded by impassable seas to the east and south, deep jungles in the south toward Vietnam, high mountain ranges in the west toward the Indian subcontinent, and endless deserts and steppes to the west and north. Its leaders have thus always focused on maintaining social order at home rather than expanding beyond their core area. Fairbank believed that the strategic culture was also a result of Chinese philosophy. Confucius stressed that war was generally undesirable, while Sun Tzu (Master Sun) in *The Art of War* advocated the goal of "winning without fighting." Finally, Fairbank argued that Chinese strategic culture had been shaped by two thousand years of raids by nomads from the north, culminating in Genghis Khan's bloody invasion in the thirteenth century. These experiences had created a deep-rooted defensive mind-set, a "Chinese-wall mentality." The nomads of the Asian interior could not be defeated, so the Chinese built a wall to protect themselves. Only in the nineteenth century—when China was ruled by another nomadic people, the Manchu, who had guns—was the Mongol threat eliminated.

However, one should not buy the argument from Beijing—and from the old sinologists—that the Chinese lack a warrior culture.

Historical literature, written by members of the elite, esteems those who adhered to Confucian values, but ordinary Chinese people have always looked up to strong and skilled fighters. Examples of such heroes are Zhuge Liang, a legendary military strategist of the Three Kingdoms period, and Tai Gong, a legendary Hangzhou general who was the architect of the conquest of the mighty Shang Empire. Other examples are warriors who proved their bravery on the battlefield, such as Guan Gong, Zhang Fei, and Tang Taizong. All three have been praised in folktales, operas, and books. Guan Gong has even been worshiped as a god of war.[4]

In recent times, China's Communist Party has also celebrated warriors from the battles against the Japanese and the Nationalists and the wars in Korea and Vietnam.[5] Today's popular culture cultivates warrior heroes in books, comics, and especially movies, such as *Hero, House of Flying Daggers*, and *Crouching Tiger, Hidden Dragon*.

Alastair Iain Johnston, professor at Harvard University and an expert on China's foreign policy, has shown that Chinese strategic culture in no way rejects the use of military force.[6] Based on a study of strategic thinking during the Ming Dynasty, Johnston shows that the policies of the mighty emperors vis-à-vis their enemies were influenced not by Confucianism but rather by what in the West is known as realpolitik. This thinking is captured in the following rule of thumb: if you want peace, prepare for war. Johnston cites many Ming Dynasty thinkers who regarded military force as the most appropriate way to deter and combat nomadic tribes on the border in the north.

In his study of the strategic culture of the People's Republic, Andrew Scobell comes to a similar conclusion:[7] China has shown willingness to use aggressive military force and to take significant risks in war and in border disputes with neighboring countries, including Korea, Taiwan, India, the Soviet Union, Vietnam, and the Philippines. Whereas Fairbank approaches strategic culture as a static phenomenon, Scobell sees it as dynamic. Mao developed his doctrine of the people's war in the context of the Cold War and possible world war and American invasion. Unable to withstand an attack from the United States conventionally, China would mobilize its large population and benefit from its strategic depth. The enemy was to be absorbed and defeated through guerrilla warfare. The scenario underlying the current doctrine of limited people's war under modern, high-tech conditions is, by contrast, conceived as an intensive and time-limited war in China's border areas, primarily against Taiwan. The underlying premise is that China still cannot match the United States military and so should seek to acquire weapons that make it difficult for the Americans to come to the aid of Taiwan.

Chinese strategic culture is not more defensive than that of other great powers—quite the contrary. A study shows that the People's Republic used military force in eight out of eleven (72 percent) foreign policy crises from 1949 to 1985. By comparison, the figures for the same period were 27 percent for the Soviet Union, 18 percent for the United States, and 12 percent for the United Kingdom.[8] It is during territorial disputes in particular that China has sought military solutions. Furthermore, the study concludes that the Chinese use of military force was usually of high intensity, characterized by large confrontations or full-scale war. China has not been involved in armed conflicts with any of its neighbors since the war against Vietnam ended in 1979. But the government's handling of protesters in Tiananmen Square in 1989, in Tibet in 2008, and in Xinjiang in 2009 show that it is prepared and willing to use military force against its own people.

China is likely to continue to present itself as a pacifist giant, hoping to avoid confrontations with the outside world. But this does not mean that the country will never go to war. The benefits of war will be weighed against the costs, defensive mentality be damned. In plain language, this means that China—like other great powers—will not rule out use of military force.

Notes

1. "China's National Defense in 2004," Information Office of the State Council of the People's Republic of China, http://www.china.org.cn/e-white/20041227/index.htm.

2. Several historians have pointed out that the early Chinese used gunpowder to fire weapons; see, inter alia, Kenneth Chase, *Firearms: A Global History to 1700* (New York: Cambridge University Press, 2003), 33–35, 39; Stephen Turnbull, *Genghis Khan and the Mongol Conquests, 1190–1400* (Oxford: Osprey Publishing, 2003), 33; Timothy May, *The Mongol Art of War* (Yardley, UK: Westholme, 2007), 103.

3. See, e.g., John K. Fairbank, "Introduction: Varieties of the Chinese Military Experience," in *Chinese Ways in Warfare*, ed. Frank A. Kierman Jr. and John K. Fairbank (Cambridge, MA: Harvard University Press, 1974), 1–26.

4. Ralph D. Sawyer, "Chinese Strategic Power: Myths, Intent, and Projections," *Journal of Military and Strategic Studies* 8, no. 4 (summer 2006): 12–13.

5. Ibid., 13.

6. Alastair Iain Johnston, *Cultural Realism: Strategic Culture and Grand Strategy in Chinese History* (Princeton, NJ: Princeton University Press, 1998).

7. Andrew Scobell, *China's Use of Military Force: Beyond the Great Wall and the Long March* (Cambridge: Cambridge University Press, 2003).

8. Jonathan Wilkenfeld, Michael Brechter, and Sheila Moser, *Crisis in the Twentieth Century*, vol. 2: *Handbook of Foreign Policy Crises* (Oxford: Pergamon Books, 1988).

Myth 39

CHINESE HISTORY GOES IN CIRCLES

This dynasty could turn out to be very short-lived.
——Western ambassador to China, referring to the
Communist Party state

Chinese and Western historians alike have propounded a theory of "dynastic circles" (*chaodai xunhuan*). According to this theory, all Chinese dynasties go through the following phases: A new ruler unites China, establishes a new dynasty, and claims the "mandate of heaven" (*tian ming*). He is chosen by heaven to govern. China becomes prosperous, and the population increases. Then follow corruption, natural disasters, overpopulation, and peasant rebellions. All this is taken as certain evidence that the emperor has lost the mandate of heaven. An emperor will lose the mandate of heaven if he turns out to be an incompetent ruler. Then follows a period of chaos and violence, during which warlords control a fragmented empire. Finally one warlord defeats the others, and a new dynasty emerges with a ruler who has the mandate of heaven. The cycle begins anew.

In the classic fourteenth-century novel *Romance of the Three Kingdoms* (*Sanguo Yanyi*), it is stated that after years of discord comes unity and after a long period of cohesion comes dissolution. China's little big man, Deng Xiaoping, believed so strongly in this theory that he studied how the politics of the last imperial dynasty, the Qing (1644–1911), had contributed to its downfall. He hoped to avoid making the same mistakes.

Chinese and Western historians have different reasons for tracing these dynastic cycles. Many Chinese historians wish to emphasize continuity and China's long uninterrupted history. Tradition and history are important components of Chinese nationalism and national pride. Western scholars have presented a similar analysis to show that China—as opposed to the West—has been stagnant for thousands of years, moving in circles without any real progress.

But it is untrue that Chinese history simply repeats itself.

When we study the history of each dynasty, we find that each had a unique downfall. The ability of the Mongol conquerors, led by Genghis Khan and later by his successors, to subjugate China in the thirteenth century was unique. Never before had foreigners gained full control of the empire. Several of the key factors that brought about the fall of the last dynasty, the Qing, in 1911, were also unique. European imperialism had had catastrophic consequences for China. Particularly damaging were the Opium Wars—military conflicts between China and the United Kingdom in the nineteenth century caused by China's ban of the harmful substance and Britain's refusal to end the profitable trade. Another significant circumstance was the fact that the Qing rulers were from Manchuria, which had not yet become a part of China. When the country was in dire straits, antiforeign sentiments were turned against the Manchurian rulers and used to whip up the revolutionary mood. A third unique phenomenon was Chinese intellectuals' skepticism of the empire as a form of government and interest in trying out Western models, such as constitutional democracy.

Many dynasties were felled by simple tricks of fate—such as insane, stupid, or lazy emperors. One of them was the king of Zhou, the last in a series of thirty-one emperors during the Shang Dynasty (ca. 1600–1045 BCE). He was a stubborn and arrogant tyrant, best known for having forced the only one who dared to oppose him, Count Ji Chang, to eat one of his own sons. Another of Ji Chang's sons later got his revenge and overthrew the despotic Zhou. The king burned himself to death, and that was the end of the Shang Dynasty.

The mismanagement of Toghon Temur, the last emperor of the Mongol Yuan Dynasty (1271–1368), is also legendary. At one point he had the idea to kill all Chinese with the five most common surnames—Zhang, Wang, Liu, Li, and Zhao—constituting 80 percent of the population. Fortunately, the diabolical plan was never implemented. Otherwise he was so busy with tantric sex orgies that he completely forgot to run the country. He was not particularly motivated to fight against what would become the Ming Dynasty (1368–1644) and escaped to the Mongolian steppes when troops approached the capital. With that, Mongol control of China was lost.

Of course, one must read these narratives with a big pinch of salt. History is always written by later dynasties, and many have probably succumbed to the temptation of slandering their predecessors—in order to appear in a better light themselves. Yet there is no doubt that some emperors have shaped the historical developments of dynasties by the power of their personalities, for better and for worse.

It is important to remember that historical developments in many cases continued independently of changing dynasties. One example is the impressive golden age of the so-called Tang-Song transition, with its political reform, economic growth, emergence of protoindustry, and advances in culture, agriculture, science, technology, and education. Developments from the mid-Tang (618–907) continued into the Song (960–1279), despite power shifts.

Many are so seduced by the idea of dynastic circles that they genuinely believe the notion to be a correct representation of history. To quote the Bible, "Seek and you will find!" Bookstores in airports around the world make good money on books comparing contemporary America to the late Roman Empire. History is a complex subject, and there are countless sources. If you wish to unveil patterns and similarities, you will be able to—but you will be obliged to ignore significant differences, choices made by individual actors, and simple chance.

A cyclic understanding of history easily becomes deterministic; one assumes that development must move in a certain direction, and this has consequences. The theory establishes the idea that China is a prisoner of history, caught in a circle or cycle that is difficult to break. Today, some use this perspective to foresee the inevitable fall of the Communist Party. They do this by highlighting what they think are similarities with imperial dynasties and concluding that the People's Republic is at a certain point in such a cycle—and thus will fall. There tends to be a large element of wishful thinking in such analysis. At the other end of the spectrum, we see how official China also occasionally promotes a circular understanding of history before 1949—when the Communist Party assumed power and broke the cycle. In this reading, China has escaped from the "trap," thanks to the party.

Books that advocate dynastic circles are truly fascinating, if for no other reason than the illusion they provide that it is easy to become an expert on Chinese history. But if one really wants to understand this subject—as indeed one should!—then such theories are more of a hindrance than a help.

Myth 40

TIBET WAS A SHANGRI-LA UNTIL THE CHINESE CAME

> I think it was a system that was an experiment of extraordinary cou-
> rage where institutions were created to foster great human beings,
> loving human beings, responsible human beings.
> —Richard Gere on the old Tibet [1]

Tibet evokes strong emotions in the West. Books and movies convey the idea that the region was once a paradise: civilized, nonviolent, ruled by peace and wisdom, a place where everyone was happy—until the Chinese invaded in 1950. James Hilton's novel *Lost Horizons* (1933) established the myth of Shangri-la, a fictional place in the Tibetan mountains where a British diplomat finds peace of mind, love, and the meaning of life. In recent decades, blockbuster movies like *Kundun* and *7 Years in Tibet*, both from 1997, show that even Hollywood sees its chance to make money from Westerners' fascination with Tibet and its recent history. Pro-Tibet organizations are active in all corners of the world.

Today, the harmonious Tibetan order of old is presented in stark contrast to the current Chinese rule. Restrictions on worship and political activity are enforced more strictly in Tibet than anywhere else in China. Pictures of police manhandling Tibetan demonstrators are presented in news media throughout the world, confirming the perception (which is largely true) that Tibet is controlled in an authoritarian and inhumane way. The pictures tend to be accompanied by descriptions of the old Tibet as a society in which freedom, spirituality, peace, and love prevailed.

Lee Feigon, professor of Chinese and Tibetan history, holds that Western portrayals of Tibet are a far cry from reality. Each new version settles on the previous ones like a layer of fresh snow, obscuring what came before until the ground is totally covered. We can no longer see the reality, according to him.[2] Donald Lopez, professor of Buddhist and Tibetan studies, argues that the West's romanticized Tibet impairs our understanding of Tibet's past and present both. He even claims that the idealization of Tibet harms its struggle for independence.[3]

Many may be surprised to learn that Tibetans were traditionally a warrior people. Tibet's military strength was so great that in certain periods it ruled parts of China, India, Nepal, Central Asia, and the Middle East. The leaders of neighboring states were forced to send valuable items and beautiful princesses to Tibet as signs of submission. Tibetan arms and armor, like those found in Tibetan monasteries, belie the image of a peace-loving people. They are evidence of a society in which war formed a part of everyday life and was given great importance.[4]

One major reason Westerners associate Tibetan culture with unconditional peace is the emphasis on nonviolence of the current Dalai Lama, number fourteen. The fact that he has insisted on refraining from violence in the struggle against Chinese rule and has stuck to his guns (or, rather, lack thereof) for decades is indeed impressive. But Tibetan leaders condemning violence is in fact a new phenomenon. Pacifism is not a traditional Tibetan value.

Independent Tibet was a religious dictatorship, at least in parts of its history. Per Kværne, professor of religious studies at the University of Oslo and an expert on Tibet, has described how monasteries were centers of power,[5] economic and political as well as religious. The monasteries held great economic power through their monopoly on trade in important groceries such as barley, butter, and tea. Another Tibet expert, Peter Bishop, has described the dark undertones of spiritual and political absolutism in the lamas, the chief priests, before 1950. At first glance the country appeared naively content, but a web of political and religious intrigue spread from Lhasa.[6] The central government was characterized by power struggles, and serving as the Dalai Lama was at times highly risky.

Tibet was a feudal society—a fact greatly exaggerated and exploited by the Chinese to legitimize the occupation. However, Kværne holds that "feudal society" is the correct term when describing pre–People's Republic Tibet.[7] The aristocracy of ancient Tibet has been described by Professor Lopez.[8] Rich noble families owned large properties and made up the civil service in the nineteenth century. Monasteries were the highest local authority, and noble families sent their sons to monasteries to ensure the family's position. Many noble families had slaves. China has probably exaggerated the extent of slavery, again to legitimize its occupation. But Western researchers have also documented slavery throughout Tibet's history.

Physical punishments, such as cutting off hands and feet, removing eyes, flogging, and the death penalty, are said to have been a part of the justice system until 1913, but it is unclear how widespread they were in different areas and different periods. A Tibetan poem from the fifth century describes how spies were to be treated. It is uncertain whether the text was ever implemented in practice:

> The blood from the liver escapes through the mouth,
> Without damaging the skin,
> We remove the guts through the mouth,
> The man will be alive, even if his heart comes to his mouth.

Tibet has become so politicized that it is difficult to find balanced historical sources about the region. The Chinese depict incomparably dire straits and despotic religious rulers—in order to justify the invasion and the suppression of religion. The Tibetan side exaggerates the positive aspects of the old life and holds forth on the negative consequences of Chinese domination. Western Tibet activists do the same, but with the volume turned up.

This phenomenon is linked to what Edward Said described as "Orientalism," the Western tendency to romanticize and essentialize Asian cultures.[9] Many Westerners find it exotic and alluring to dwell on the idea of a society characterized by spirituality and peace—so unlike their own, not to mention a China stereotyped as inhuman and uncaring. The fact that American celebrities, such as the American actor Richard Gere, actively support a free Tibet undoubtedly helps to spread this vision.

1. "Dreams of Tibet," PBS, 28 October 1997,http://www.pbs.org/wgbh/pages/frontline/shows/tibet/interviews/gere.html.

2. Lee Feigon, *Demystifying Tibet: Unlocking the Secrets of the Land of the Snows* (Chicago: Ivan R. Dee, 1996).

3. Donald S. Lopez Jr., *Prisoners of Shangri-la: Tibetan Buddhism and the West* (Chicago: University of Chicago Press, 1998).

4. More on this in ibid.

5. Per Kværne, "Annerledeslandet" (The Country of Difference), Morgenbladet, 18 April 2008, http://morgenbladet.no/samfunn/2008/annerledeslandet#.VCXF9RZUg32.

6. Quoted in Feigon, *Demystifying Tibet*.

7. Kværne, "Tibet Images among Researchers on Tibet."

8. Lopez, *Prisoners of Shangri-la*.

9. Edward Said, *Orientalism* (New York: Vintage Books, 1979).

Myth 41

MAO WAS A MONSTER

Mao discovered in himself a love for bloodthirsty thuggery. This gut enjoyment, which verged on sadism, meshed with, but preceded, his affinity for Leninist violence.

—Jung Chang and Jon Halliday [1]

Jung Chang and Jon Halliday's 832-page biography of Mao Zedong—the man who established the People's Republic of China in 1949 and ruled the country until his death in 1976—has become a best seller. Reviewers have praised the book as "the most thoroughly researched and richly documented piece of synthetic scholarship yet to appear on the rise of Mao and the [Chinese Communist Party]," stating that it "will most likely change forever the way modern Chinese history is understood and taught." [2] Said to "blow away the miasma of deceit and ignorance which still shrouds Mao's life from many Western eyes," [3] the book opens with an assertion that Mao, during his decades in power, was responsible for the deaths of as many as 70 million people [4]—more murders than attributed to even Hitler and Stalin. Mao's goal "was a completely arid society, devoid of civilization, deprived of representation of human feelings, inhabited by a herd with no sensibility. . . . He wanted the nation to be brain-dead in order to carry out his big purge—and to live in this state permanently." [5]

The "Let a Hundred Flowers Bloom, Let a Hundred Schools of Thought Contend" campaign from 1956 to 1957 shows Mao's evil and scheming ways, argue Chang and Halliday. In order to trick scholars into revealing their true, counterrevolutionary attitudes, Mao encouraged them to freely express their views. Academics knew better than to take this at face value. But when Mao repeated his request for criticism, they walked right into the trap. Within a few weeks, several million letters had reached the party leadership. After the campaign had lasted one year, Mao believed that he had a good enough view of the "poisonous weeds," and the trap snapped shut.

Critics were executed or mercilessly punished in labor camps.

The Great Leap Forward from 1958 is cited as another example of Mao's evil. The chairman knowingly starved 38 million people to death, according to Chang and Halliday. Mao was ready and willing to let even more people die.[6] The starting point for the campaign was the need for large amounts of steel for Mao's superpower ambitions, and 90 million people across the country were put to work. In the cities, all of six hundred thousand furnaces were built and placed in backyards; to feed the furnaces, people were forced to sacrifice all their metal possessions. In rural areas, people had to work on large public projects. The result was disastrous. Large areas of forest were cut down, causing flooding in many places. Poor families were left without the most basic and necessary tools. No one worked on the harvest during the spring of 1959—instead they fed the furnaces or worked on slave projects in the countryside. And all was in vain: the steel produced turned out to be useless.[7]

Even Mao's closest were made to suffer. The fact that Mao punished Liu Shaoqi, his second in command, because he had the nerve to criticize the Great Leap Forward, is not news. But the fact that Mao withheld the death penalty because he wanted Liu to suffer a slow and painful death is not generally known. The chairman was allegedly continuously updated on Liu's torment and disease—complete with pictures. The book suggests that this was something Mao enjoyed.[8]

These are just a few of the many examples of Mao's evil that Chang and Halliday produce.

Mao undoubtedly caused great suffering for the Chinese people, but the book has major flaws.[9] The first is that the authors ascribe to Mao exclusively malicious intent. Documenting the disastrous consequences of Mao's projects is not difficult. But entering the mind of a man who died forty years ago is not so easy. The "Hundred Flowers" campaign was not necessarily a "devious plan" and a "trap" to remove intellectuals.[10] It is unclear what Mao's intentions really were. His aims at the outset may have been noble enough. One cannot rule out that he genuinely hated bureaucracy and wanted a continuous revolution through criticism and debate, then became overwhelmed by the scale of criticism and the fact that it was directed at the Communist Party and the lack of freedom and democracy. This must have frightened him, leading him to persecute the critics. Moreover, there is little evidence to suggest that Mao intentionally created the famine during the Great Leap Forward. In hindsight it is easy to see that the reforms were disastrous and that the chairman's judgment was—to put it mildly—poor. But if one wants to understand how such a tragedy could happen, one must take into consideration that Mao was ill informed. Local party representatives were afraid to report that the areas under their control had failed to reach production goals. Mao can certainly be blamed for setting the tone; yet it is doubtful that he planned the tragic outcome. The fact that Mao punished his closest advisors speaks volumes about his paranoia and greed for power. But Chang and Halliday go further, saying that he was motivated by sadism. This is pure speculation.

Chang and Halliday also ignore the historical context, both within China and internationally. China in 1949 was an impoverished country with poorly developed infrastructure. The country had suffered for almost a century, enduring first the ravages of European colonial powers and then decades of civil war between the Nationalists and the Communists, interrupted only by the Japanese occupation. Failing to take into account such factors when analyzing the conditions under which Mao made his decisions oversimplifies to the point of misleading. The claim that Mao killed 38 million people during the Great Leap Forward is questionable. Many suffered from malnutrition even before the People's Republic was established. The campaign undoubtedly exacerbated the situation but cannot take all the blame for every death by starvation during this period. Equally questionable is the claim that Mao started the Korean War to satisfy his own hunger for power.[11] Most historians maintain that Mao was dragged into the Korean War as a result of Kim Il-sung's attack on South Korea and the subsequent American military intervention.

The authors are convinced that everything Mao touched turned into a disaster and portray only the negative aspects of his rule. In producing such a tremendous piece of work—really vast—it is peculiar that they have failed to spot any positive and long-term consequences of Mao's policies. He succeeded in unifying China after decades of occupation and civil war. Mao developed China's industry and infrastructure, thereby laying a foundation for the economic growth that has taken place under his successors. The more recent and more balanced *Mao: The Real Story*, by contrast, points out that while there was no shortage of suffering under Mao's rule, he nonetheless should be credited with transforming China from a semicolony into an independent and powerful state.[12]

Nor do Chang and Halliday mention his social reforms, despite the fact that they had great effects. Literacy among the population skyrocketed after the People's Republic was established. In 1949 only two out of ten Chinese people could read; thirty years later, 65.5 percent could.[13] Under Mao life expectancy doubled, from thirty-five to sixty-three years.[14] These accomplishments are important parts of his story, if only to make clear why so many Chinese people today remember this period more positively than Chang and Halliday's portrayal suggests.

Mao deserves a tough historical judgment. And attempts to penetrate his psyche are a sure way of selling books. But they do not contribute much to our understanding of this pivotal period of China's history or of Mao.

Notes

1. Jung Chang and Jon Halliday, *Mao: The Unknown Story* (London: Jonathan Cape, 2005), 41.

2. Sophie Beach, "CDT Bookshelf: Richard Baum Recommends *Mao: The Unknown Story*," *China Digital Times*, 5 September 2005, http://web.archive.org/web/20070406133636/http://chinadigitaltimes.net/2005/09/cdt_bookshelf_r.php.

3. Max Hastings, "The Long March to Mass Murder," *Telegraph*, 5 June 2005, http://www.telegraph.co.uk/culture/books/3643215/The-long-march-to-mass-murder.html.

4. Chang and Halliday, *Mao*, 21.

5. Ibid., 509.

6. Ibid., 457.

7. For a recent analysis of the hardship suffered by the Chinese people during this period, see Yang Jisheng, *Tombstone: The Great Chinese Famine, 1958–1962* (New York: Farrar, Straus & Giroux, 2012).

8. Ibid., 554–56.

9. For a collection of good academic reviews of the book, see Gregory Benton and Lin Chun, eds., *Was Mao Really a Monster?* (London: Routledge, 2010).

10. Chang and Halliday, *Mao*, 434, 435.

11. Ibid., 371–81.

12. Alexander V. Pantsov and Steven I. Levine, *Mao: The Real Story* (New York: Simon & Schuster, 2012).

13. Zhang Tiedao, "Literacy Education in China," United Nations Educational, Scientific, and Cultural Organization, 2005, http://ddp-ext.worldbank.org/EdStats/CHNgmrpro05a.pdf.

14. Gao Mobo, *The Battle for China's Past: Mao and the Cultural Revolution* (London: Pluto Press, 2008), 81.

Myth 42

THE CHINESE DO NOT CARE ABOUT THEIR OWN HISTORICAL HERITAGE

As a foreigner in China, one is struck by how few historical monuments there are, given the country's long history, and all the more surprised by how carelessly those that remain are treated. Visiting Beijing, it is a shock to walk along Qianmen Street, which was first developed during the Ming Dynasty (1368–1644). The historical street, which stretches south from Tiananmen Square, was for centuries the center of the capital's cultural life, with a myriad of stores and as many as one hundred thousand inhabitants. In 2008, just before the opening of the Beijing Olympics, Qianmen Street underwent "protective demolition"—government speak for tearing down old buildings and rebuilding them "according to [the street's] original expression and form." In reality this meant erecting modern copies, often with a view to attracting revenue from tourists. Only nine original buildings survive among the sixty-six new ones. One gets the unpleasant feeling of finding oneself in a Chinese Disneyland.

Sadly, this grim example is far from unique. Beijing's traditional neighborhoods, known as *hutongs*, are demolished in order to build skyscrapers. All over the capital are houses bearing a painted circle with the character 折 (*chai*), meaning "tear down"; in other words, the government has decided that the house is to be demolished to make room for new construction. In the Forbidden City, placards about Chinese history read, "Made possible by the American Express Company." The authorities apparently did not see fit to pay themselves for the renovation of the Imperial Palace—home to twenty-four emperors and their administrations for five hundred years, a UNESCO World Heritage Site, and one of the country's premier tourist attractions. The Great Wall, China's most famous historical construction, is in many places in dire condition. Only sections near Beijing, the ones most visited by tourists, have been renovated. Numerous old temples have been leveled only to be rebuilt, some twice as large as the original, using modern materials—in order to attract tourists.

The legendary city of Kashgar, the center of Muslim culture in China and a key point on the Silk Road, is about to be razed. The authorities have decided that 85 percent of what remains of the historic center is to be demolished. The official explanation is that the buildings are unsafe in the face of earthquakes, to which Xinjiang is indeed exposed. This is, however, a convenient pretext for a politically motivated project. Beijing sees a link between historic Uyghur culture and many Uyghurs' struggle for independence or more autonomy for Xinjiang; thus it sees advantages in erasing symbols of that culture.

Out of a total of 766,722 registered historical monuments in China, 44,000 had disappeared by the end of 2011, announced the State Administration of Cultural Heritage. [1]

Few Chinese object when historical monuments or buildings are demolished. Those who do run the risk of retaliation. The legal framework intended to protect historic sites is not fully implemented—like many of China's laws—and practice varies from place to place around the country. [2] Consequently, one easily gets the impression that modernization is the only thing that matters to the Chinese authorities and that material historical legacy must yield.

Not that much is left anyway. The events of China's dramatic last two hundred years took their toll on the country's historical heritage: the Opium Wars of 1839 to 1842 and 1856 to 1860; European raids in the late nineteenth and early twentieth centuries; the chaos that followed the last emperor's retirement in 1912, when a fragmented China was ruled by various warlords; the war against Japan from 1937 to 1945; and the Red Guards who went berserk during the Cultural Revolution, ruining monasteries, temples, and other monuments.

But it is certainly not the case that the Chinese do not care about their historic heritage.

They are far more concerned with taking care of their stories than their physical historical heritage, according to Pierre Ryckmans (best known by his pen name, Simon Leys). [3] He believes that Chinese rulers, unlike their European counterparts, were not obsessed with building monuments to their own greatness—palaces, temples, and the like—to serve as everlasting visible memories. What mattered to the Chinese was passing on the stories about their rulers. Only the intangible—written or memorized words—lasts forever, while physical things disintegrate with time.

There is also a highly pragmatic aspect to prioritizing historical knowledge over historical objects; the expression "Use history as a mirror" (*Yishi weijian*) recommends looking to and learning from history when faced with a difficult situation.

Nonmaterial cultural heritage and history are very present, cherished sources of pride in China. Television and film companies produce grand—and expensive—historical soap operas and movies, and ratings go through the roof. The characters in the most popular TV series also appear in commercials—for example, for the national liquor *baijiu*. History is also highly present in the Chinese language; many common idioms make no sense unless one knows Chinese history. If a Chinese colleague describes your work style as "waiting for a hare by the stump" (*shou zhu dai tu*), you have to be acquainted with Chinese literary history to know if this is praise or criticism. It is the latter. The idiom refers to a story about a man in whose fields there was a tree stump. One day a hare hopped into the stump and broke its neck. Dinner was practically served to the man on a platter. He decided that it was obviously a waste of time and effort to cultivate the land, what with dinner falling into his lap. So he stopped—but his stump never felled a hare again. Now the expression connotes naive laziness.

It might also be a challenge to empathize with the Chinese who laments about a situation being "Chu songs from four sides" (*si mian Chu ge*) unless we know the history of the war between the states of Chu and Han in about 200 BCE. Xiang Yu led the Chu troops, with few soldiers and little food, and was terrified when one night he heard the opposing troops singing Chu songs. He realized then that the Chu land had already fallen and that the people of Chu had joined the enemy. His situation was hopeless.

Chinese interest in material historical legacy is also rising. Appreciating pre–People's Republic artifacts hasn't been politically incorrect for a long time—not since the Mao era.

In 2011, China leapfrogged the United States to become the world's largest art and antiques market. [4] In the last ten to fifteen years, collecting antiques has become a popular hobby, and several Chinese auction houses have been established. European auction houses have in recent years turned bigger profits than ever, despite the financial crisis, thanks in no small part to Chinese buyers. Wealthy Chinese outbid each other in pursuit of Chinese antiques outside China. At Sotheby's, the number of Chinese buyers tripled during the first decades of the twenty-first century. The customers at the Hong Kong International Art and Antique Fair have gone from 90 percent Western at the beginning of the millennium to 95 percent Chinese today. [5] Chinese antique collectors are driven by their nationalistic desire to bring stolen cultural treasures home, a desire for investment objects and status symbols, and the sheer joy of collecting.

Increased interest in antique collecting has also caused problems in terms of illegal excavation and destruction in archaeological contexts.

The Chinese government, too, is increasingly concerned with the country's material cultural heritage. At the local level this is apparent in the many historical museums in the provinces. Almost four hundred new museums opened across the country in 2011.[6] Local authorities have pulled out all the stops and invested large sums of money, and many of the museums are excellent. Exhibitions tend to focus on unique local heritage and findings from archaeological excavations. The presentations are usually very professional, with texts in English and Chinese.

The government's concern that tourism might damage cultural heritage makes itself felt in a museum being constructed in Dunhuang, Gansu province. Unlike most museums, its purpose is not to attract crowds for its own sake. Instead it is meant to keep hordes of careless tourists away from the area's ancient and rapidly deteriorating Buddhist cave murals.[7]

The central authorities have also become more interested in what they perceive to be stolen art treasures outside China.[8] Government representatives have visited the British Museum in London and New York's Metropolitan Museum of Art, among other institutions, and demanded the return of antiquities that ended up there by questionable means. It is easy to disapprove of the fact that Europeans took so many cultural treasures out of China throughout history, and one does not blame the Chinese for wanting them back. However, given the situation described above, one wonders if they would have survived if they had stayed in China.

Notes

1. "Census Reveals Loss of 44,000 Heritage Sites," China.org.cn, 30 December 2011, http://www.china.org.cn/china/2011-12/30/content_24289241.htm.

2. Marina Svensson, "Protection of the Cultural Heritage in the PRC: Preservation Policies, Institutions, Laws, and Enforcement," Centre for East and South-East Asian Studies, University of Lund, http://www.ace.lu.se/o.o.i.s/5933.

3. Pierre Ryckmans, "The Chinese Attitude towards the Past," *China Heritage Quarterly*, no. 14 (June 2008), http://www.chinaheritagequarterly.org/articles.php?searchterm=014_chineseAttitude.inc&issue=014.

4. *News China Magazine*, 1 September 2013, 4.

5. See, e.g., "China's Antique Collectors Driving Prices through the Roof," *Independent*, 16 March 2010, http://www.independent.co.uk/news/world/asia/chinarsquos-antique-collectors-driving-prices-through-the-roof-1921932.html; "Chinese Tycoons Trawl UK Antiques Market for Treasures," *Guardian*, 16 January 2011, http://www.guardian.co.uk/artanddesign/2011/jan/16/chinese-antiques-record-prices.

6. "A Building Boom as Chinese Art Rises in Stature," *New York Times*, 20 March 2013, http://www.nytimes.com/2013/03/21/arts/artsspecial/a-prosperous-china-goes-on-a-museum-building-spree.html.

7. Ibid.

8. See, e.g., James Cuno, *Who Owns Antiquity? Museums and the Battle over Our Ancient Heritage* (Princeton, NJ: Princeton University Press, 2008); Richard Kraus, "The Politics of Art Repatriation: Nationalism, State Legitimation, and Beijing's Looted Zodiac Animal Heads," in *Chinese Politics: State, Society, and the Market*, ed. Peter Hays Gries and Stanley Rosen (New York: Routledge, 2010), 199–221.

Part VI

The Future

Myth 43

THE INTERNET WILL TOPPLE THE COMMUNIST PARTY

By the end of 2013, 618 million Chinese were online, according to the China Internet Network Information Center.[1] Everyone has a mobile phone in his or her pocket. So popular are the new means of communication that the Chinese sacrifice pictures of iPads and iPhones to their ancestors to ensure that relatives stay connected after death. "[The Internet age] is an era where the leaders perform, and the people are the audience," says Professor Guo Weiqing at Sun Yatsen University in Guangzhou.[2] The Web provides easy access to information, making it harder for Beijing to implement censorship and conceal power abuses. Besides, social media make it far easier for disgruntled Chinese to share their frustrations with each other and to organize protests. Many people believe that it is only a matter of time before the widespread dissatisfaction of today explodes online and the Communist Party falls.

Focusing on social media in political analysis is very trendy—even for the authors of this book, who were raised in the mid-1970s, before the advent of the Internet. But one must be careful not to exaggerate the importance of the Web. Although social media have a significant mobilizing potential, this does not necessarily make revolution more likely or easier to carry out.

The Web is a "Janus phenomenon," according to *Observer* writer and *Spectator* blogger Nick Cohen.[3] The Internet may make it easier to connect and organize people, but it may also increase the risks associated with participation in political opposition activities. As they surf, Web users leave behind traces that authoritarian regimes can use to track down dissidents. Iran provides a sad example of this. When the regime stifled the Green Movement in the wake of the highly disputed presidential election in 2009, the Iranian security apparatus started searching for those who had participated in the riots. The tool that had been so helpful in mobilizing and coordinating was now used against the protesters. The security forces read blogs and tweets, resulting in thousands of activists being arrested, imprisoned, and in some cases sentenced to death.

The authorities in China have the exact same opportunity.

The journalist Shi Tao was sentenced to ten years in prison after Yahoo! agreed to give the Chinese government access to his e-mail, which showed that he had forwarded so-called sensitive information. The case got international attention only due to the embarrassing role Yahoo! had played.

The Internet also provides the government with new channels through which it can spread its own message. Beijing has invested tremendous resources in getting the party newspapers online, all the while striving to censor purveyors of alternative worldviews, using what has become known as the "Great Firewall."[4] Although the wall is full of cracks—proxy sites like Hide My Ass! are one way to break through—it does to some extent prevent exposure to "undesirable" ideas from Western critics and Chinese dissidents. Local and central governments alike seek to ensure that the government is the dominant voice behind the firewall and pay small amounts of cash to those willing to post regime-friendly comments online. These commenters are referred to as members of the "50 Cent Party," after the amount of money they supposedly receive per post. International Web portals like Google also make good money in China; they know that if they want to stay in business, they must delete content Chinese authorities deem subversive.

Andrew J. Nathan, professor of political science at Columbia University, points out that the Internet and social media flood citizens with information. All Chinese today are familiar with issues like corruption, land grabbing, uneven distribution of wealth, and environmental degradation. Nathan argues that this has led to information overload, making it less likely that a single event will rouse the Chinese enough to trigger mass mobilization against the regime.[5]

It is also important to consider the ways in which the Chinese actually use the Internet.

When reading Western analysis of Internet censorship in China, one gets the impression that Chinese youth are mostly looking for Western news sources and stories that are critical of the Chinese government, such as the websites of Amnesty International and Human Rights Watch, but are constantly running up against the "Great Firewall." The reality is a bit different. Chinese youth use the Internet much as Western youth do, for entertainment, gaming, and social media.

Change requires political activism. The basis for activism is deep dissatisfaction with social, economic, and political conditions among those with the courage to do something. In the presence of these basic preconditions, people have always found ways to communicate with each other and organize protests—even without the Internet. Illegal pamphlets circulated during the American Revolution in the eighteenth century, cassette tapes were distributed during the 1978–1979 revolution in Iran, and faxes were used during the protests in China in 1989. People do not riot because of a blog or a tweet. The Internet does not create revolution itself; it is only a tool.

Chinese authorities perceive the Web as a threat; otherwise they wouldn't try to censor it. But as long as people do not pour into the streets, the Internet will never topple China's Communist Party.

Notes

1. "CNNIC Released the 33rd Statistical Report on Internet Development in China," CNNIC, January 17, 2014, http://www1.cnnic.cn/AU/MediaC/rdxw/hotnews/201401/t20140117_43849.htm.

2. Calum MacLeod, "China Shuts Down 16 Websites in Effort to Curb Rumors," *USA Today*, 2 April 2012, 7.

3. Nick Cohen, *You Can't Read This Book: Censorship in an Age of Freedom* (London: Fourth Estate, 2012).

4. This term was first mentioned in Geremie R. Barmé and Sang Ye, "The Great Firewall of China," *Wired*, June 1997, http://www.wired.com/wired/archive/5.06/china_pr.html.

5. Andrew J. Nathan, "China at the Tipping Point?" *Journal of Democracy* 24, no. 1 (January 2013): 22.

Myth 44

THE END OF THE COMMUNIST REGIME IS NEAR

The two dynasties in Chinese history that most resemble the Communist episode are the Qin (221–207 B.C.) and the Sui (A.D. 589–618). Both oversaw huge new construction and great increases in wealth but also ruthless tyranny, deaths from forced labor, and horrors such as burning of books and burying of scholars (the "dissidents" of another era). Both were well short.

—Perry Link[1]

When Will China Collapse? Within this decade—in other words, by 2011.

—Gordon G. Chang[2]

The Chinese Communist Party's Eighteenth Congress in November 2012—which was especially important because the once-per-decade leadership succession would be determined—was marked by an atmosphere of crisis. The party had just been deeply shaken by the Bo Xilai scandal. Many Western analysts argued that the Communist Party was doomed. But this was not the first time observers had forecasted the death of the regime. Many thought the 1989 Tiananmen crisis would topple the party. In the early 1990s, China watchers expected the Soviet Union's collapse to prove contagious. Communist regimes were a thing of the past, they said. At the turn of the millennium, many again declared the party to be on its deathbed, this time as a result of the obligations of World Trade Organization (WTO) membership: market liberalism required democratization. In 2001, Gordon G. Chang published *The Coming Collapse of China*, in which he predicted that the People's Republic would implode within a decade. As the son of a Chinese man who immigrated to the United States in search of a better life, the author seems to have a deep well of aversion to his ancestral homeland, which explodes between the covers.

And yet the Communist Party is still with us today.

Despite considerable dissatisfaction, the pressure from below for change appears to be weak in China. There are few signs of an emerging political movement with the potential to unite possibly disaffected groups—workers, migrants, farmers, women, students, intellectuals, ethnic minorities, and environmentalists.[3] Thus, a new broad mobilization à la 1989 fails to arise. The reason is partly that many Chinese accept the rule of the Communist Party. In *Accepting Authoritarianism*,[4] Teresa Wright, a professor at California State University, argues that key segments of Chinese society, including businessmen and entrepreneurs who were allowed to join the party in 2002, see their interests best served by the existing order. Wider segments of society do not want to rock the boat either, as in recent decades the current regime has ensured economic prosperity for most people. In 2012, according to figures from the Chinese government, as many as 85 percent of people living in urban areas owned their own homes,[5] and 200 million households in rural areas had use of their own plots of land.[6] Although the real figures are probably somewhat lower, a large percentage of the Chinese have an interest in maintaining the status quo.

At the same time, the government has made organizing political opposition difficult and risky. Civil society is tightly controlled by the state, dissidents are monitored and harassed, and real opposition parties are banned. The security forces suppress all attempts at demonstrations and unrest—particularly in provinces dominated by non-Han minorities. In addition, the government has a wide range of subtler methods to undermine critics. For example, responsibility for everything that goes wrong often falls, rightly or wrongly, on local or regional authorities, shielding the central government from criticism. The rulers in Beijing exist in clouds of ignorance. "If only the Emperor knew about this, he would surely intervene," the Chinese complained during the imperial era. In many ways, not much has changed. The government also seeks to diminish sources of instability by, for example, increasing investment in rural areas, reducing agricultural taxes, and cracking down on local party officials who put the squeeze on farmers.

There are few signs that substantial policy changes will be initiated from above—by the political elite. An authoritarian regime might introduce political reforms in order to ease pressures, as was done in Taiwan in the 1980s. So far there are few indications that the leaders in Beijing want to democratize or see any need to. The former prime minister Wen Jiabao, during the party's national congress in March 2012, mentioned the word "reform" (*gaige*) seventy times and stated that the time was ripe for democracy.[7] But what did he mean by democracy? The outgoing prime minister probably thought that political reform was required, but there is little reason to believe that he had in mind a genuine multiparty system and free elections of legislative and executive powers. Most likely he was thinking of "democracy with Chinese characteristics"—in other words, changes that would not weaken the Communist Party's grip on power.

As long as the leadership remains united, it is also unlikely that rivalries within the ruling elite will bring democracy to China. Conceivably, a faction within the party could seek to strengthen its position by building alliances with groups outside the elite through promises of political participation. But given that the mechanisms for holding the elite together seem to be in good working order, this is not a very likely scenario.

One variation of elite conflict is a military coup—military officers forcing civilian leaders to step aside. This is also unlikely in today's China for many reasons. The complex organization of the Chinese military, in which the party exercises control at all levels, makes it difficult for officers to take power, even if they want to. One can hardly imagine the top officers conspiring without the civilian leadership finding out. Moreover, China is large—very large—and it is difficult to move troops around without being detected. More importantly, there is little to suggest that the military wishes to seize power. On the contrary, over the past decades, officers have sought to distance themselves from politics in order to become a professional military force.[8]

Pressure from outside also appears to have limited impact on the Chinese leadership. The United States, other Western countries, and financial institutions like the International Monetary Fund, the World Bank, and the WTO repeat calls for human rights and democratization like a mantra. But these demands fall on deaf ears, interpreted by Beijing as attempts to undermine China's stability and growth. The leaders' harsh reprisals against Norway after the 2010 Nobel Peace Prize went to Liu Xiaobo show that they do not intend to be moved by external pressure.

Of course, the Communist Party will not rule forever. No political regime does—not even in China, as the long list of dynasties clearly demonstrates. Depending on how we count, China has been governed by anywhere between fourteen and forty dynasties. If we buy into the myth that China's history spans five thousand years, then the People's Republic has governed for only 1 percent of this time. History shows that political upheavals tend to be sudden and unexpected, in China as elsewhere. Still, it seems too early to write an obituary for the Communist regime in Beijing.

Notes

1. Perry Link, "America's Outdated View of China," *Washington Post*, 10 May 2012, http://www.washingtonpost.com/opinions/the-us-governments-outdated-view-of-china/2012/05/10/gIQAUvgaGU_story.html.

2. Gordon G. Chang, *The Coming Collapse of China* (New York: Random House, 2001), http://www.gordonchang.com/qanda.htm.

3. Vivienne Shue, "Legitimacy Crisis in China?" in *Chinese Politics: State, Society, and the Market*, ed. Peter Hays Gries and Stanley Rosen (New York: Routledge, 2010), 42.

4. Teresa Wright, *Accepting Authoritarianism: State Society Relations in China's Reform Era* (Stanford, CA: Stanford University Press, 2010).

5. See, e.g., "China's Home Ownership Rate Much Higher than International Standard," *Global Times*, 14 May 2012, http://www.globaltimes.cn/NEWS/tabid/99/ID/709329/Chinas-home-ownership-rate-much-higher-than-international-standard.aspx.

6. "OECD Review of Agricultural Policies—China," OECD, 2011, http://www.oecd.org/document/57/0,3746,en_2649_33797_35557433_1_1_1_1,00.html.

7. Michael Sainsbury, "Wen Jiabao's Remarkable Road to Reform," *Australian*, 17 March 2012, http://www.theaustralian.com.au/news/world/wen-jiabaos-remarkable-road-to-reform/story-fnb1brze-1226301929918.

8. Andrew J. Nathan and Andrew Scobell, *China's Search for Security* (New York: Columbia University Press, 2012), ch. 11.

Myth 45

THE CHINESE ARE MASTERS OF LONG-TERM THINKING

In Beijing, leaders think in time frames of one hundred years.
—Often heard among Western diplomats, journalists, and researchers

"**H**e who is prudent and lies in wait for an enemy who is not will be victorious," advised Sun Tzu (Master Sun) more than 2,500 years ago in *The Art of War*.[1] "It is too early to tell,"[2] Prime Minister Zhou Enlai famously said when asked to assess the impact of the French Revolution during a 1971 dinner with Henry Kissinger, then foreign policy advisor to President Richard Nixon. Mao Zedong's time horizon was no less modest. "We can do without Taiwan for the time being, and let [the reunion] come after one hundred years,"[3] the chairman declared in a meeting with Nixon. In another context Mao said China would build nuclear submarines "even if it takes us 10,000 years."[4] Such quotes—which often have unclear origins and are removed from their original contexts—are repeated by Western observers to support the idea that patience and long-term thinking are deeply rooted traits of Chinese strategy and diplomacy.[5]

In *On China*, Henry Kissinger reveals his admiration for Chinese diplomacy—and the Chinese leaders he got to know during secret talks leading up to President Nixon's meeting with Mao in 1972.[6] Kissinger portrays leaders such as Mao, Zhou Enlai, and Deng Xiaoping as products of an ancient strategic tradition stretching back to Master Sun. Western short-term political maneuvers were totally eclipsed by Chinese diplomacy, according to the old statesman. Reading between the lines, one can practically hear Kissinger's teeth grinding in frustration with American foreign and security policy.

Kissinger's book touches upon another factor conducive to long-term planning—namely, the one-party system. Exempt from worries about the next election, the leaders in Beijing are free to think long-term and big. They can act effectively and make unpopular decisions, unlike democratically elected Western politicians, who rarely think beyond today's news cycle.[7] "The typical time horizon in Washington hovers somewhere between the daily spin for the evening talk shows and the next election cycle. In Beijing the clear focus is on where China wants to be in fifty years," if we are to believe Kishore Mahbubani, dean of the Lee Kuan Yew School of Public Policy in Singapore.[8]

The twenty-first century will belong to China, thanks to its capacity for long-term thinking, continues Mahbubani. He emphasizes the self-discipline of Deng and his successors, who since 1978 have worked purposefully and patiently to restore China to its historically prominent position. The leaders in Beijing have never been led astray by the promise of short-term gains, says Mahbubani. They know that China has the world's largest population and will bend global power structures to its own advantage by virtue of this alone. The West, on the other hand, is blind to longer development trends and a slave to the election cycle. The most shortsighted is the United States—a country with a short history and a short memory, according to Mahbubani.[9]

There are undoubtedly elements of long-term thinking in Chinese politics, and such thinking is institutionalized. The authorities still use one- to five-year plans as a management tool in most areas, including economics, science, defense, and culture. Such plans ensure continuity from one generation to the next at the top of the Communist Party.

But the claim that Chinese leaders are inherently better than others at long-term thinking is questionable.

"Crossing the river by feeling the stones" was Deng's recipe for China's reform and opening up. He privileged experimentation and flexibility over long-term thinking. This policy of improvisation has been guiding Chinese politics ever since, and Chinese leaders have emphasized not being bound by long-term plans. As rulers of the world's largest country, they have no choice but to adapt policy to pressure from below and outside. They must deal with an infinite variety of internal and external challenges, a never-ending game of whack-a-mole. Instead of planning they must constantly put out fires, which often break out in the most unexpected places.

Further, processes steal much time, just as in Western political systems. In today's China, decision-making processes have become complex and timeconsuming. Ministries, the military, provincial governments, state-owned companies, and many other actors have their own interests and seek to influence the leaders in Beijing. They often set their own interests before those of the nation. The result is suboptimal compromises made with little regard for the long term.

Political processes also take more time now because the party is no longer dominated by one strong man, like Mao or Deng. A core of party oligarchs makes decisions on the basis of compromise and consensus. The senior leadership is divided on many issues, and the political game thus drags on and on. Furthermore, there is a never-ending struggle for positions and influence among different interest groups within the Communist Party. The winners (thus those who reach the top) have mastered the game of power politics and are not necessarily the greatest policy strategists. In other words, the system produces leaders who think in the short term and are more focused on the political game than on long-term national goals, just as in the West.

These are not optimal conditions for long-term planning.

The idea that the Chinese think in hundred-year increments is an example of the Western tendency to see the Chinese as "different"—as one big Sun Tzu. In reality, Chinese politicians are not that different from Western politicians. When the Chinese refer to one hundred, one thousand, or ten thousand years, this means simply "at some point in the future" and should not be interpreted literally. When Zhou Enlai replied, "It is too early to tell," about the French Revolution, he was probably referring to the student riots in Paris in 1968 and not the revolution of 1789, despite what storytellers want to believe. [10]

Notes

1. Tzu Sun, *The Art of War* [*Sunzi bingfa*], trans. Samuel B. Griffith (New York: Oxford University Press, 1963), 83.

2. Citation borrowed from "Zhou Enlai," BBC News, http://news.bbc.co.uk/2/shared/spl/hi/asia_pac/02/china_party_congress/china_ruling_party/key_people_events/html/zhou_enlai.stm.

3. Quote taken from Henry Kissinger, *On China* (New York: Penguin Press, 2011), 280.

4. Quoted in Andrew S. Erickson et al., eds., *China's Future Nuclear Submarine Force* (Annapolis, MD: Naval Institute Press, 2007), 69.

5. See, e.g., Kishore Mahbubani, "Smart Power, Chinese-Style," *American Interest* (March–April 2008): 68–77; Martin Jacques, *When China Rules the World: The End of the Western and the Birth of a New Global Order* (New York: Penguin Press, 2009); Henry Kissinger, *On China* (New York: Penguin Press, 2011); Zbigniew Brzezinski, *Strategic Vision: America and the Crisis of Global Power* (New York: Basic Books, 2012).

6. Kissinger, *On China*.

7. Several other pundits have also pointed out that the Chinese one-party system has advantages when it comes to designing a consistent foreign and defense policy; see, e.g., Mahbubani, "Smart Power, Chinese-Style."

8. Ibid., 68.

9. Ibid.

10. See, e.g., Richard McGregor, "Zhou's Cryptic Caution Lost in Translation," *Financial Times*, 10 June 2011, http://www.ft.com/intl/cms/s/0/74916db6-938d-11e0-922e-00144feab49a.html.

Myth 46

THE RMB WILL ECLIPSE THE DOLLAR AS THE WORLD'S RESERVE CURRENCY

Not only may the Chinese economy soon be larger than America's—if measured in purchasing power—but the renminbi could displace the dollar as the premier, reserve currency within the next decade or soon thereafter.

—Arvind Subramanian, senior fellow at the Peterson Institute for
International Economics and author of *Eclipse: Living in the Shadow
of China's Economic Dominance*[1]

Many argue that the renminbi (RMB) could displace the US dollar (USD) as the world's reserve currency in the not too distant future. American observers are alarmed. Since World War II, the dollar has been the world's reserve currency. This has given the United States several advantages. For example, the country can borrow money more cheaply than others, and US banks and companies avoid currency exchange costs and can easily operate overseas. Whereas 90 percent of the United States' import and even more of its export are paid for in dollars, only a small part of China's trade is settled in RMB. If the dollar were unseated, the United States would lose much of its economic freedom of maneuver, weakening its global dominance.

Beijing makes no secret of its ambition to internationalize its currency so as to challenge the dollar's position. Since China is the world's leading exporter of goods and is likely to become the world's largest importer of goods in a few years, it seems natural that more of the country's international trade should be settled in RMB. Strengthening its currency's international position could give China some of the same benefits the United States currently enjoys. In addition, China wants to become more independent from the dollar. And then there is obviously an element of prestige here. Chinese authorities have taken steps toward internationalizing their currency—for example, by establishing bilateral currency swap arrangements with some key trading partners, mostly in Asia, enabling these countries to bypass the US dollar. The BRICS (Brazil, Russia, India, China, and South Africa) countries have similarly agreed to promote trade in local currencies. Moreover, Beijing has established Hong Kong as an offshore RMB market—a move that has helped increase use of the renminbi in trade settlements.

But to establish the RMB as the world's reserve currency is no easy task. Using the currency in trade settlements will not suffice.

If the renminbi is to challenge the dollar "within the next decade or soon thereafter," the Chinese government must act quickly to open up China's capital markets. Other countries will consider the RMB a more attractive reserve currency if it becomes easier to trade RMB for investment purposes. In order to become a global reserve currency, the RMB must become a true global trade and investment currency as well. Today the RMB cannot freely be used for investments because the Chinese authorities maintain restrictions on capital flows. With the new, seemingly reform-friendly leadership that came to power in 2012–2013, the internationalization of the RMB might gain momentum. The governor of the central bank, Zhou Xiaochuan, is among those pushing for more flexible capital markets and RMB internationalization. The fact that Chinese confidence in the dollar has weakened suggests that the new leaders will be even more eager to establish the RMB as a world currency. Nevertheless, the authorities will be forced do this in a gradual and controlled way to avoid the risks associated with opening China's capital markets, such as capital flight and "hot money inflow"—flow of capital from one country to another in order to earn a short-term profit on interest rate differences or anticipated exchange rate shifts. Allowing the Chinese to freely move their domestic savings abroad would probably harm China's banking system. Furthermore, capital liberalization could lead to excessive external borrowing as well as a volatile exchange rate, which could create an unpredictable situation for the export sector. To benefit from a freer flow of capital, Beijing must first have in place regulations and a supervisory apparatus that make it possible to deal with capital transactions properly. New regulations for moving RMB back onshore from offshore (and vice versa) must be implemented so that non-Chinese will feel comfortable about holding the currency. Theoretically the government could simply open up its capital markets overnight. But that would be most unwise, and in practice doing so takes a long time.

Another factor suggesting that the RMB will not overtake the US dollar as the world's dominant currency reserve is that Chinese authorities will be reluctant to phase out their dollar reserves rapidly. A rush by China to sell off USD holdings on a large scale might lead to a significant weakening of the dollar. A weakened dollar would harm China's economy because the Chinese have invested their savings in the currency. As mentioned earlier in this book, about two-thirds of China's massive reserve of $3.3 trillion is in dollars.[2] In addition, a weak dollar would reduce demand for Chinese goods in the United States, China's single most important export market. This would be bad news for a Chinese export industry that is already struggling. In 2012, China's export to the United States was worth as much as $425.58 billion.[3]

Last, but not the least, the lack of international confidence in the Chinese economy makes it unlikely that the RMB will eclipse the dollar as the world's reserve currency in the short to medium term. As China shows clear signs of slowing growth in gross domestic product (GDP), many economists warn about bubble tendencies in the Chinese economy and a possible debt crisis. There are good reasons to question whether China's current growth model is sustainable. Hence, many of the world's countries will likely refrain from phasing out their dollar reserves and replacing them with RMB in the near future.

Undoubtedly, the dollar's dominance looks less convincing than before. Meanwhile, the circulation of RMB has widened. Also, it speaks in favor of the RMB as a global reserve currency that so much world economic output comes from China. Still, it is important to keep perspective. The US dollar overtook the pound as the principal global currency fifty years after the United States became the largest world economy. And the RMB is not yet one of the top five payment currencies in the world; it ranks fourteenth in global payment volumes. The RMB will gradually gain more significance in Asia, as the euro has in Europe. We are most likely moving toward a world with several world currencies. But it will take a very long time for the RMB to replace the US dollar as the dominant currency reserve—if indeed it ever does.

Notes

1. Arvind Subramanian, "Coming Soon: When the Renmibi Rules the World," *Financial Times*, 11 September 2011, http://www.ft.com/intl/cms/s/0/ 098adcf6-daea-11e0-a58b-00144feabdc0.html.

2. "China Reserves Ample to Buy World's Gold Twice," *Bloomberg*, 3 March 2013, http://www.bloomberg.com/news/2013-03-03/china-reserves- ample-to-buy-world-s-gold-twice-chart-of-the-day.html.

3. "Trade in Goods with China," US Census Bureau, http://www.census. gov/foreign-trade/balance/c5700.html.

Myth 47

CHINA IS A MILITARY THREAT

The Middle East is just a blip. The American military contest with China in the Pacific will define the twenty-first century. And China will be a more formidable adversary than Russia ever was.

—Robert Kaplan[1]

China could become the most powerful adversary the United States has ever faced. Over the next 20 years, China's GDP and defense budget could exceed those of the United States. If it chose, China could therefore become a more capable opponent than either the Soviet Union or Nazi Germany at their peak, neither of which ever approached America's economic might.

—James Dobbins[2]

China's military modernization sets alarms ringing, especially among American researchers, analysts, and politicians. Each year, the Pentagon releases a report on military developments in the People's Republic. The reports question the intentions behind Chinese modernization. Beijing is criticized for a lack of transparency, and the Chinese authorities are accused of underreporting the amount they spend on military upgrades. "Of the major and emerging powers, China has the greatest potential to compete militarily with the United States," warns the Pentagon.[3]

The fear is even stronger among China's Asian neighbors, particularly Taiwan, which Beijing considers part of China, and countries like Japan, Vietnam, and the Philippines, which have territorial disputes with the Chinese in the South and East China seas. New Delhi and Moscow also harbor concerns about Chinese military developments.

And not without reason.

In March 2012, the National People's Congress approved a defense budget that for the first time exceeded $100 billion. Over the past fifteen years, China's defense budget has experienced—if we are to believe the official figures—13 percent annual growth on average, which means that the Chinese spend five times more on the military today than they did in 1997.[4] And the official figures do not tell the whole story. As a rule of thumb analysts multiply the official budget by 1.5 to get a number approximating actual defense spending.[5] The Chinese defense budget is now the world's second largest, behind that of the United States; it is twice as large as the individual defense budgets of Britain, France, and Russia, which share third place, and three times larger than India's.[6] Beijing explains this increase with the need to improve working conditions for its 2.3 million military personnel and also points out that the budget measured as a proportion of GDP is modest, only 1.4 percent (or 2 percent, if one considers the approximate actual defense spending obtained by multiplying the official numbers by 1.5). This is lower than what other major powers spend; the United States, by comparison, spends 4.5 percent of its GDP on the military.[7]

Nevertheless, the Chinese defense budget is still formidable, and the Chinese military is rapidly acquiring new capabilities. A significant part of Chinese defense spending is earmarked for research, and over the years the Chinese have developed new weapons systems such as antiship missiles—an obvious threat to American aircraft carriers—and high-speed catamarans and aircraft fighters with stealth technology. In August 2011, the Chinese aircraft carrier originally named *Shi Lang* (later *Liaoning*) completed its maiden voyage. Shi Lang was an admiral and national hero who conquered Taiwan on behalf of the Qing Dynasty in the late seventeenth century.

The worries of Asian neighbors are understandable. But seen from a Western perspective—more precisely, from that of Washington—concerns about Chinese military buildup seem exaggerated.

China is still clearly militarily inferior to the United States in budget, training, and technology. In 2012, the Americans spent seven times more on defense than the Chinese did (four and a half times if we use the approximate actual Chinese defense spending): $707.5 billion.[8] The American defense budget was as large as all other defense budgets in the world combined. In a speech given during the Tenth Shangri-La Dialogue in Singapore in 2011, China's defense minister, General Liang Guanglie, said that Chinese military power was twenty years behind that of the United States.[9] This was not falsely modesty. Chinese forces have not been in combat since the war against Vietnam ended in 1979, while the United States has gained valuable experience from numerous wars all over the world. The Americans have fought twice as many wars since the

Cold War as they did during it. Technologically speaking, China's military apparatus has been held back by the Western countries' arms embargo, which was implemented after the Tiananmen massacre in 1989. According to Dennis J. Blasko, former US Army military intelligence and foreign area officer, in 2010 only 25 percent of the Chinese air force's aircraft fleet and about 50 percent of its aircraft fighters were modern, while in the Chinese navy 26 percent of surface vessels and 56 percent of the submarine fleet were combat capable.[10] The US Navy is still the largest in the world, with a total tonnage exceeding that of the next thirteen nations combined (eleven of which are American allies).[11]

Furthermore, Chinese defense largely focuses on internal enemies, while American forces are aligned against external threats. While the United States has divided the world into five military regions, Chinese forces are organized by seven military regions within China. Internal threats are perceived as numerous and dangerous. The authorities themselves often speak of their enemies as the "five poisons" (*wu du*): separatists (Taiwanese, Tibetan, and Uyghur), the Falun Gong movement, and democracy activists. In 2011, the National People's Congress for the first time approved a budget for maintenance of internal order that exceeded the official defense budget. Much of the money went to the People's Armed Police. Despite this paramilitary force's increased resources, internal security remains a major task for the military as well. This responsibility is even enshrined in the Chinese constitution. On several occasions, the People's Armed Police have had to ask for assistance from the military—for instance, during the protests in 1989 and the unrest in Tibet in 2008 and after the 2008 earthquake in Sichuan.

The Chinese military is also tied up in the Taiwan Strait, whereas American forces are highly mobile. Even though Beijing wants a peaceful reunification with Taiwan, it is seen as politically important for the Chinese leadership to present a credible military threat to the island. In addition, border defense is an important task for Chinese forces. The country has unresolved border disputes with several of its fourteen neighbors, including India. China also borders several potentially unstable countries, such as North Korea, Myanmar, and Kyrgyzstan. Whereas the United States has 662 military bases abroad, including several in China's neighbor countries,[12] China has none. The United States has more than fifty formal military alliances, while China has only one: a friendship agreement with North Korea. With friends like that, who needs enemies? The United States has eleven operational aircraft carrier groups, six of them sailing in the Pacific, while China is years from having its first group.

Military Power of China versus the United States

	China	United States
Defense budget (official figures for 2012)	US$106.5 billion	US$707.5 billion
Operational aircraft carrier groups	0	11
Military bases abroad (official figures for 2011)	0	662
Formal military alliances	1	50+

As the Chinese defense minister noted, China will not be able to compete with the American military for decades to come, despite increased budgets and new capabilities. As long as there is danger of rebellion at home and the Taiwan conflict remains unresolved, the global ambitions of the Chinese armed forces will be limited. Just as importantly, the People's Republic has not been a revolutionary regime with a willingness to change the global status quo for decades. Today China's interests are best served by the existing international political and economic system, which is guaranteed by the United States. The authorities in Beijing will be careful not to enter an armed conflict with Washington.

Notes

1. Robert Kaplan, "How We Would Fight China," *Atlantic Magazine*, June 2005, http://www.theatlantic.com/magazine/archive/2005/06/how-we-would-fight-china/3959.

2. James Dobbins, "War with China," *Survival* 54, no. 4 (August–September 2012): 7–24.

3. "Quadrennial Defense Review Report," US Department of Defense, 2006, http://www.defense.gov/qdr/report/report20060203.pdf, 29.

4. Figures taken from Stockholm Peace Research Institute (SIPRI), cited in Richard Bitzinger, "China's New Defense Budget: What Does It Tell Us?" RSIS Commentaries, no. 060/2012, 4 April 2012, http://www.rsis.edu.sg/publications/Perspective/RSIS0602012.pdf.

5. For example, SIPRI adds 50 percent.

6. Figures taken from SIPRI, referred in Bitzinger, "China's New Defense Budget."

7. Figures taken from "Military Expenditure (% of GDP)," World Bank, http://data.worldbank.org/indicator/MS.MIL.XPND.GD.ZS.

8. Figures taken from "National Defense Budget: Estimates for FY 2012," US Department of Defense, http://comptroller.defense.gov/defbudget/fy2012/FY12_Green_Book.pdf, 17.

9. See, e.g., Wendell Minnick, "PLA 20 Years behind U.S. Military: Chinese DM," *DefenseNews*, 7 June 2011, http://www.defensenews.com/article/20110607/DEFSECT02/106070309/PLA-20-Years-Behind-U-S-Military-Chinese-DM.

10.   Dennis J. Blasko, lecture at the Norwegian Institute for Defence Studies, 8 March 2013.

11.   Robert M. Gates, "A Balanced Strategy: Reprogramming the Pentagon for a New Age," *Foreign Affairs* 88, no. 1 (January–February 2009): 32.

12.   Department of Defense, "Base Structure Report: Fiscal Year 2010 Baseline," ACQWeb, 2011, http://www.acq.osd.mil/ie/download/bsr/bsr2010baseline.pdf.

Myth 48

CHINESE WILL REPLACE ENGLISH AS THE WORLD'S LANGUAGE

> Imagine that your monthly mortgage bill arrives, unremarkable except that it's suddenly written in Mandarin.
> —Bruce Fuller, professor, University of California, Berkeley[1]

Many argue that the Chinese language will spread far and fast as a result of China's growing influence. English became the world language as a result of Britain's global dominance during the colonial era and, after that, the superpower status of the United States. Thus, it seems natural to assume that the same will happen with Chinese. The science fiction television series *Firefly* promotes this idea. Its American characters use Chinese slang, profanities, and exclamations—much as many Europeans today use English expletives. Bibb County, Georgia, in the United States is preparing for the arrival of the Chinese language by making Mandarin mandatory from kindergarten to secondary school.[2]

As many as 900 million people are native Mandarin speakers, in addition to a few hundred million Chinese whose native language is another local dialect, but who learn Mandarin in school and so speak it as a second language, some fluently. This is the largest language group in the world—nearly three times bigger than those for native English or Spanish speakers. For Japanese and Koreans it tends to be easier to learn Chinese than English. And in Europe and the United States, the number of students who learn Chinese has increased dramatically over the past two decades.

Yet there is ample reason to be skeptical about the assumption that Chinese will become the new number one world language.

First, it is hard to see why one would replace English. English is well established as a second language and as the first international language. Significant resources have already been devoted to teaching and learning it worldwide. In India, which has the world's second-largest population, English is the official language and is widely used. At an international academic conference or on a safari in Tanzania, English is likely the common language. Whereas Chinese is not very common outside China and Chinese communities in other countries, English is the official language of more than fifty countries scattered around the globe.

Second, the fact that Latin and French lost their international status does not mean that English will do the same. This is the first time in world history that we have a truly global language. Latin was the liturgical and scientific language, and French was the language of diplomacy, but neither was ever as widespread as English is today. No language ever has been, so there are really no historical examples to go by.

Third, if we decide that we do need a new world language, Chinese is not particularly well suited for the task. It is difficult to learn for several reasons: The largest dictionaries have between forty thousand and one hundred thousand characters, and you must know three to four thousand of these before you can read anything other than textbooks. The English alphabet consists of only twenty-six letters and is therefore easy to learn well enough to be able to pronounce the vast majority of English words. When we come across an unknown Chinese character, by contrast, it is virtually impossible to guess how to pronounce it or what it means.

Another factor making Chinese unsuitable is that it contains few sounds. This makes it difficult to incorporate foreign words by approximation. It is not easy to see that *Sidegeermo* (斯德哥尔摩) means Stockholm, *Bali* (巴黎) means Paris, or that the person asking for a *jin tangli* (金汤力) wants a gin and tonic. This is as close as one gets in Chinese, but it does not sound much like the original. English, on the other hand, incorporates words from Greek, Hindi, Dutch, and Italian, among other languages, without major problems or changes.

Chinese has only four hundred different sounds (syllables)—too few to express tens of thousands of characters. The Chinese language also has four tones, which can give the same sound different meanings. If we say a word in the wrong tone (such as the upward *xing* instead of the downward *xing*), the listener will have difficulty understanding what we are trying to say. The wrong tone means as much in Chinese as a wrong letter in English: man/mad, back/sack, box/cox, tan/tad, ten/pen, tout/pout, land/sand. *Xing*, in fact, has numerous different meanings: star (星), to wake up (醒), punishment (刑), and orangutan (猩), to mention a few. Those of us who did not grow up in a Chinese-language environment must memorize each tone. Even with tones to differentiate sounds, Chinese has considerably fewer sounds than many other languages, and many words are pronounced exactly the same. It is thus impossible to guess the meaning of a word based on the sound alone. Therefore, Babylonian confusion would arise if Chinese characters were abolished and Chinese was instead written with Latin characters (Pinyin).

An expatriate Chinese family is likely to learn the language of the country they've moved to in the course of a generation or even within a few years, whereas few Westerners do the same in China. This says something about the difficulty of learning Chinese. Even Asians appear to be more interested in learning English than Chinese. Written Japanese includes Chinese characters, but schoolchildren only learn about two thousand characters in elementary school, and pronunciation and usage are different from Chinese. In Korea, Chinese was the written language until the fifteenth century. Today, the knowledge of Chinese characters is falling in the general population in South Korea, although interest in studying Chinese as a foreign language is slightly on the rise.

Computers complicate matters for Chinese as well. Typing Latin letters is both easier and faster than typing Chinese characters. Typing Chinese is a double operation: we first write the word in Latin letters (or abbreviations for the most common words) or specify the strokes of the character in the correct order, then choose the right character from the list suggested by the computer. Computers and the Internet have become indispensable parts of modern life, our constant companions; until someone finds an easier way to type Chinese characters (and it is hard to imagine what that would be), the typing disadvantage can only become more significant. Because the number of Chinese sounds is so low, looking ahead one might even have problems finding enough URLs.

Finally, there is no particular interest, either within or outside China, in promoting Chinese as the number one world language. Granted, Confucius Institutes are being set up all over the world—there are around seven hundred if we include the small ones—but their goal is not to establish Chinese as a world language. The Chinese authorities hope the centers will spread Chinese language to anyone with a special interest—just as Goethe Institutes and the Alliance Française spread German and French—in addition to imparting Chinese culture, attitudes, and values.

Indeed, the authorities' primary interest today is teaching English to the Chinese. It is estimated that there are more people studying English in China than there are studying English in the Unites States. The market for English teachers in China seems to be insatiable. Any native English speaker can get a job teaching English on the spot (as can anyone whose native language is assumed to be English, including Finns, Belgians, and Norwegians). The same is not true for Chinese in the West. Chinese who study abroad easily find attractive jobs when they return home, largely because they speak good English. The same is not the case for Europeans and Americans who have studied in China.

English will remain the most important international language. But Chinese may well come in second.

Notes

1. Editors, "Will Americans Really Learn Chinese?" *New York Times*, 7 February 2010, http://roomfordebate.blogs.nytimes.com/2010/02/07/will-americans-really-learn-chinese.

2. Mark Mcdonald, "Making Mandarin Mandatory—in U.S. Kindergartens," *New York Times*, 10 September 2012, http://rendezvous.blogs.nytimes.com/2012/09/10/making-mandarin-mandatory-in-u-s-kindergartens/?ref=world.

Myth 49

THE TWENTY-FIRST CENTURY BELONGS TO CHINA

> I believe the 21st century will belong to China because most centuries
> have belonged to China.
>
> —Niall Ferguson[1]

In the 550 easy-to-read pages of the best-selling *When China Rules the World: The End of the Western World and the Birth of a New Global Order*,[2] Martin Jacques describes China's rise and how this new superpower will change the world. He imagines a future in which the world is characterized by a Chinese kind of modernity, deeply rooted in China's distinct culture and tradition. "By drawing extensively on Chinese history, Jacques reveals how the widespread belief that China is becoming more like the West is deeply mistaken—in fact, an increasingly powerful China will seek to shape the world in its own image," promises the book's cover. Thus Jacques joins the ranks of writers who ask not if but when China will become the world's new superpower—and what a twenty-first century dominated by China will be like.[3]

The backdrop to such predictions is the perceived relative stagnation of the West, particularly the United States.[4] China's impressive economic growth adds fuel to the argument. The Chinese economy has in recent years grown faster than the predictions of even the most optimistic analysts. In 2003, Goldman Sachs made headlines by forecasting that China's economy would be bigger than that of the United States by 2041. In 2009 the company moved that year up to 2027.[5] More recent studies conclude that China's GDP will overtake that of the United States as early as 2020.[6] In December 2012, the Organization for Economic Cooperation and Development presented a report concluding that China would overtake the United States as early as 2016, becoming the world's largest economy.[7]

As George Orwell once observed, "Whoever is winning at the moment will always seem to be invincible." But it is not necessarily the case that China will replace the United States as the world's leading superpower. Economic indicators are important, but they must not blind us. Money is not always easily convertible into global political influence. Japan, which for decades was the world's second-largest economy, hardly managed to convert money into power. Special historical reasons may have hampered Japan's international status, but the Chinese may also come to find that money and influence do not necessarily go hand in hand.

China lacks "soft power"—the ability to get other countries to "want what you want."[8] Countries who wield soft power have a kind of national charisma, inspiring other countries with their values, cultures, policies, and institutions. China might eventually grow to become a global superpower, but it is not becoming more popular as it becomes more powerful, if we are to believe a global survey published by the Pew Research Center in 2013. Most respondents, including half of the Americans surveyed, expected China to overtake the United States. However, only half of the forty thousand respondents in thirty-nine countries had a favorable view of China, compared to 63 percent for the United States. Moreover, a far higher number responded that they regarded the United States as a "partner."[9] In other words, China has a global image problem.

The authorities in Beijing are aware of this problem and are now discussing openly the need to strengthen the country's international reputation. They have invested significant resources in an international charm offensive. Through diplomacy, favorable trade terms, the use of international media, and cultural and student exchanges, they have sought to promote good "Chinese values," such as collectivism, self-control, hard work, altruism, and morality.[10]

But the campaign has had limited impact so far. Polls show that there is still considerable skepticism about China around the world.[11]

The reason for this, explains Professor Yan Xuetong at the Qinghua University in Beijing, is the gap between the values that the authorities trumpet and China's real authoritarian tendencies, corruption, and obsession with money. Only when the government demonstrates its ability to govern in accordance with good values at home can it hope to inspire people in other countries, advises Yan. According to him, money makes it easy for the Chinese to buy friends in all corners of the world, but "such 'friendship' does not stand the test of difficult times."[12] One may also criticize the United Stated for the gap between its ideals and its actions. Still, America's rhetoric of freedom and individualism is more attractive than the Chinese values Beijing trumpets (morality, hard work, collecti-vism).

Many argue that the Chinese authoritarian capitalism model (the "Beijing Consensus") has trumped the Western model, based on ideas about democracy and market liberalism (the "Washington Consensus"), as a model for developing countries.[13] Annual economic growth of nearly 10 percent over three decades, coupled with political stability, is obvious-ly an inspiration to poor countries around the world—especially for elites who hope to stay in power forever. But there is no evidence that the Chinese are actually trying to export their model or that other regimes are actually seeking to adopt it. No state can or will adopt the Chinese model in its entirety. It is a result of China's unique historical development, which has produced an intricate political system and an even more com-plex economic system. What's more, the Chinese model is constantly evolving, making it even more difficult to adopt.

China's historical comeback is truly impressive. But until Beijing finds a way to make Chinese characteristics more attractive to other coun-tries, the twenty-first century's belonging to China remains unlikely.

Notes

1. Rudyard Griffiths and Patrick Luciani, eds., *Does the 21st Century Belong to China?* (Toronto: House of Anansi Press, 2011), 7.

2. Martin Jacques, *When China Rules the World: The End of the Western World and the Birth of a New Global Order* (New York: Penguin Press, 2009).

3. See, e.g., Arvind Subramanian, "The Inevitable Superpower: Why Chi-na's Rise Is a Sure Thing," *Foreign Affairs* 90, no. 5 (September–October 2011): 66–78; Wu Xinbo, "Understanding the Geopolitical Implications of the Global Financial Crisis," *Washington Quarterly* 33, no. 4 (October 2010): 155–63.

4. See, inter alia, Subramanian, "The Inevitable Superpower"; Gideon Rach-man, "American Decline: This Time It's for Real," *Foreign Policy*, no. 184 (January–February 2011): 59–65; Stefan Halper, *The Beijing Consensus: How China's Authoritarian Model Will Dominate the Twenty-First Century* (New York: Basic Books, 2010); Christopher Layne, "The Waning of U.S. Hegemo-ny—Myth or Reality? A Review Essay," *International Security* 34, no. 1 (sum-mer 2009), 147–72; Robert A. Pape, "Empire Falls," *National Interest*, no. 99 (January–February 2009), 21–34; Niall Ferguson, *Colossus: The Rise and Fall of the American Empire* (New York: Penguin Press, 2005).

5. See, e.g., "The Long-Term Outlook for the BRICs and N-11 Post Crisis," Goldman Sachs, 4 December 2010, http://www2.goldmansachs.com/our-thinking/brics/brics-at-8/brics-the-long-term-outlook.pdf.

6. See, inter alia, "Dating Game: When Will China Overtake America?" *Economist*, 16 December 2010, http://www.economist.com/node/17733177; "Convergence, Catch-Up and Overtaking: How the Balance of World Economic

Power Is Shifting," PricewaterhouseCoopers, January 2010, http://www.
ukmediacentre.pwc.com/imagelibrary/downloadMedia.ashx?MediaDetailsID=
1626; "The Super-Cycle Report," Standard Chartered Bank, 2010, http://www.
standardchartered.com/id/_documents/press-releases/en/The%20Super-
cycle%20Report-12112010-final.pdf.

7. Josephine Moulds, "China's Economy to Overtake US in Next Four
Years, Says OECD," *Guardian*, 9 November 2012, http://www.guardian.co.uk/
business/2012/nov/09/china-overtake-us-four-years-oecd.

8. Joseph S. Nye, *Soft Power: The Means to Success in World Politics* (New
York: Public Affairs, 2004), 36.

9. "America's Global Image Remains More Positive than China's," Pew
Research Council, 18 July 2013, http://www.pewglobal.org/2013/07/18/
americas-global-image-remains-more-positive-than-chinas.

10. See, e.g., Joshua Kurlantzick, *Charm Offensive: How China's Soft Power
Is Transforming the World* (New Haven, CT: Yale University Press, 2007).

11. For views on China in various places around the world, see "Chapter 4.
Views of China," Pew Global Attitudes Project, 2011, http://www.pewglobal.
org/2011/07/13/chapter-4-views-of-china; for American views on China in the
period from 1989 to 2008, see "General Attitudes toward China," World Public
Opinion, 2008, http://www.americans-world.org/digest/regional_issues/china/
china1.cfm; for 2008 survey-based reports by Public Agenda, see "More than
Half Say the Development of China as a Superpower Is a Critical Threat to the
U.S. and Majorities Say China Will Play a Greater Role in the Next 10 Years,"
http://www.publicagenda.org/charts/more-half-say-development-china-
superpower-critical-threat-us-and-majorities-say, and "Americans Are Divided
on Whether China Is a Friend of the U.S., but Few Say China Is an Enemy,"
http://www.publicagenda.org/charts/americans-are-divided-whether-china-
friend-us-few-say-china-enemy.

12. Yan Xuetong, "How China Can Defeat America," *New York Times*, 20
November 2011, http://www.nytimes.com/2011/11/21/opinion/how-china-can-
defeat-america.html. For a more detailed elaboration on this point, see Yan Xue-
tong, "Xunzi's Thoughts on International Politics and Their Implications," in
China Orders the World: Normative Soft Power and Foreign Policy, ed. William
A. Callahan and Elena Barabantseva (Baltimore: Johns Hopkins University
Press, 2012), 54–88.

13. See, e.g., Halper, *Beijing Consensus*.

NOTES ON TRANSLITERATION

We have made a point of introducing the reader to some key words, phrases, and proper nouns in modern Chinese. We have aimed for consistent transliteration according to the Pinyin system. We hence write "Mao Zedong" instead of "Mao Tse-tung," "Beijing" instead of "Peking," and "Guomindang" instead of "Kuomintang"; the latter examples are all the standard of the Wade-Giles system. We have omitted tones.

For certain proper nouns that are established in English with a different spelling and whose Pinyin version might confuse the reader, we have made exceptions to the Pinyin standard. We do not adjust the spelling of names like Sun Tzu, Chiang Kai-shek, Peking University, or Yangtze River.

BIBLIOGRAPHY

Adler, Joseph A. "Daughter/Wife/Mother or Sage/Immortal/Bodhisattva? Women in the Teaching of Chinese Religions." *ASIANetwork Exchange* 14, no. 2 (winter 2006), http://www2.kenyon.edu/Depts/Religion/Fac/Adler/Writings/Women.htm.

Amnesty International. "China: Falun Gong Practitioner Missing in China." 10 May 2010, http://www.amnesty.org/en/library/asset/ASA17/021/2010/en/df9220a8-a89f-4d86-93a8-28ed2f15e915/asa170212010en.html.

Antholis, William. "New Players on the World Stage: Chinese Provinces and Indian States." *Brookings Essay*, 22 October 2013, http://www.brookings.edu/research/essays/2013/new-players-on-the-world-stage?utm_campaign=brookings-essay&utm_source=hs_email&utm_medium=email&utm_content=10654531&_hsenc=p2ANqtz-9JQ-JdYk1x05moCQfxCWawIBP5cz1JtlXlXUuzdMccGbnBZSAjxQhr5wsCtfVqLPOtVqtiPho WVYTGCXbIQF5pyMuqZQ&_hsmi=10654531.

Bardhan, Pranab. *Awakening Giants, Feet of Clay: Assessing the Economic Rise of China and India.* Princeton, NJ: Princeton University Press, 2012.

Barmé, Geremie R., and Sang Ye. "The Great Firewall of China." *Wired*, June 1997, http://www.wired.com/wired/archive/5.06/china_pr.html.

Beach, Sophie. "CDT Bookshelf: Richard Baum Recommends *Mao: The Unknown Story.*" *China Digital Times*, 5 September 2005, http://chinadigitaltimes.net/2005/09/cdt-bookshelf-richard-baum-recommends-mao-the-unknown-story/.

Benton, Gregory, and Lin Chun, eds. *Was Mao Really a Monster?* London: Routledge, 2010.

Bitzinger, Richard. "China's New Defense Budget: What Does It Tell Us?" RSIS Commentaries, no. 060/2012, 4 April 2012, http://www.rsis.edu.sg/publications/Perspective/RSIS0602012.pdf.

Brown, Kerry. *Ballot Box China: Grassroots Democracy in the Final Major One-Party State.* London: Z Books, 2011.

Brush, Peter. "Vietnam, China and the Boat People." Jean and Alexander Heard Library, 2007, http://www.library.vanderbilt.edu/206central/Brush/BoatPeople.htm#_edn4.

Brzezinski, Zbigniew. *Strategic Vision: America and the Crisis of Global Power.* New York: Basic Books, 2012.

Calamia, Joseph. "China Rising: International Patent Applications." *IEEE Spectrum* 48, no. 7 (2011): 68.

Cartier, Carolyn, and Luigi Tomba. "Chapter 2: Symbolic Cities and the 'Cake Debate.'" *China Story Yearbook 2012: Red Rising, Red Eclipse.* Canberra: Australian National University, 2012, http://www.thechinastory.org/yearbooks/yearbook-2012/chapter-2-symbolic-cities-and-the-cake-debate.

Chang, Gordon G. *The Coming Collapse of China.* New York: Random House, 2001.

Chang, Jung, and Jon Halliday. *Mao: The Unknown Story.* London: Jonathan Cape, 2005.

Chang, Maria Hsia. *Falun Gong: The End of Days.* New Haven, CT: Yale University Press, 2004.

Chase, Kenneth. *Firearms: A Global History to 1700.* New York: Cambridge University Press, 2003.

"China's Rural Growth Spurs Copper Demand." *Businessweek*, 2 November 2010, http://www.businessweek.com/globalbiz/content/nov2010/gb2010112_326953.htm.

Chow, Rey. *Women and Chinese Modernity: The Politics of Reading between West and East.* Minneapolis: University of Minnesota Press, 1991.

Chua, Amy. *World on Fire: How Exporting Free Market Democracy Breeds Ethnic Hatred and Global Instability.* New York: Doubleday, 2003.

Clinton, Hillary R. "America's Pacific Century." *Foreign Policy,* 11 October 2011, http://www.foreignpolicy.com/articles/2011/10/11/americas_pacific_century.

Cohen, Nick. *You Can't Read This Book: Censorship in an Age of Freedom.* London: Fourth Estate, 2012.

Cordesman, Anthony H., and Martin Kleibe. *Chinese Military Modernization: Force Development and Strategic Capabilities.* Washington, DC: Center for Strategic and International Studies, 2007.

Cuno, James. *Who Owns Antiquity? Museums and the Battle over Our Ancient Heritage.* Princeton, NJ: Princeton University Press, 2008.

Daouda, Cisse. "Cultural Differences in Business Relations: The Case of China and Africa." Chinainvests.org, 30 December 2010, http://chinainvests.org/2010/12/30/cultural-differences-in-business-relations-the-case-of-china-and-africa.

Dikötter, Frank. *The Discourse of Race in Modern China.* London: Hurst and Company, 1992.

Dobbins, James. "War with China." *Survival* 54, no. 4 (August–September 2012): 7–24.

Economist. "Dating Game: When Will China Overtake America?" *Economist,* 16 December 2010, http://www.economist.com/node/17733177.

Erickson, Andrew S., Lyle J. Goldstein, William S. Murray, and Andrew R. Wilson, eds. *China's Future Nuclear Submarine Force.* Annapolis, MD: Naval Institute Press, 2007.

Esherick, Joseph. "How the Qing Became China." In *Empire to Nation: Historical Perspectives on the Making of the Modern World,* edited by Joseph Esherick, Hasan Kayalı, and Eric Van Young. Lanham, MD: Rowman & Littlefield, 2006.

Fairbank, John K. "Introduction: Varieties of the Chinese Military Experience." In *Chinese Ways in Warfare,* edited by Frank A. Kierman Jr. and John K. Fairbank, 1–26. Cambridge, MA: Harvard University Press, 1974.

Fan, Xiujuan. "Shehui zhuanxingqi zongjiao jiazhiguan yanjiu" [A Study of Religious Values during the Period of Social Change], *Jiangxi kexue xueyuan xuebao* [*Journal of Jiangxi Technological University*], 12 August 2011.

Farrer, James. "From 'Passports' to 'Joint Ventures': Intermarriage between Chinese Nationals and Western Expatriates Residing in Shanghai." *Asian Studies Review,* March 2008, http://sophia.academia.edu/JamesFarrer/Papers/590164/From_Passports_to_Joint_Ventures_Intermarriage_between_Chinese_Nationals_and_Western_Expatriates_Residing_in_Shanghai.

Fei, Xiaotong. *From the Soil: The Foundations of Chinese Society.* Berkeley: University of California Press, 1992.

Ferguson, Niall. *Colossus: The Rise and Fall of the American Empire.* New York: Penguin Press, 2005.

Finance Degree Center. "Foreign Aid around the World." Finance Degree Center, http://www.financedegreecenter.com/foreign-aid.

Fincher, Leta Hong. "Women's Rights at Risk." *Dissent* (spring 2013), http://www.dissentmagazine.org/article/womens-rights-at-risk.

Foroohar, Rana. "Everything You Know about China Is Wrong." *Newsweek,* 17 October 2009, http://www.newsweek.com/id/21890/output/print.

Fraser Institute, "Economic Freedom of the World 2011: Annual Report." 2011, http://www.freetheworld.com/cgi-bin/freetheworld/getinfo.cgi.

Freeman, Will. "The Accuracy of China's 'Mass Incidents.'" *Financial Times,* 2 March 2010, http://www.ft.com/cms/s/0/9ee6fa64-25b5-11df-9bd3-00144feab49a.html#axzz1raquJDvr.

French, Howard W. "The Next Empire." *Atlantic,* May 2010, http://www.theatlantic.com/magazine/archive/2010/05/the-next-empire/308018.

Fuller, Pierre. "China's Charitable Past." *New York Times,* 28 September 2010, http://www.nytimes.com/2010/09/29/opinion/29iht-edfuller.html.

Gabriele, Alberto. "The Role of the State in China's Industrial Development: A Reassessment." *Munich Personal RePEc Archive,* 5 April 2009, http://mpra.ub.uni-muenchen.de/14551/1/MPRA_paper_14551.pdf, 2.

Gao, Mobo. *The Battle for China's Past: Mao and the Cultural Revolution.* London: Pluto Press, 2008.

Gao, Zugui. "Constructive Involvement and Harmonious World: China's Evolving Outlook on Sovereignty in the Twenty-First Century." Friedrich Ebert Stiftung, Briefing Paper 13, October 2008, http://library.fes.de/pdf-files/iez/05923.pdf.

Gates, Robert M. "A Balanced Strategy: Reprogramming the Pentagon for a New Age." *Foreign Affairs* 88, no. 1 (January–February 2009): 28–40.

Gilley, Bruce. "The Meaning and Measure of State Legitimacy: Results for 72 Countries." *European Journal of Political Research* 45, no. 3 (2006): 499–525.

Goebel, R. J. "China as an Embalmed Mummy: Herder's Orientalist Poetics." *South Atlantic Review* 60, no. 1 (January 1995): 111–29.

Goldman Sachs. "The Long-Term Outlook for the BRICs and N-11 Post Crisis." Goldman Sachs, 4 December 2010, http://www2.goldmansachs.com/our-thinking/brics/brics-at-8/brics-the-long-term-outlook.pdf.

Goldstein, Steven M. "The Future: Introduction." In *The Chinese: Adapting the Past, Building the Future*, edited by Robert F. Dernberger et al., 701–10. 4th ed. Ann Arbor: Center for Chinese Studies, University of Michigan, 1996.

Gries, Peter Hays. *China's New Nationalism: Pride, Politics and Diplomacy.* Berkeley: University of California Press, 2004.

Guadalupi, Gianni. *China: Through the Eyes of the West.* Vercelli, Italy: White Star Publishers, 2003.

Halper, Stefan. *The Beijing Consensus: How China's Authoritarian Model Will Dominate the Twenty-First Century.* New York: Basic Books, 2010.

Halsall, Paul. "Qian Long: Letter to George III, 1793." *Internet Modern History Sourcebook*, August 1997, http://www.fordham.edu/halsall/mod/1793qianlong.asp.

Hastings, Max. "The Long March to Mass Murder." *Telegraph*, 5 June 2005, http://www.telegraph.co.uk/culture/books/3643215/The-long-march-to-mass-murder.html.

Haugen, Heidi Østbø. "Afrikanere redder Kinas handel" [Africans Come to the Rescue of Chinese Trade], *Ny Tid*, 24 July 2009.

———. "Globaliseringens fotsoldater" [The Footsloggers of Globalization]. *Aftenposten Innsikt*, October 2009.

Hegel, Georg Wilhelm Friedrich. *Philosophy of History.* New York: Barnes & Noble, 2004.

Heggelund, Gørild, Steinar Andresen, and Inga Fritzen Buan. "Chinese Climate Policy: Domestic Priorities, Foreign Policy, and Emerging Implementation." In *Global Commons, Domestic Decisions*, edited by Kathryn Harrison and Lisa McIntosh Sundstrom, 239–61. Cambridge, MA: MIT Press, 2010.

Hewitt, Duncan. *China: Getting Rich First: A Modern Social History.* New York: Pegasus, 2009.

Hill, Joshua. "Voting as a Rite: A History of Elections in Twentieth Century China." Unpublished PhD diss., Harvard University, 2011.

Hirschman, Albert O., and Michael Rothschild. "The Changing Tolerance for Income Inequality in the Course of Economic Development; with a Mathematical Appendix." *Quarterly Journal of Economics* 87, no. 4 (1973): 544–66.

Hochs, G. L., and S. C. Redding. "The Story of the East Asian 'Economic Miracle': Part Two: The Cultural Connection." *Euro-Asia Business Review* 2, no. 4 (1983).

Horioka, Charles Yuji. "An International Comparison of Altruism and Bequest Motives: The Case of China, India, Japan, and the United States." Institute of Economics, Academica Sinica, Taipei, 3 July 2010, http://www.econ.sinica.edu.tw/upload/file/0817.pdf.

Horn, John, Vivien Singer, and Jonathan Woetzel. "A Truer Picture of China's Export Machine." *McKinsey Quarterly*, September 2010, http://www.mckinseyquarterly.com/Strategy/Globalization/A_truer_picture_of_Chinas_export_machine_2676.

Hsee, Christopher K., and Elke U. Weber. "Researching Risk Preference." *Capital Ideas* 1, no. 3 (1998), http://www.chicagobooth.edu/capideas/sum98/hsee.htm.

Hsiao, Russell. "Hu Confers Hardliner Top Military Rank." *China Brief* 9, no. 15 (23 July 2009), http://www.jamestown.org/single/?no_cache=1&tx_ttnews%5Btt_news%5D=35306.

Huntington, Samuel P. *The Third Wave.* Norman: University of Oklahoma Press, 1991.

Hvistendahl, Mara. *Unnatural Selection: Choosing Boys over Girls and the Consequences of a World Full of Men.* New York: Public Affairs, 2011.

Hwa, Erh-Cheng. "Progress in Reforming China's Banks." Paper presented during the "China's Policy Reforms: Social Services, Regulation and Finance" conference, Stanford University, Stanford, California, 22–24 October 2008, http://scid.stanford.edu/group/siepr/cgibin/scid/?q=system/files/shared/Hwa_10-3-08.pdf.

Information Office of the State Council of the People's Republic of China. "China's National Defense in 2004." Information Office of the State Council of the People's Republic of China. http://www.china.org.cn/e-white/20041227/index.htm.

Jacques, Martin. *When China Rules the World: The End of the Western World and the Birth of a New Global Order.* New York: Penguin Press, 2009.

Jie, Chen. *Popular Political Support in Rural China.* Washington, DC: Woodrow Wilson Center Press, 2004.

Johnson, Ian. "China Gets Religion!" *New York Review of Books*, 22 December 2011, http://www.nybooks.com/articles/archives/2011/dec/22/china-gets-religion.

Johnston, Alastair Iain. *Cultural Realism: Strategic Culture and Grand Strategy in Chinese History.* Princeton, NJ: Princeton University Press, 1998.

Kane, Daniel C., introduction to *Au Japon: Memoirs of a Foreign Correspondent in Japan, Korea, and China, 1892–1894*, by A. B. de Guerville. West Lafayette, IN: Parlor Press, 2009.

Kaplan, Robert. "How We Would Fight China." *Atlantic Magazine*, June 2005, http://www.theatlantic.com/magazine/archive/2005/06/how-we-would-fight-china/3959.

Kingston, Jeff. "What You Must Understand Is We Chinese All Hate Japanese." *Japan Times*, 27 February 2011, http://www.japantimes.co.jp/text/fl20110227x1.html.

Kissinger, Henry. *On China*. New York: Penguin Press, 2011.

Ko, Dorothy. *Cinderella's Sisters: A Revisionist History of Footbinding*. Berkeley: University of California Press, 2005.

———. *Teachers of the Inner Chambers: Women and Culture in Seventeenth Century China*. Stanford, CA: Stanford University Press, 1994.

Kraus, Richard. "The Politics of Art Repatriation: Nationalism, State Legitimation, and Beijing's Looted Zodiac Animal Heads." In *Chinese Politics: State, Society, and the Market*, edited by Peter Hays Gries and Stanley Rosen, 199–221. New York: Routledge, 2010.

Kristof, Nicholas D. "China Sees 'Market-Leninism' as Way to Future." *New York Times*, 6 September 1993, http://www.nytimes.com/1993/09/06/world/china-sees-market-leninism-as-way-to-future.html.

Kumar, Sanjeev. "Rural Development through Rural Industrialization: Exploring the Chinese Experience." *Asian Scholarship*, http://www.asianscholarship.org/asf/ejourn/articles/Sanjeev%20Kumar2.pdf.

Kurlantzick, Joshua. *Charm Offensive: How China's Soft Power Is Transforming the World*. New Haven, CT: Yale University Press, 2007.

Kværne, Per "Annerledeslandet" (The Country of Difference). Morgenbladet, 18 April 2008. http://morgenbladet.no/samfunn/2008/annerledeslandet#.VCXF9RZUg32.

———. "Tibet Images among Researchers on Tibet." In *Imagining Tibet: Perceptions, Projections and Fantasies*, edited by Thierry Dodin and Heinz Räther, 47–63. Boston: Wisdom Publications, 2001.

Lam, Ching Man. *Not Grown Up Forever: A Chinese Conception of Adolescent Development*. New York: Nova Science Publishers, 1997.

Lam, Willy. "PLA's 'Absolute Loyalty' to the Party in Doubt." *China Brief* 9, no. 9 (30 April 2009), http://www.jamestown.org/single/?no_cache=1&tx_ttnews%5Btt_news%5D=34920.

Layne, Christopher. "The Waning of U.S. Hegemony—Myth or Reality? A Review Essay." *International Security* 34, no. 1 (summer 2009): 147–72.

Lee, Feigon. *Demystifying Tibet: Unlocking the Secrets of the Land of the Snows*. Chicago: Ivan R. Dee, 1996.

Lee, Yun Kuen. "Building the Chronology of Early Chinese History." *Asian Perspective* 41, no. 1 (2002): 15–42.

Lee Kuan Yew School of Public Policy and Asia Society. "Rising to the Top? A Report on Women's Leadership in Asia." Asia Society, April 2012, http://sites.asiasociety.org/womenleaders/wp-content/uploads/2012/04/Rising-to-the-Top-Final-PDF.pdf.

Lei, Xie. "China's Environmental Activism in the Age of Globalization." Working Papers on Transnational Politics, City University, London, May 2009.

Li, Zhisui. *The Private Life of Chairman Mao: The Memoirs of Mao's Personal Physician*. New York: Random House, 1994.

Lin, Justin Yifu, Tao Ran, Liu Mingxing, and Zhang Qi. "Urban and Rural Household Taxation in China: Measurement and Stylized Facts." Chinese University of Hong Kong Paper Collection, July 2002, http://www.usc.cuhk.edu.hk/PaperCollection/webmanager/wkfiles/1722_1_paper.pdf.

Link, Perry. "America's Outdated View of China." *Washington Post*, 10 May 2012, http://www.washingtonpost.com/opinions/the-us-governments-outdated-view-of-china/2012/05/10/gIQAUvgaGU_story.html.

Loewe, Michael, and Edward L. Shaughnessy. *The Cambridge History of Ancient China: From the Origins of Civilization to 221 BC*. New York: Cambridge University Press, 1999.

Lopez, Donald S., Jr. *Prisoners of Shangri-la: Tibetan Buddhism and the West*. Chicago: University of Chicago Press, 1998.

Lowrie, William. *Fundamentals of Geophysics*. Cambridge: Cambridge University Press, 2007.

Luttwak, Edward N. *The Rise of China vs. the Logic of Strategy*. Cambridge, MA: Belknap Press of Harvard University Press, 2012.

Lynas, Mark. "How Do I Know China Wrecked the Copenhagen Deal? I Was in the Room." *Guardian,* 22 December 2009, http://www.guardian.co.uk/environment/2009/dec/22/copenhagen-climate-change-mark-lynas.

Ma, Rong. "Ethnic Relations in Contemporary China: Cultural Tradition and Ethnic Policies since 1949." *Policy and Society* 25, no. 1 (2006): 85–108.

Mahbubani, Kishore. "Smart Power, Chinese-Style." *American Interest* (March–April 2008): 68–77.

Mann, Susan, and Yu-Yin Cheng, eds. *Under Confucian Eyes: Writings on Gender in Chinese History*. Berkeley: University of California Press, 2001.

May, Timothy. *The Mongol Art of War*. Yardley, UK: Westholme, 2007.

McGregor, Richard. *The Party: The Secret World of China's Communist Rulers.* New York: HarperCollins, 2010.

———. "Zhou's Cryptic Caution Lost in Translation." *Financial Times,* 10 June 2011.

Menzies, Gavin. *1421: The Year China Discovered the World.* London: Bantam Press, 2002.

Meyer, Erin, and Elisabeth Yi Shen. "China Myths, China Facts." *Harvard Business Review,* 2010, http://hbr.org/2010/01/china-myths-china-facts/ar/pr.

Mitter, Rana. *Modern China: A Very Short Introduction.* Oxford: Oxford University Press, 2008.

Monson, Jamie. *Africa's Freedom Railway.* Bloomington: Indiana University Press, 2011.

Mosher, Steven W. *Hegemon: China's Plan to Dominate Asia and the World.* New York: Encounter Books, 2000.

Moyo, Dambisa. "Beijing, a Boon for Africa." *New York Times,* 27 June 2012, http://www.nytimes.com/2012/06/28/opinion/beijing-aboon-for-africa.html.

Mullaney, Thomas. *Coming to Terms with the Nation: Ethnic Classification in Modern China.* Berkeley: University of California Press, 2010.

Nathan, Andrew J. "China at the Tipping Point?" *Journal of Democracy* 24, no. 1 (January 2013): 20–25.

Nathan, Andrew J., and Andrew Scobell. *China's Search for Security.* New York: Columbia University Press, 2012.

National Bureau of Statistics of China. "Communiqué of the National Bureau of Statistics of the People's Republic of China on Major Figures of the 2010 Population Census." 29 April 2011, http://www.stats.gov.cn/english/newsandcomingevents/t20110429_402722516.htm.

Nye, Joseph S. *Soft Power: The Means to Success in World Politics.* New York: Public Affairs, 2004.

O'Brien, Kevin J., and Lianjiang Li. *Rightful Resistance in Rural China.* Cambridge: Cambridge University Press, 2006.

Organisation for Economic Co-operation and Development (OECD). "OECD Review of Agricultural Policies—China." OECD, 2011, http://www.oecd.org/document/57/0,3746,en_2649_33797_35557433_1_1_1_1,00.html.

Pan, Lynn. *Shanghai Style: Art and Design between the Wars.* San Francisco: Long River Press, 2008.

Pantsov, Alexander V., and Steven I. Levine. *Mao: The Real Story.* New York: Simon & Schuster, 2012.

Pape, Robert A. "Empire Falls." *National Interest,* no. 99 (January–February 2009): 21–34.

Pardos, John. *The Blood Road: The Ho Chi Minh Trail and the Vietnam War.* New York: John Wiley & Sons, 2000.

Perry, Elizabeth J. *Challenging the Mandate of Heaven.* New York: M. E. Sharpe, 2002.

Petre, Silviu. "Returning to West: China's Long Road Developmental Domestic Policy." Scribd.com. http://www.scribd.com/doc/44846441/Returning-to-West-de-Silviu-Petre.

Pew Charitable Trust. "Who's Winning the Clean Energy Race? 2012 Edition." Pew Charitable Trusts, 16 April 2013, http://www.pewtrusts.org/uploadedFiles/wwwpewtrustsorg/News/Press_Releases/Clean_Energy/clen-G20-report-2012-FINAL.pdf.

Pew Global Attitudes Project. "Chapter 4. Views of China." Pew Global Attitudes Project, 13 July 2011, http://www.pewglobal.org/2011/07/13/chapter-4-views-of-china.

———. "22-Nation Pew Global Attitudes Survey." Pew Global Attitudes Project, 17 June 2010, http://www.pewglobal.org/files/2011/04/Pew-Global-Attitudes-Spring-2010-Report2.pdf.

Ping, Zhou, and Loet Leydesdorff. "The Emergence of China as a Leading Nation in Science." Cornell University Library, 2009, http://arxiv.org/ftp/arxiv/papers/0911/0911.3421.pdf, 84.

Polo, Marco. *The Travels of Marco Polo, the Venetian.* London: Forgotten Books, 2012.

PricewaterhouseCoopers (PWC). "Convergence, Catch-Up and Overtaking: How the Balance of World Economic Power Is Shifting." PWC, January 2010, http://www.ukmediacentre.pwc.com/imagelibrary/downloadMedia.ashx?MediaDetailsID=1626.

Pritchard, Jack. "China Is Key to N. Korea." *Choson Ilbo,* 6 February 2010, http://english.chosun.com/site/data/html_dir/2010/02/06/2010020600241.html.

Public Agenda. "Americans Are Divided on Whether China Is a Friend of the U.S., but Few Say China Is an Enemy." Public Agenda, 2008, http://www.publicagenda.org/charts/americans-are-divided-whether-china-friend-us-few-say-china-enemy.

———. "More than Half Say the Development of China as a Superpower Is a Critical Threat to the U.S. and Majorities Say China Will Play a Greater Role in the Next 10 Years." Public Agenda, 2008, http://www.publicagenda.org/charts/more-half-say-development-china-superpower-critical-threat-us-and-majorities-say.

Qian, Gang. "China's Reporters Push the Boundaries." *Wall Street Journal,* 3 August 2011, http://online.wsj.com/article/SB10001424053111903520204576483811379409124.html.

Rachman, Gideon. "American Decline: This Time It's for Real." *Foreign Policy,* no. 184 (January–February 2011): 59–65.

Rahn, Patsy. "The Falun Gong: Behind the Headlines." *Cultic Studies Journal* 17, no. 1 (2000): 168–86.
Ramo, Joshua Cooper. *The Beijing Consensus*. London: Foreign Policy Centre, 2004.
Rand Corporation. "China's Foreign Aid and Government-Sponsored Investment Activities." Rand Corporation, 2013, http://www.rand.org/pubs/research_reports/RR118.html.
Randers, Jørgen. *2052: A Global Forecast for the Next Forty Years*. White River Junction, VT: Chelsea Green Publishing, 2012.
Raphals, Lisa. *Sharing the Light: Representations of Women and Virtue in Early China*. Albany: State University of New York Press, 1998.
Reese, Lyn. "Gender Equity and Texts." *Social Studies Review* 33, no. 2 (1994): 12–15.
Reporters without Borders. "World Report—China." Reporters without Borders, 29 August 2011, http://en.rsf.org/report-china,57.html.
Rohmer, Sax Gabriel. *The Insidious Dr. Fu Manchu*. London: Forgotten Books, 2008. First published 1913.
Royal Society Science Academy. "Knowledge, Networks and Nations: Global Scientific Collaboration in the 21st Century." Royal Society Science Academy, 27 March 2011, http://royalsociety.org/uploadedFiles/Royal_Society_Content/Influencing_Policy/Reports/2011-03-28-Knowledge-networks-nations.pdf.
Rupert, G. G. *The Yellow Peril; or, the Orient versus the Occident as Viewed by Modern Statesmen and Ancient Prophets*. Choctaw, OK: Union Publishing, 1911.
Ryckmans, Pierre. "The Chinese Attitude towards the Past." *China Heritage Quarterly* no. 14 (June 2008), http://www.chinaheritagequarterly.org/articles.php?searchterm=014_chineseAttitude.inc&issue=014.
Sæther, Elin. "The Conditional Autonomy of the Critical Press in China." PhD diss., University of Oslo, 2008.
Said, Edward. *Orientalism*. New York: Vintage Books, 1979.
Sainsbury, Michael. "Wen Jiabao's Remarkable Road to Reform." *Australian*, 17 March 2012, http://www.theaustralian.com.au/news/world/wen-jiabaos-remarkable-road-to-reform/story-fnb1brze-1226301929918.
Sautman, Barry. "African Perspectives on China-Africa Links." Center on China's Transnational Relations, 14 May 2009, http://www.cctr.ust.hk/materials/conference/.../18/20090514-bsautman.ppt.
Sawyer, Ralph D. "Chinese Strategic Power: Myths, Intent, and Projections." *Journal of Military and Strategic Studies* 8, no. 4 (summer 2006).
Scobell, Andrew. *China's Use of Military Force: Beyond the Great Wall and the Long March*. Cambridge: Cambridge University Press, 2003.
Seligsohn, Deborah. "China at Durban: First Steps toward a New Climate Agreement." *WRI Insights*, 16 December 2011, http://insights.wri.org/news/2011/12/china-durban-first-steps-toward-new-climate-agreement.
Shen, Simon, and Shaun Breslin, eds. *Online Chinese Nationalism and China's Bilateral Relations*. Lanham, MD: Rowman & Littlefield, 2010.
Shue, Vivienne. "Legitimacy Crisis in China?" In *Chinese Politics: State, Society, and the Market*, edited by Peter Hays Gries and Stanley Rosen, 46–51. New York: Routledge, 2010.
Song, R. "China's Coastal Population and Economic Development: Summary of the Symposium." *China Journal of Popular Science* 4, no. 2 (1992), http://www.ncbi.nlm.nih.gov/pubmed/12317925.
Standard Chartered Bank. "The Super-Cycle Report." Standard Chartered Bank, http://www.standardchartered.com/id/_documents/press-releases/en/The%20Super-cycle%20Report-12112010-final.pdf.
State Council Information Office. "China's Foreign Aid." State Council Information Office, April 2011, http://english.gov.cn/official/2011-04/21/content_1849913_3.htm.
Stensdal, Iselin. "Chinese Climate-Change Policy, 1988–2013: Moving On Up." *Asian Perspective* 38, no. 1 (2014): 111–36.
Stiglitz, Joseph E. "China: Forging a Third Generation of Reforms." World Bank, Beijing, China, 23 July 1999, http://unpan1.un.org/intradoc/groups/public/documents/APCITY/UNPAN004886.pdf.
Subramanian, Arvind. *Eclipse: Living in the Shadow of China's Economic Dominance*. Washington, DC: Peterson Institute for International Economics, 2011.
———. "The Inevitable Superpower: Why China's Rise Is a Sure Thing." *Foreign Affairs* 90, no. 5 (September–October 2011): 66–78.
Sun, Tzu. *The Art of War [Sunzi bingfa]*. Trans. Samuel B. Griffith. New York: Oxford University Press, 1963.
Sun, Yun. "Chinese Public Opinion: Shaping China's Foreign Policy, or Shaped by It?" Brookings Institution, 13 December 2011, http://www.brookings.edu/research/opinions/2011/12/13-china-public-opinion-sun.

Svensson, Marina. "Protection of the Cultural Heritage in the PRC: Preservation Policies, Institutions, Laws, and Enforcement." Centre for East and South-East Asian Studies, University of Lund, http://www.ace.lu.se/o.o.i.s/5933.
Thompson, Larry Clinton. *William Scott Ament and the Boxer Rebellion: Heroism, Hubris, and the Ideal Missionary.* Jefferson, NC: McFarland, 2009.
Tong, Yanqi, and Lei Shaohua. "Large-Scale Mass Incidents in China." EAI Background Brief 520 (15 April 2010), http://www.eai.nus.edu.sg/BB520.pdf.
Trump, Donald. *Time to Get Tough: Making America #1 Again.* Washington, DC: Regnery Publishing, 2011.
Tsang, Shu-ki, and Cheng Yuk-shing. "China's Tax Reforms of 1994: Breakthrough or Compromise?" *Asian Survey* 34, no. 9 (1994), http://www.sktsang.com/ArchiveIII/China_tax_1994.pdf.
Turnbull, Stephen. *Genghis Khan and the Mongol Conquests, 1190–1400.* Oxford: Osprey Publishing, 2003.
US Census Bureau. "Trade in Goods with China." US Census Bureau, http://www.census.gov/foreign-trade/balance/c5700.html.
US Department of Defense (DoD). "Annual Report to Congress: Military and Security Developments Involving China." DoD, 2011, http://www.defense.gov/pubs/pdfs/2011_cmpr_final.pdf.
———. "Base Structure Report." DoD, 2011, http://www.acq.osd.mil/ie/download/bsr/bsr2010baseline.pdf.
———. "National Defense Budget: Estimates for FY 2012." DoD, 2012, http://comptroller.defense.gov/Portals/45/Documents/defbudget/fy2012/FY12_Green_Book.pdf.
———. "Quadrennial Defense Review Report." DoD, 2006, http://www.defense.gov/qdr/report/report20060203.pdf.
———. "Sustaining U.S. Global Leadership: Priorities for 21st Century Defense." DoD, January 2012, http://graphics8.nytimes.com/packages/pdf/us/20120106-PENTAGON.PDF.
Ungar, E. S. "The Struggle over the Chinese Community in Vietnam, 1946–1986." *Pacific Affairs* 60, no. 4 (winter 1987–1988): 596–614.
UNICEF. "Gender Equality." UNICEF. http://www.unicef.cn/en/index.php?m=content&c=index&a=lists&catid=135.
United Nations Development Programme (UNDP). "UNICEF and U.N. Human Development Report." UNDP, http://hdrstats.undp.org/en/indicators/103.html.
———. "The United Nations Human Development Report, 2007–08." UNDP, http://hdr.undp.org/sites/default/files/reports/268/hdr_20072008_en_complete.pdf.
Wade, Geoff. "Most Outrageous Claims by Mr. Menzies in *1421*." 1421 Myth Exposed, http://www.1421exposed.com/html/most_outrageous_claims.html.
Waldron, Arthur. "The Soviet Disease Spreads to China." *Far Eastern Economic Review* (October 2009): 24–27.
Wang, Irene. "Incidents of Social Unrest Hit 87,000 in 2005." *South China Morning Post*, 20 January 2006.
Wang, Xiaobing, and Jenifer Piesse. "Inequality and the Urban-Rural Divide in China: Effects of Regressive Taxation." *China and World Economy* 18, no. 6 (November–December 2010): 36–55.
Wang, Yi. "Women's Situation in China during the Social Transition." Paper presented during the Nordic Association for China Studies biannual conference, Oslo, Norway, 19 June 2011.
Wang, Yizhou. "Guanjian reng zai neizheng" [Domestic Policy Is Still the Crucial Point], 360doc.com, 25 June 2010, http://www.360doc.com/content/12/0104/20/322140_177285699.shtml.
Wang, Zhengxu. "Political Trust in China: Forms and Causes." In *Legitimacy: Ambiguities of Political Success or Failure in East and Southeast Asia*, edited by Lynn White. Singapore: World Scientific, 2005.
Wasserstrom, Jeffrey N. *China in the 21st Century: What Everyone Needs to Know.* Oxford: Oxford University Press, 2010.
———. *China's Brave New World: And Other Tales of Global Times.* Bloomington: Indiana University Press, 2007.
———. "Student Protests in Fin-de-Siècle China." *New Left Review*, September–October 1999, https://newleftreview.org/I/237/jeffrey-wasserstrom-student-protests-in-fin-de-siecle-china.
Whitney, Christopher B., and David Shambaugh. "Soft Power in Asia: Results of a 2008 Multinational Survey of Public Opinion." Chicago Council of Foreign Affairs, 2008, http://www.thechicagocouncil.org/hottopics_details.php?hottopics_id=110.
Whyte, Martin King. "Do Chinese Citizens Want the Government to Do More to Promote Equality?" In *Chinese Politics: State, Society, and the Market*, edited by Peter Hays Gries and Stanley Rosen, 129–59. New York: Routledge, 2010.
———. *Myth of the Social Volcano: Perceptions of Inequality and Distributive Injustice in Contemporary China.* Stanford, CA: Stanford University Press, 2010.

Wilkenfeld, Jonathan, Michael Brechter, and Sheila Moser. *Crisis in the Twentieth Century.* Vol. 2: *Handbook of Foreign Policy Crises.* Oxford: Pergamon Books, 1988.
Wilsdon, James, and James Keeley. "China: The Next Science Superpower?" Naider, 2007, http://www.naider.com/upload/82_China_Final.pdf, 30–31.
Wood, Frances. *Did Marco Polo Go to China?* Boulder, CO: Westview Press, 1995.
World Bank. "Exports of Goods and Services (% of GDP)." World Bank. http://data.worldbank.org/indicator/NE.EXP.GNFS.ZS.
———. "GINI Index." World Bank. http://data.worldbank.org/indicator/SI.POV.GINI.
———. "Military Expenditure (% of GDP)." World Bank. http://data.worldbank.org/indicator/MS.MIL.XPND.GD.ZS.
———. "World Development Indicators." World Bank. http://databank.worldbank.org/ddp/home.do?Step=12&id=4&CNO=2.
World Public Opinion. "General Attitudes toward China." World Public Opinion, 2008, http://www.americans-world.org/digest/regional_issues/china/china1.cfm.
Wright, Teresa. *Accepting Authoritarianism: State Society Relations in China's Reform Era.* Stanford, CA: Stanford University Press, 2010.
Wu, Xinbo. "Understanding the Geopolitical Implications of the Global Financial Crisis." *Washington Quarterly* 33, no. 4 (October 2010): 155–63.
Wu, Yisan. "Internet Censorship in China." *Epoch Times*, 10 November 2006, http://www.theepochtimes.com/news/6-11-10/47995.html.
Wübbeke, Jost. "China's Climate Change Expert Community—Principles, Mechanisms and Influence." *Journal of Contemporary China* 22, no. 82 (2013): 712–31.
Yan, Hairong, and Barry Sautman. "Chasing Ghosts: Rumours and Representations of the Exports of Chinese Convict Labour to Developing Countries." *China Quarterly* 210 (June 2012): 398–418.
Yan, Xuetong. "How China Can Defeat America." *New York Times*, 20 November 2011, http://www.nytimes.com/2011/11/21/opinion/how-china-can-defeat-america.html.
———. "Xunzi's Thoughts on International Politics and Their Implications." In *China Orders the World: Normative Soft Power and Foreign Policy*, edited by William A. Callahan and Elena Barabantseva, 54–88. Baltimore: Johns Hopkins University Press, 2012.
Yang, C. K. *Religion in Chinese Society.* Berkeley: University of California Press, 1961.
Yang, Jisheng. *Tombstone: The Great Chinese Famine, 1958–1962.* New York: Farrar, Straus & Giroux, 2012.
Yu, Hua. *China in Ten Words.* New York: Anchor Books, 2011.
Zakaria, Fareed. "Don't Feed China's Nationalism." *Daily Beast*, 12 April 2008, http://www.thedailybeast.com/newsweek/2008/04/12/don-t-feed-china-s-nationalism.html.
Zhang, Longxi. "The Myth of the Other: China in the Eyes of the West." *Critical Inquiry* 15, no. 1 (autumn 1988): 108–31.
Zhang, Tiedao. "Literacy Education in China." United Nations Educational, Scientific, and Cultural Organization, 2005, http://ddp-ext.worldbank.org/EdStats/CHNgmrpro05a.pdf.
Zhang, Zhiming. "Inside the Growth Engine: A Guide to China's Regions, Provinces and Cities." HSBC Global Research, December 2010, http://www.research.hsbc.com/midas/Res/RDV?p=pdf&key=nmMuQ3lvVa&n=284797.PDF.
Zhao, Suisheng. "China's Pragmatic Nationalism: Is It Manageable?" *Washington Quarterly* 29, no. 1 (winter 2005): 131–44.
Zheng, Yongnian. *De Facto Federalism in China: Reforms and Dynamics of Central-Local Relations.* Singapore: World Scientific, 2007.
Zhu, Xufeng. "China's National Leading Group to Address Climate Change: Mechanism and Structure." EAI Background Brief 572, East Asian Institute, National University of Singapore, 22 October 2010, http://www.eai.nus.edu.sg/BB572.pdf.

INDEX

abortion, 64
Africa, 139–141; racial issues and, 128–129; Zheng He and, 169
aircraft carrier groups, 217, 218
Ai Weiwei, 9, 83
alliances, 217, 218
altruism, 55–57
Anderson, Jonathan, 96
antiques, 193–194
Arouet, François-Marie. *See* Voltaire
art: in Beijing and Shanghai, 82–83; copying and, 107; and heritage, 193–194, 194
Asia: gender balance in, 64; military issues in, 215–216
atheism, 77–79

Baidu, 109
Beijing, openness in, 81–84
Beijing Consensus, 226–227
Biggers, Earl Derr, 6
birth planning, 63–66
Bishop, Peter, 184
Blasko, Dennis J., 217
Boxer Rebellion, 5
Bo Xilai, 21, 23–24, 203
Brecht, Bertolt, 55
Britain, 180; defense budget, 216
Buddhism, 39, 67–68, 77, 78
Bush, George W., 8

business: Chinese people and, 99–101; export/import balance, 95–97, 97; innovation and, 107–110; reach of, 87–89; state control and, 113–116; and United States, 91; *See also under* economic

carbon dioxide emissions, 143, 145
cartography, Chinese, 167–169
Catholicism, 77–78
CCTV (China Central Television), 43
censorship, 41–44; and Internet, 200; in Shanghai, 81, 82, 83
central control, 17–20
Central Military Commission, 30
Central Party School, 15
Chan, Charlie, 6
Chang, Gordon G., 203–204
Chang, Jung, 187–190
Charter 08, 49
checkbook diplomacy, 154
Chen Daoming, 9
Chen Duxiu, 49
Chen Guangcheng, 9, 64
Cheonan, 150
Chiang Ching-kuo, 49
Chiang Kai-shek, 49
China: demographics of, 19, 63; economic relationship with United States, 91–93; fears regarding, types of, x–xi; geography of, 68; *See also under*

ABOUT THE AUTHORS

Marte Kjær Galtung is a senior China analyst at the Norwegian Defence Staff. She is a social anthropologist with China as her specialty and speaks fluent Chinese. She has previously worked on China with the Norwegian Ministry of Foreign Affairs, as a cultural attaché at the Norwegian embassy in Beijing, and subsequently on the Norwegian government's China strategy. She is author of *China: The History, Culture, People, and Politics*.

Stig Stenslie is head of the Asia Branch of the Norwegian Defence Staff. He has been visiting scholar at, among others, the Norwegian Institute for Defence Studies, National University in Singapore, and Columbia University in New York. He holds a doctorate in political science from the University of Oslo. He is author of several books on contemporary China and the Middle East, the most recent being *Regime Stability in Saudi Arabia: The Challenge of Succession* and *Stability and Change in the Modern Middle East*.